PAT GETZ-PREZIOSI received her doctor-
ate from Harvard University and has lived
and studied in Greece. She is an internation-
ally recognized authority on Cycladic art,
and is the author of numerous publications.

Sculptors of the Cyclades

Pat Getz-Preziosi

SCULPTORS OF THE CYCLADES:

INDIVIDUAL AND TRADITION

IN THE THIRD MILLENNIUM B.C.

Published in Association with the J. Paul Getty Trust

THE UNIVERSITY OF MICHIGAN PRESS

Ann Arbor

Published in the United States of America by
The University of Michigan Press and simultaneously
in Markham, Canada, by Fitzhenry & Whiteside, Ltd.
Manufactured in the United States of America

1990   1989   1988   1987   4   3   2   1

Library of Congress Cataloging-in-Publication Data on page 258

For Ali and Tarquin, companions in the Cyclades

Οἱ πέτρες μουσκεύουν στὸ φῶς καὶ στὴ μνήμη.

RITSOS

PREFACE

T H E recording of modern interest in the sculpture of the Cyclades begins perhaps with the publication in 1818 of a figure unearthed by the Earl of Aberdeen in a grave near Athens. Exploration of the Cyclades themselves by serious travelers, scholars, and treasure seekers began in earnest in the second half of the nineteenth century and since then has continued unabated, providing a corpus of several thousand objects for study.

For nearly five thousand years Cycladic figures, or *idols* as they are freely called, have held a strange fascination. During the period of their manufacture in the third millennium B.C., when they were buried with the dead, they were also exported beyond the Cyclades (which explains the Earl's good fortune in Attica) and were even imitated on the Greek mainland and on Crete. Chance finds, usually fragmentary, treasured as magically charged relics of the dim past, are occasionally found in later Bronze Age contexts and beyond: one little torso was buried beside an adolescent in a grave at Argos almost two thousand years after it was made, while the head of a similar figure was found in a remote Hellenistic watchtower on Siphnos.

In recent times Cycladic sculptures were at first considered, pejoratively, primitive – at best images to be conserved as curiosities from the furthest reaches of Greek history. In the twentieth century they have come to be treasured for the compelling combination of their moon-bright marble and their essential forms – their aesthetic magic – and for the mystery that envelops them. They are frequently compared to the works of Brancusi or Modigliani. Picasso is said to have remarked about a Cycladic figure in his own possession: "Better than Brancusi. Nobody has ever made an object stripped that bare."[1] Today the works of the Early Bronze Age Cycladic sculptors span the millennia, taking their places with equal presence and power beside objects of ancient, ethnographic, and contemporary art.

Cycladic sculpture is scattered in museums and private collections throughout the world. Not a few of these are primarily collections of modern or tribal art. This widespread popularity, which has intensified dramatically in the last twenty years, has had serious consequences for the study of Cycladic art and culture, affecting both the scope and the very nature of possible art historical research. For, to meet the strong demand, unauthorized excavation of Cycladic sites has flourished uncontrollably and, unless strict measures are taken soon, it appears that it will end only when the sources are forever exhausted. As a result, for the great majority of the known pieces of sculpture the precise find-places have been lost (or, worse, falsified) and nothing is known about the circumstances or the contexts of their discovery.

Archaeologists, for various reasons, have been powerless to keep pace with these clandestine activities. Only a relatively small number of figures have been recovered in sanctioned excavations. Without wishing to minimize their importance, it must be said that most of these excavations are problematical in some way. In the earlier ones (e.g., those of Bent on Antiparos and Stephanos on Naxos) much important information was not recorded and in some cases the finds are now no longer traceable. More recent excavations (e.g., those of Doumas on Naxos and Paros), while very careful, have taken place in cemeteries already partially plundered so that the picture we have of them is necessarily incomplete. Some sites had been disturbed already in antiquity either by subsequent occupation (e.g., Aplomata on Naxos) or possible geologic change (e.g., the site on Keros opposite the islet of Daskaleio). Some investigations remain incomplete (e.g., those on Keros). Some remain altogether unpublished (e.g., those of Kontoleon conducted on Naxos nearly four decades ago), while others await final publication, which will free the finds for further study by others (e.g., those of Zapheiropoulou on Ano Kouphonisi and of Kontoleon and Lambrinoudakis at Aplomata).[2]

Serious study of the finds and even of the sites has been further bedeviled as a direct result of the popularity enjoyed by Cycladic sculpture outside Greece: forgeries have been introduced,[3] unpublished objects have been stolen, and access to certain sites has been made difficult for security reasons.

The very fragmentary state of the archaeological record has provided ample opportunity for pure speculation to take wing, particularly with regard to a determination of the meaning and purpose of the figures and other finds. On quite a different level, one that directly affects the present study, the lack of provenances and knowledge of associated finds for so many pieces has wrought havoc with our understanding of the distribution patterns of the various sculptural types and of the works of individual sculptors.

By adopting a largely visual approach to the subject of Cycladic sculpture, I have managed to circumvent some of these problems. My primary concern has been to learn as much as possible from an examination of the sculptures themselves, both those with and those without documented provenances. Following a general introduction in which I do touch on such questions as why these figures were carved and in what order (chap. 1), I turn my attention to how they were designed and fashioned (chap. 2) and by "whom" (chaps. 3 through 6), and I conclude with a brief discussion of where they were made (chap. 7). My main interest here has been to isolate pieces attributable to particular sculptors who lived some four-and-a-half thousand years ago and to speculate about their development as artists working within the strict conventions of a sophisticated traditional craft.

My own serious study of Cycladic art dates back to the early 1960s when I was a fellow at the American School of Classical Studies in Athens. At that time I began to gather material for a doctoral dissertation called *Traditional Canon and Individual Hand in Early Cycladic Sculpture*, which was presented to Harvard University in 1972. Since then I have elaborated on certain aspects of the dissertation in a number of articles published in scholarly journals. The present book, written for a much wider readership, goes beyond these earlier writings, incorporating much new material as well as certain basic information for the reader who might not be familiar with the subject.

Note: The bracketed numbers found throughout the book refer to specific works I have to date attributed to sixteen sculptors discussed in detail in chapters 4 through 6. Checklists enumerating the works of each of these artists can be found in Appendix 1.

ACKNOWLEDGMENTS

M A N Y people and institutions have been enormously helpful, patient, and indulgent during the more than twenty years that this work was in progress. I am of course especially indebted to the archaeologists, to the museum curators and their associates, and to the private collectors who generously made their objects available and provided information and/or photographs, graciously complying whenever possible with requests for particular views, clearer photographs, or photographs taken without bases or supports. Many more people were helpful to me than I can possibly mention by name. Here I would particularly like to thank the following individuals and, where appropriate, the institutions with which they are or were affiliated at the time the research and writing were carried out: Lila Marangou (Greek Archaeological Service, Amorgos); Christos Doumas (National Archaeological Museum, Athens); Dolly Goulandris (Athens); Olga Tzachou-Alexandri (National Archaeological Museum, Athens); Photeini Zapheiropoulou (Ephor of the Cyclades, Greek Archaeological Service, Athens); Herbert Cahn (Basel); Marie-Louise Erlenmeyer (Basel); Elisabeth Rohde (Staatliche Museen zu Berlin, Antikensammlung, E. Berlin); Ulrich Gehrig and Wolf-Dieter Heilmeyer (Staatliche Museen Preussischer Kulturbesitz, W. Berlin); Adriana Calinescu (Indiana University Art Museum, Bloomington); J. Gy. Szilágyi (Szépmüvészeti Múzeum, Budapest); Richard Nicholls (Fitzwilliam Museum, Cambridge); Michael Lloyd (Australian National Gallery, Canberra); B. C. Holland (Chicago); Jane Biers (Museum of Art and Archaeology, University of Missouri, Columbia); Søren Dietz (Antiksamlingen, Nationalmuseet, Copenhagen); Hans Rost (Staatliche Kunstsammlungen, Skulpturensammlung, Dresden); David Robb and Ruth Sullivan (Kimbell Art Museum, Fort Worth); Irène de Charrière (Musée Barbier-Müller, Geneva); Nicholas Koutoulakis (Geneva); Ioannis Sakellarakis (Archaeological Museum, Herakleion); Dominique de Menil (Houston); Mary

Jane Victor (Menil Foundation, Houston); Uri Avida (Israel Museum, Jerusalem); Jürgen Thimme (Badisches Landesmuseum, Karlsruhe); the late John Caskey (Director, University of Cincinnati excavations on Kea); the late Marianne Schuster (Lausanne); Brian Cook and J. Lesley Fitton (British Museum, London); Felicity Nicholson (Sotheby's, London); Sir Robert Sainsbury (London); Robin Symes (London); Paolo Morigi (Lugano); Sylvia Törnkvist (Klassiska Institutionen och Antikmuseet, Lund); Jiří Frel and Marion True (J. Paul Getty Museum, Malibu); Klaus Vierneisel (Staatliche Antikensammlungen und Glyptothek, Munich); Olga Hadjianastasiou (Greek Archaeological Service, Naxos); Vasilis Lambrinoudakis (Greek Archaeological Service, Naxos); Annika Barbarigos (New York); Christos Bastis (New York); Maurice Bonnefoy (New York); Gregory Callimanopulos (New York); André Emmerich (New York); Richard Keresey (Sotheby's, New York); George Lois (New York); Edward Merrin (New York); Joan Mertens and Dietrich von Bothmer (Metropolitan Museum of Art, New York); Alan Safani (New York); Alexandra Stafford and Mrs. Frederick Stafford (New York); Paul and Marianne Steiner (New York); Michael Ward (New York); Andrea Woodner and Ian Woodner (New York); Graham Beal and Alan Borg (Sainsbury Centre for Visual Arts, University of East Anglia, Norwich); Ann Brown and Michael Vickers (Ashmolean Museum, Oxford); Sophie Descamps, Françoise Gaultier, Marie Montembault, Alain Pasquier, and François Villard (Musée du Louvre, Paris); Carlo Fallani (Rome); Renée Beller Dreyfus (Fine Arts Museums of San Francisco, San Francisco); Marie-Louise Winbladh (Medelhavsmuseet, Stockholm); Saburoh Hasegawa (National Museum of Western Art, Tokyo); Polly Roulhac and Frances Smyth (National Gallery of Art, Washington, D.C.); Francie Woltz (Hirshhorn Museum and Sculpture Garden, Washington, D.C.); Hansjörg Bloesch (Winterthur); Elly and Isidor Kahane (Zürich); Heidi Vollmoeller (Zürich); and a number of other people who prefer not to have their names mentioned. The present locations of a few of the pieces illustrated here are not known to me. Photographs, as well as permission to publish them, were provided by former owners.

For sharing their ideas with me, for offering welcome suggestions or important information, for help and encouragement in manifold ways practical or spiritual or both, I would like to thank Gibson Danes, Jack Davis, Christos Doumas, Efstathios Eleftheriou, Karen Foster, Ilse Getz-Danes, Dolly Goulandris, Olga Hadjianastasiou, Norman Herz, Martha Joukowsky, Mary Laing, Joan Mertens, David Mitten, Sarah Morris, Elizabeth Oustinoff, Colin Renfrew, Jeremy Rutter, Klaus Sommer, Manya Stamatopoulou, Jürgen Thimme, Saul Weinberg, and Photeini Zapheiropoulou.

Because of the focus of the text and out of a desire to keep the notes to a minimum, I have not always acknowledged my colleagues' ideas or discussed their differing opinions, although this work owes much to them. The pertinent contributions to the field of these scholars are, however, cited in the bibliography.

I am grateful, too, to the Archaeological Institute of America for awarding me the Olivia James Traveling Fellowship in 1974−75 to undertake a study of the large collection of sculpture fragments known as the "Keros hoard" that figures prominently in this book; and to the American Council of Learned Societies for selecting me in 1981 for a fellowship funded under a gifts-and-matching grant from the National Endowment for the Humanities to write the book, and in 1984 for a grant-in-aid for further research in the Cyclades.

Finally, I would like to thank a few of the people involved in preparing *Sculptors of the Cyclades* for publication: Lydia Duff and Elizabeth Oustinoff for their careful typing of the manuscript, and Eugenia Joyce Fayen for patiently making drawings to my often confusing specifications; for their guidance and help at various stages leading to publication I am also indebted to Jiří Frel and Sandra Knudsen Morgan of the J. Paul Getty Museum, Deborah Marrow of the J. Paul Getty Trust, and John Griffiths Pedley of the University of Michigan.

CONTENTS

Chapter One
The Marble Isles:
An Introduction to the Early Bronze Age Cyclades   3

Chapter Two
The Sculptural Tradition   35

Chapter Three
Isolating the Individual Hand   57

Chapter Four
Three Archaic Sculptors   71

Chapter Five
Eight Classical Sculptors   83

Chapter Six
Five Late Classical Sculptors   115

Chapter Seven
Ending on a Geographical Note   131

EPILOGUE   141

ABBREVIATIONS   143

NOTES   145

APPENDIXES

Appendix One
Checklists of Figures Attributed to Sixteen Sculptors   155

Appendix Two
Size Range of Works Attributed to Sixteen Sculptors   165

BIBLIOGRAPHY   167

INDEX   173

PLATES   177

ILLUSTRATIONS

Plates
(following p. 177)

Color

I. Plastiras-type figures of the Early Cycladic I phase

II. Special figures of the Early Cycladic II phase

III. Musician figures

IV. Marble vases of the Early Cycladic I phase

V. Figure with "cradle" and three marble vases of the
Early Cycladic II phase

VI. Figures with painted details

VII. Figures with painted (*A, C, D*) or unusual carved detail (*B*)

VIII. Musician groups of the Early Cycladic II phase

IX. Works attributed to the Goulandris Master

X. A nearly life-size figure

XI. Head of an unusually large, elongated figure

Black and White

1. One-piece compositions with two and three figures

2. Groups of figures from graves of the Early Cycladic I phase

3. Groups of figures from graves of the transitional phase

4. Groups of figures from graves of the Early Cycladic I phase

5. Two of three figures said to be from a grave on Naxos

6. The pair of figures from grave 10 at Spedos on Naxos

7–8. A pair of harp players said to have been found together

9. A pair of harpers said to have been found in a grave on Thera

10. The double pipes player and harper from a grave on Keros

11 – 12. A group of four figures said to have been found together
on Naxos (A) and two related figures (B, C)

13. The pair of figures from grave 14 at Dokathismata on Amorgos

14 – 15. Works attributed to the Doumas Master

16 – 17. Works attributed to the Metropolitan Museum Master

18 – 20. Works attributed to the Athens Museum Master

21 – 22. Works attributed to the Kontoleon Master

23. Works attributed to the Israel Museum Master

24 – 25. Works attributed to the Copenhagen Master

26 – 27. Works attributed to the Fitzwilliam Master

28 – 30. Works attributed to the Steiner Master

31 – 33. Works attributed to the Naxos Museum Master

34 – 37. Works attributed to the Goulandris Master

38 – 39. Works attributed to the Bastis Master

40 – 41. Works attributed to the Schuster Master

42 – 43. Works attributed to the Ashmolean Master

44 – 45. Works attributed to the Berlin Master

46 – 47. Works attributed to the Stafford Master

48 – 50. Works attributed to the Dresden Master

Figures

1. The Cyclades   2

2. The Aegean basin, with find-places of Cycladic sculpture outside
the Cyclades   6

3. The typological development of the female figure in Cycladic art   8

4. Late Neolithic and Early Bronze I approaches to the female
form compared   10

5. Stages in the development of Cycladic sculpture showing the
gradual reduction of risk in the treatment of the legs   12

6. Precanonical figures: points in the development of the folded
arrangement of the arms   14

7. The development of the profile   15

8. Some figures with arm perforations   16

9. Chalandriani-variety figures: departures from the canonical
folded arrangement of the arms   18

10. The Koumasa variety: a) angular; b) rounded   19

11. Some male figures   21
12. Some fragmentary two-figure (and three-figure?) compositions   22
13. Figure with "cradle" showing the manner in which the figure may have been secured   24
14. The Cyclades with major find-places of Neolithic and Early Bronze Age marble sculpture   28
15. The planning of archaic figures of the Plastiras type: *a*) the traditional three-part canon; *b*) an unusual early example of the four-part canon   37
16. The planning of classical figures of the Spedos variety: the four-part canon applied identically on figures carved by different sculptors   37
17. The planning of late classical figures of the Dokathismata variety: the four-part canon applied by means of a compass (*a*) and by means of a straight edge (*b*)   38
18. The planning of late classical figures of the Chalandriani variety: *a*) a five-part design; *b*) a three-part design   38
19. The planning of a "tandem" two-figure composition   40
20. The planning of a standing woodwind player   40
21. The planning of two harp players   42
22. The harmonic system: *a*) "golden triangle"; *b*) Minoan double axe sign; *c*) Minoan masons' marks; *d*) suggested schema for an Early Bronze Age protractor   43
23. Examples of the harmonic system   44
24. The planning of the three-figure group   46
25. The folded-arm arrangement: asymmetrical (*a, b*) and symmetrical (*c, d*) renderings   48
26. The folded-arm arrangement and the depiction of pregnancy   49
27. Some figures with abdominal bands   50
28. The depiction of fingers   51
29. Detail of a figure with elaborate painted detail   55
30. One of two seated female figures from grave 15 at Aplomata   61
31. Find-places of figures attributed to the Doumas Master   73
32. Comparison of the proportions of the three figures attributed to the Metropolitan Museum Master   75
33. The planning of figures attributed to the Metropolitan Museum Master   76
34. The planning of the Athens Museum Master's name-piece   79
35. The planning of figures attributed to the Kontoleon Master   84
36. The planning of figures attributed to the Israel Museum Master   87

37. The planning of figures attributed to the Fitzwilliam Master   91
38. The planning of figures attributed to the Steiner Master   93
39. The planning of figures attributed to mature phases of the Naxos Museum Master's career   97
40. The planning of figures attributed to the Goulandris Master   102
41. The effect of the harmonic system on the design of figures attributed to the Goulandris Master: *a*) an early work; *b*) a mature work   103
42. Painted facial detail on figures attributed to the Goulandris Master   105
43. Painted details on the sides and/or backs of the heads of figures attributed to the Goulandris Master   106
44. Possible painted detail on a name-piece of the Goulandris Master   107
45. Painted detail on the forearms of a figure attributed to the Goulandris Master   107
46. The planning of figures attributed to the Bastis Master   109
47. A comparison of figures attributed to the Goulandris and Bastis masters   111
48. Find-places of works attributed to the four late Spedos-variety masters discussed in chapter 5   112
49. The planning of figures attributed to the Ashmolean Master   118
50. The planning of figures attributed to the Berlin Master   121
51. The planning of a figure attributed to the Stafford Master (*a*) and the effect of the hypothetical harmonic system (*d*) on the design of the sculptor's name-piece (*b, c*)   125
52. The planning of a figure attributed to the Dresden Master   127
53. The distribution of works attributed to the sculptors discussed in chapters 5 and 6   132

Sculptors of the Cyclades

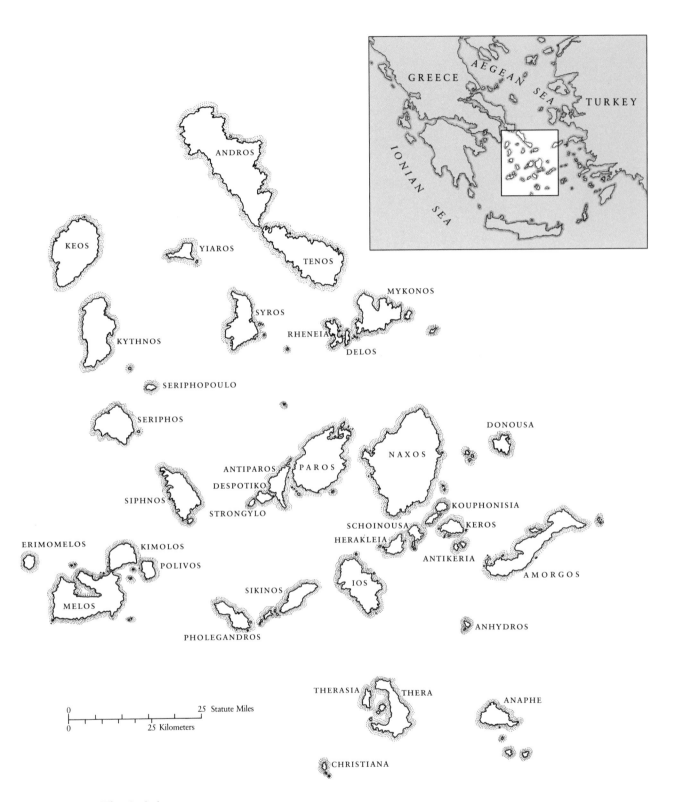

FIG. 1. The Cyclades

Chapter One

The Marble Isles:
An Introduction to the Early
Bronze Age Cyclades

Barren rockpiles rising out of the sea – sun-baked, wind-buffeted: these are the Cyclades on first acquaintance. An archipelago of some thirty small islands, innumerable islets, and stray rocks, they consist essentially of the exposed summits of two submerged mountain ridges that extend in two south / southeasterly curves from Attica and Euboia. The more westerly string includes Keos, Kythnos, Seriphos, Siphnos, Pholegandros, Sikinos, Ios, and Amorgos; while the eastern string is composed of Andros, Tenos, Mykonos, Rheneia, and Delos. The largest, most central islands in the group, Naxos and Paros, with some of their smaller neighbors as well as Syros, lie between these two chains. The volcanic islands, Melos and Thera (Santorini), and remote Anaphe lie somewhat beyond and to the south. The total land mass of the Cyclades is roughly 2,580 square kilometers. About 10 percent of this area is arable (fig. 1).

Initially these islands appear stark and forbidding, every detail of the rocky landscape illuminated by the crystal clear light for which the Aegean is famous, but their terrain is really quite varied – in places even Arcadian, with olive groves and terraced vineyards and fields of grain. Hidden from view as one approaches from the sea are fertile valleys and upland hollows covered with thistle and scrub for grazing hardy flocks. The coastlines of the islands are irregular and for the most part precipitous, with few sandy coves, though nearly every island possesses at least one deep bay that affords a sheltered anchorage. Many of these bays are rimmed by small patches of fertile plain or gently sloping hillsides.

The climate of the Cyclades is generally temperate and reliable for crops, but during periods of calm in summer it can be extremely hot, while the damp winter can be uncomfortably cold, especially in the higher altitudes. The islands are not infrequently blasted by severe windstorms that can whip the usually mild-mannered Aegean into a sudden frenzy,

3

making journeys in small craft treacherous, and even today can effectively strand the traveler and cut off communications with the mainland or with other islands for days at a time.

Although especially sere in summer, in the damper winter and spring months the Cyclades are green and carpeted with wildflowers and aromatic herbs. In prehistoric times the vegetation was probably somewhat more abundant. Indiscriminate tree cutting and over-grazing by the ubiquitous goat from antiquity on have combined with the winds to exact their toll in soil erosion and deforestation. There also was once plenty of small game to hunt on the islands and, before the nefarious practice of dynamiting took hold a century or more ago, many fish in the sea.

In antiquity Paros was renowned for her figs; Naxos and Tenos for wine; Tenos also for garlic; Delos for doves and Anaphe for partridges; while Paros and Naxos were famous for their marble; Siphnos for her gold and silver mines; and Melos and Thera for a variety of volcanic minerals. Each of the islands in the archipelago has its own special physical character. Each varies in relative productivity according to its size, elevations, geology, and soils, but even on those endowed with the most fertile fields and mineral resources life has always been hard, requiring equal measures of fortitude, industry, and ingenuity to wrest from them even a modest living. The remark made by the men of Andros to Themistocles that two deities, Poverty and Want, had never left their island (Herodotus 8.111.2–3) was doubtless applicable earlier than the fifth century B.C. and to other islands besides Andros. Probably few islanders were ever able to acquire more than the bare necessities of life.

The Early Bronze Age Culture

In classical times the Cyclades (Kyklades) comprised those islands that were thought to form a circle (kyklos) around the holy island of Delos, birthplace of Apollo and Artemis. The rest of the islands now grouped under this name were then included in the southern Sporades ("scattered ones"). We do not know what the prehistoric inhabitants might have called the archipelago, or if they even had a collective name for their islands. But we do know that in the third millennium B.C. the Cyclades provided the environment for a vigorous independent pre-Greek culture to take hold and flourish. Some of the islands were already populated, although sparsely, in the Middle and Late Neolithic ages, probably due in part to their proximity to Melos, the major Aegean source of obsidian. This highly prized volcanic glass was used to make all sorts of tools and weapons and was preferred for these purposes even long after the introduction of metalworking. (It was in fact still used in modern times on threshing sleds.) By the beginning of the third millennium B.C. the population had grown, most of the islands in the group had been settled, and now the Cyclades became an important force in the shaping of the Early Bronze Age civilization of the Aegean basin.

Situated to the north of Crete, these islands form a natural bridge of stepping-stones between Crete (which eventually overshadowed the Cyclades later in the Bronze Age), main-

land Greece, and Asia Minor. Yet, with the exception of Keos and Andros close to the mainland, the Cyclades were, despite their central position at the crossroads of the Aegean, essentially remote and inward looking. Apart from one cylinder seal inspired by north Syrian
models found on Amorgos and the impressions of what might have been an Egyptian stamp
seal on a clay jar from Syros,[4] there is no tangible evidence of any foreign influence or presence in the Cyclades from outside the Aegean at this time. Nor are there any objects that
could definitely be called imports from nearby regions.[5] Still, by the middle of the millennium there must have been a lively trade in goods and raw materials and an exchange of ideas
going on among the Cyclades and the neighboring cultures of Minoan Crete, Helladic
Greece, and the coast and offshore islands of Asia Minor. (Certain pottery forms, orna-
ments, and implements are common to all the Aegean subcultures at this time even though
each of these regions maintained an individual character by preserving its own cultural traditions.) What the islanders received in exchange for finished objects (sculpture, pottery), and
raw materials (obsidian and metal ores and perhaps emery) traded beyond their own orbit
must have been largely perishable in any case (fig. 2).

Although they had boats that were well suited for traveling the Aegean waterways, it is
likely that most of the islanders were, as they are now, more at home on land than on water.
In the Cyclades, although one is almost always aware of the presence of the surrounding sea,
the landscape is one of hills and highlands, and with the exception of the fishermen, mer-
chants, and middlemen who hug the perimeters of the islands and maintain outside contacts,
Cycladic people have essentially always been uplanders in spirit, with neither great fondness
for nor familiarity with the sea about them. Even today it is not uncommon to find an older
farmer or shepherd who has never left his island.

Easily accessible to each other over short sea passages – one is never out of sight of land
for long – yet rather detached from the world at large by the absence of daily contact by
many with it, the Cycladic people resourcefully created their own world in response to their
particular insular setting. Little is known of the material manifestations of daily life in the
small fishing, farming, and herding communities of the Early Bronze Age Cyclades. Much
like the fieldstone houses and chapels on the islands today, which if not attended to regularly
simply fall apart, their homes and shrines – along with their simple tools and utensils – have
for the most part vanished, their crumbled walls reclaimed by the stony fields.

The products of the Early Cycladic culture left to us are for the most part those which
the islanders buried with their dead. Given a life of hard work and little comfort, death may
have been regarded as the most enduring part of their existence and when possible they pre-
pared themselves for it with objects specially fashioned. For figurative sculpture and for vessels the preferred substance was marble. Chalk-white and gleaming, it is common to nearly
all the Cyclades. So common is it, in fact, and so widely used by these early islanders that
they might well have thought to call their archipelago "the marble isles." Their cramped
boxlike graves have yielded an assortment of items crafted in local materials: tools and weapons of Melian (and occasionally Antiparian) obsidian and of bronze; jewelry (pins, rings,

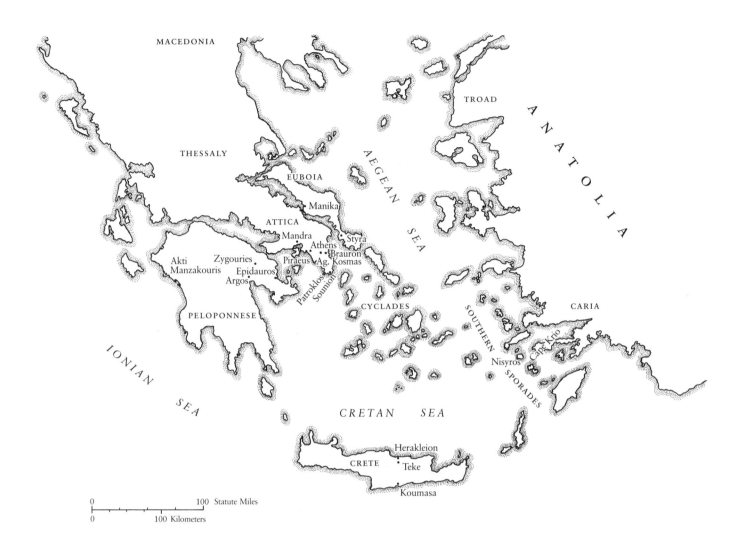

MACEDONIA

TROAD

A N A T O L I A

THESSALY

A E G E A N

EUBOIA

Manika

S E A

ATTICA

Mandra   Styra

Athens

Zygouries   Brauron

Akti   Piraeus Ag. Kosmas

Manzakouris   Epidauros   Patroklos

Argos   Sounion

CARIA

CYCLADES

PELOPONNESE

SOUTHERN

Cape Krio

I O N I A N   Nisyros   SPORADES

S E A

C R E T A N   S E A

Herakleion

CRETE   Teke

Koumasa

0   100 Statute Miles

0   100 Kilometers

FIG. 2. The Aegean basin, with find-places of Cycladic sculpture outside the Cyclades

beads, amulets, diadems, etc.) fashioned in shell, stone, bone, bronze, and silver; pottery in a variety of forms; elaborately carved soapstone boxes; and other objects made of Siphnian lead, silver (probably largely from Siphnos), shell, and bone. It is, however, the objects made of marble that are the most arresting products of this sepulchral side of the Cycladic culture – the most easily recognized as Cycladic in concept and spirit.

Culture Sequence and Chronology

The Cycladic Early Bronze Age can be logically divided into three main phases. Although the material culture of each phase was remarkably homogeneous from island to island, it is quite possible that these phases may have varied in duration from place to place. It is also possible that all three phases did not occur on some islands. The chronology of the three "cultures" is relative, but the sequence is clear. It is the first two phases of the Early Cycladic period that saw the development, perfection, and eventual decline of the marble master's craft. By the third phase, marble objects had all but ceased to be made and indeed marble as an important material for sculpture is not seen in the Aegean for some fifteen hundred years when once again Cycladic sculptors excelled in its use and led the way in productivity, energy, and innovation.

There has been much argument in recent years as to whether cultural designations named after typical sites or chronological ones are preferable for describing the Cycladic sequence that is based for the most part on the excavation of unstratified sites. For the purposes of broad definition (which is all that will be necessary in this study) either system or both may be used if one bears in mind that the chronological termini may vary in different places and in any case are probably only accurate to within one or two hundred years or so. Thus, the initial phase that endured roughly from 3200 to 2800 B.C. is called the Grotta-Pelos culture (though some prefer the term Pelos-Lakkoudes) or Early Cycladic (EC) I. There followed, on some islands at least, a transitional phase (placed by some scholars at the end of the first, by others at the beginning of the second) that might be called the Kampos-Louros culture (usually it is referred to as the Kampos Group) or Early Cycladic I / II. This might have lasted a century or two. The second phase, the Keros-Syros culture, or Early Cycladic II, endured to the beginning of the Phylakopi I culture, Early Cycladic III, around 2200 B.C.

The phases of the Early Bronze Age in the Cyclades conform roughly to the divisions used for other Aegean subcultures: Early Helladic I–III on the Greek mainland and Early Minoan I–III on Crete, for example. They are based in most general terms on changes that occur in the pottery, although each culture phase has its own particular assemblage of objects in various categories. In the Cyclades the earliest sepulchral pottery features incised rectilinear decoration; that of the transitional phase introduces incised curvilinear designs; while the second phase sees the development of both stamped curvilinear patterns and dark-on-light painted wares. Plain incised and painted wares return in the third phase. Changes in

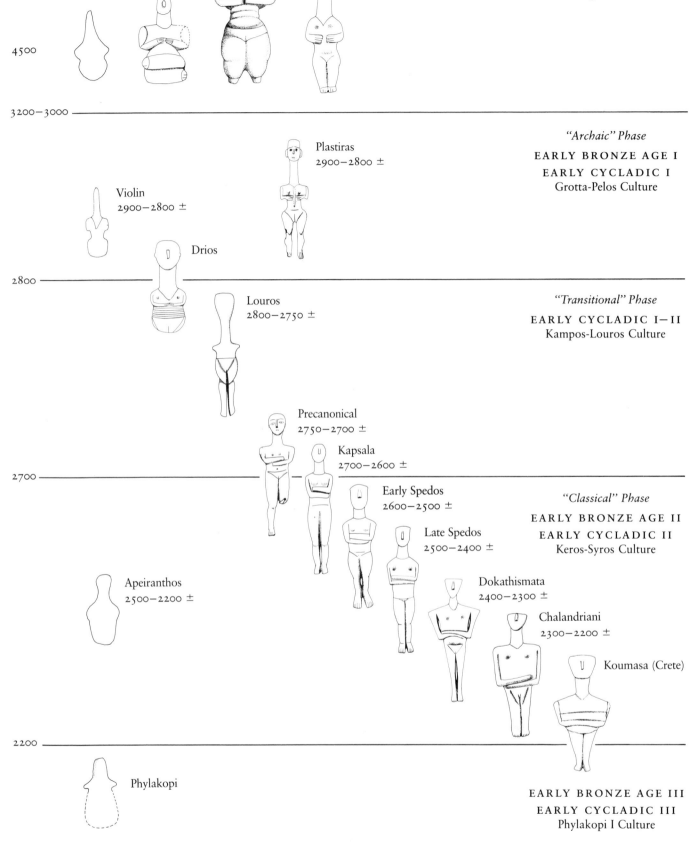

LATE NEOLITHIC AGE
Saliagos Culture

4500

3200–3000

Plastiras
2900–2800 ±

"Archaic" Phase

EARLY BRONZE AGE I
EARLY CYCLADIC I
Grotta-Pelos Culture

Violin
2900–2800 ±

Drios

2800

Louros
2800–2750 ±

"Transitional" Phase

EARLY CYCLADIC I–II
Kampos-Louros Culture

Precanonical
2750–2700 ±

Kapsala
2700–2600 ±

2700

Early Spedos
2600–2500 ±

"Classical" Phase

EARLY BRONZE AGE II
EARLY CYCLADIC II
Keros-Syros Culture

Late Spedos
2500–2400 ±

Apeiranthos
2500–2200 ±

Dokathismata
2400–2300 ±

Chalandriani
2300–2200 ±

Koumasa (Crete)

2200

Phylakopi

EARLY BRONZE AGE III
EARLY CYCLADIC III
Phylakopi I Culture

FIG. 3. The typological development of the female
figure in Cycladic art. All dates are approximate
and relative.

pottery shapes accompany each major change in decoration. The marble objects may also be divided, morphologically, into two distinct groups with, at least for the figurative sculpture, a transitional phase in between. These divisions correspond chronologically to the changes that occurred in Cycladic ceramics.

The Figurative Sculpture

As previously mentioned, the overwhelming majority of the figures that survive are made of marble. Examples in Theran pumice, shell, Siphnian lead, as well as other stones are the rare exceptions. It is, of course, possible that some if not most of the figures actually made were of wood, but it is doubtful that such a practice could ever be verified.[6] In size the figures vary from miniatures of a few centimeters to nearly life-size works; the majority do not exceed 30 cm (or 1 ft). The female form, sometimes shown pregnant, dominates throughout; male figures account for only about 5 percent of the total number known. Although in some examples no primary sexual markings are indicated, these figures are, with the exception of certain seated ones, usually assumed to represent females. In terms of naturalism, the sculptures range from simple modifications of stones shaped and polished by the sea to developed representations of the human form with subtle variations of contour and harmonious proportions.

A characteristic feature of Cycladic sculpture throughout its development, from its earliest beginnings in the Neolithic Age, was the synchronous manufacture, probably by the same sculptors, of both a shorthand version of the human form and a fully elaborated one (fig. 3). The schematic figure, derived ultimately from prototypes rendered in a sitting posture, was probably the less expensive version since it was small and could easily be shaped from a beach pebble.

Typology

Archaic Figures

The forms that Cycladic sculpture took sometime after the beginning of the Early Bronze Age appear directly related to the figures carved in much smaller numbers during the preceding Neolithic Age. From this earlier tradition the Bronze Age sculptors adopted the arm position in which the hands meet over the abdomen, fingertips touching (pl. I). Exaggerated corpulence, the hallmark of the Stone Age style, was now reduced to a two-dimensional, strongly frontal scheme: the new figure type, which is called the *Plastiras* after the site of a cemetery on Paros where four examples were recovered from a single grave, are broad across the hips, but unlike their Neolithic predecessors, their profile planes are contained within

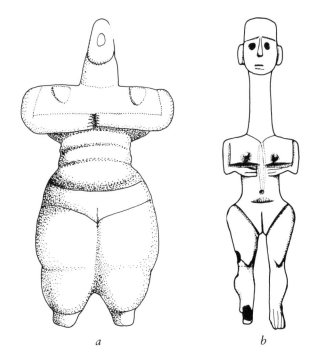

FIG. 4. Late Neolithic and Early Bronze I approaches to the female figure compared.

    a. Neolithic. Munich, Prähistorische Staatssammlung 1984, 3438 (ex Henri Smeets Collection). H. 13.5 cm. Provenance unknown. Acquired on Malta in 1935. (*ACC*, no. 3.)

    b. Plastiras type. New York, Metropolitan Museum of Art 45.11.18. H. 21.8 cm. Provenance unknown. Metropolitan Museum Master [2], pls. 16, 17.

a   *b*

narrow limits (fig. 4). It is doubtful that this fundamental change in the sculptor's approach reflects any corresponding change in religious outlook (although not enough is known about the Neolithic find contexts to be certain) nor any corresponding change in secular fashion from a reverence for adiposity to a new fondness for slenderness. It is likely, rather, that the new trend was initiated by the sculptors themselves in order to speed up the carving process. It is conceivable, too, that the gap of several centuries or more between the last Neolithic and the first Early Bronze Age marble figures was bridged by wooden statuettes, and that the forms of the new stone figures, especially their straight profiles, to a significant degree reflect such wooden prototypes.

In this early phase, which from the point of view of the sculpture could conveniently be called the "archaic," the abstract figures, often of violin shape, are characterized by a long headless termination, while their representational counterparts, the Plastiras figures, besides retaining the Neolithic arm position and standing posture, reveal a rather curious combination of exaggerated proportions and keen attention to anatomical detail, both on the face and on the body. The eyeballs were often inlaid in dark stone, another practice which may have been inherited from the Neolithic Age.[7]

Another characteristic of these archaic figures is the complete separation of the legs from the crotch (fig. 5*a*). (On the Neolithic figures normally only the feet are carved as separate entities.) Whatever the motive for this new practice, it was to carry with it a strong element of risk: in quite a few examples the legs broke, perhaps during the carving process

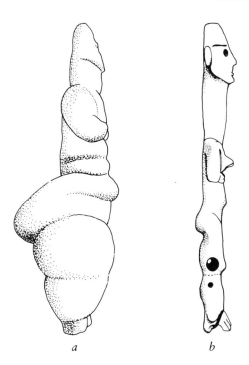

a   *b*

itself, necessitating repairs (pl. IA). Here the early sculptor brought into play one of his favor-
ite implements, a flint or obsidian(?)awl. With it he had made eye sockets, hollowed ears,
navel, buttock dimples, and even complete perforations at the elbows (pls. 16–20). With this
boring tool he now made often rather conspicuous perforations through which a string or
leather thong or bit of wire could be drawn to refasten the broken part.

Transitional Figures

Figures of *Louros* type carved during the transitional phase tend, like the figures of the preceding phase, to be quite small (fig. 5*b*). They appear to be attempts at synthesizing the
abstract and representational approaches to the human form. Certain forms, such as the
featureless face and arms that are merely angular protrusions from the shoulders, are
rendered in a shorthand schematic way, while the legs can be quite well modeled and naturalistic. These flat figures are named after the cemetery at Louros Athalassou on Naxos where
in a single grave a group of seven was found standing upright in a niche. These are the only
examples of their type for which we have a good idea of the associated finds, and it is solely
on the basis of this one unusually rich grave that the *Louros* type is identified as belonging to
the transitional phase. Other "hybrid" figures (e.g., the *Drios* type, named for a site on
Paros) in which a more or less Plastiras-type head is carved on a violin-shaped body are
probably to be similarly dated.

11

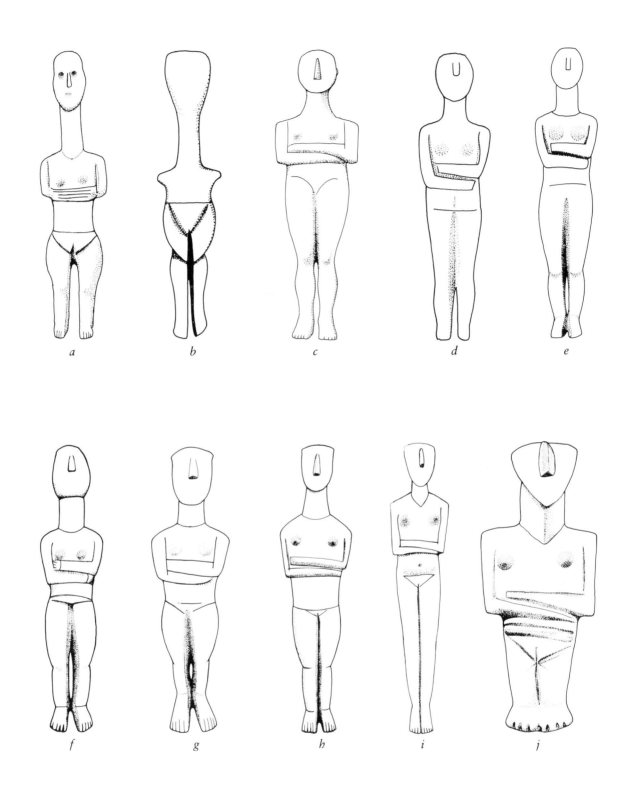

a   b   c   d   e

f   g   h   i   j

FIG. 5. Stages in the development of Cycladic sculpture showing the gradual reduction of risk in the treatment of the legs.

a. Plastiras type. Pasadena Museum of Art (Norton Simon Collection) N.75.18.3.S.A. H. 17.9 cm. Provenance unknown. (*ACC,* no. 69.)

b. Louros type. Athens, National Archaeological Museum 6140.11. H. 18 cm. Grave 26, Louros Athalassou, Naxos. (Pl. 3*A*.5)

c. Precanonical type. Menil Foundation Collection, Houston 73-01 DJ. H. 16.2 cm. Provenance unknown. (*ACC,* no. 115.)

d. Kapsala variety. Athens, National Archaeological Museum 6140.14. H./L. ca. 16 cm. Naxos.

e. Kapsala variety. Athens, National Archaeological Museum 6140.12 L. ca. 17.5 cm. Naxos. Kontoleon Master [1], pls. 21, 22.

f. Early Spedos variety. Private collection. L. 57.2 cm. Provenance unknown. Copenhagen Master [2], pls. 24, 25.

g. Early Spedos variety. New York, Christos G. Bastis Collection. L. 20.6 cm. Provenance unknown. Fitzwilliam Master [2], pls. 26, 27.

h. Late Spedos variety. Bloomington, Indiana University Art Museum 76.25. L. 60 cm. Provenance unknown. Goulandris Master [25].

i. Dokathismata variety. Oxford, Ashmolean Museum AE.176. L. 75.9 cm. "Amorgos." Ashmolean Master [4], pls. 42, 43.

j. Chalandriani variety. Private collection. L. 19 cm. Provenance unknown. Dresden Master [4], pls. 48, 49, 50.

The archaeological record is not much help at this point, and we can only guess that toward or even at the end of the transitional Kampos-Louros phase Cycladic sculptors began on what are called *precanonical* figures to try to convey more naturalistic and balanced proportions.[8] Considerable attention was still paid to individual forms and to details, but already we see this as a diminishing concern. While unknowingly paving the way for the emergence of the classic Cycladic folded-arm figure, these experimental sculptors were also finding new ways to produce full-blown (as opposed to schematic) figures in quantity while at the same time reducing the risk of fracture at key points such as the head/neck juncture and the legs. The neck was usually made shorter and the legs were carved separately for only about half their length, from the knees downward (fig. 5*c*). From now on repairs were much less frequent.

Along with the more natural proportions, which resulted in sturdier, more compressed figures, these early sculptors also seem to have sought a rendering of the arms appropriate to a normal body build. In order to assume the old Neolithic arm position, it is necessary, except in cases of extreme obesity, to hold the elbows and upper arms well away from the sides, leaving a large triangular free space (such as one finds, for example, on many roughly contemporaneous Sumerian figures of stone). An acknowledgment of this gap is indicated by the perforations at the bend of the arms on both a male and a female carved by a sculptor of Plastiras figures (fig. 8*a*).[9] Another sculptor removed a longer section of marble between the torso and upper arms of his figure (fig. 8*b*). Since such measures were fraught with considerable risk, it was probably a desire to give the arms a more realistic rendering without sacrificing safety, rather than any external influence or shift in religious meaning or ritual gesture, that set in motion the development of the folded-arm arrangement (fig. 6). This disposition

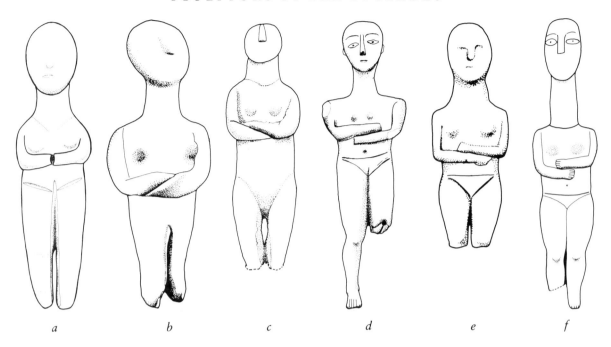

a   b   c   d   e   f

FIG. 6. Precanonical figures: points in the development of the folded arrangement of the arms.

a. Private collection. H. 15.8 cm. Provenance unknown. (*ACC*, no. 110.)

b. Norwich, University of East Anglia, Sainsbury Centre for Visual Arts, UEA 347. H. 9.6 cm. Provenance unknown. (*ACC*, no. 112.)

c. Geneva, Barbier-Müller Museum BMG 202-10. Pres. H. 7. cm. Provenance unknown. (*Classical Art*, no. 7.)

d. Geneva, Barbier-Müller Museum 202-9. H. 15.9 cm. Provenance unknown. (*ACC*, no. 144.) (Fig. 7*b*.)

e. London, British Museum 1984.12-13.10. Pres. H. 13.4 cm. Paros. (*ACC*, no. 116.)

f. Malibu, J. Paul Getty Museum 77.AA.24/ 72.AA.156. H. 28.2 cm. (PGP, *ECS*, pl. II*b*.)

of the arms was to take almost exclusive precedence over all others for most of the succeeding phase. No free space results when the arms are folded across the front of the body, especially if the elbows and upper arms are held close to the sides. Indeed, the early folded-arm figures seem to be tightly clasping themselves.

Classical Figures

The second phase of the Early Cycladic period represents the classical phase of Cycladic sculpture with the fully formed folded-arm figure emerging early on as the canonical image of the islands. This figure type occurs in essentially sequential varieties: the *Kapsala* (named for a cemetery on Amorgos), the early and late *Spedos* (after a cemetery on Naxos), the *Dokathismata* (after another burial ground on Amorgos) and the *Chalandriani* (after a necropolis on Syros). Because each of these varieties developed in a logical progression, from one to the next, probably with some chronological overlap, it is not always easy to assign a

14

figure to one particular variety. Some display separate characteristics or a blending of characteristics of two successive varieties. More simplified and streamlined than its archaic and precanonical precursors, the folded-arm figure was produced in astonishing quantity. Its abstract counterpart, called the *Apeiranthos* type after a village on Naxos, has a simple geometric or baglike body and the neck carries the suggestion of a head.

The earliest true folded-arm figures belong to the Kapsala variety. They are usually modest in size (ca. 30 cm or less) and generally have a slender build with rounded forms. Unlike the earlier figures, their profile axis is more sharply broken, particularly at the top of the head and at the bend of the knees (fig. 7c). Details tend to be modeled or painted rather than incised. The legs are worked separately from the knees or are separated by a deep cleft which is perforated along the calves (fig. 5d, e). The feet can still be held horizontally or

FIG. 7. The development of the profile.

a. Plastiras type. New York, Metropolitan Museum of Art 45.11.18. H. 21.8 cm. Provenance unknown. Metropolitan Museum Master [2], pls. 16, 17.

b. Precanonical type. Geneva, Barbier-Müller Museum BMG 202-9. H. 15.9 cm. Provenance unknown. (*ACC*, no. 114.) (Fig. 6d.)

c. Kapsala variety. Athens, National Archaeological Museum 6140.12. L. 17.5 cm. Naxos. Kontoleon Master [1], pls. 21, 22.

d. Early Spedos variety. New York, Christos G. Bastis Collection. L. 20.6 cm. Provenance unknown. Fitzwilliam Master [2], pls. 26, 27.

e. Late Spedos variety. Athens, Goulandris Collection 281. L. 63.4 cm. "Naxos." Goulandris Master [27], pls. 34, 36, 37.

f. Dokathismata variety. Athens, Goulandris Collection 206. L. 39.1 cm. "Keros." Ashmolean Master [3], pls. 42, 43.

g. Chalandriani variety. Athens, Goulandris Collection 102. L. 30.5 cm. Provenance unknown. (NG, no. 85.) (Fig. 9a.)

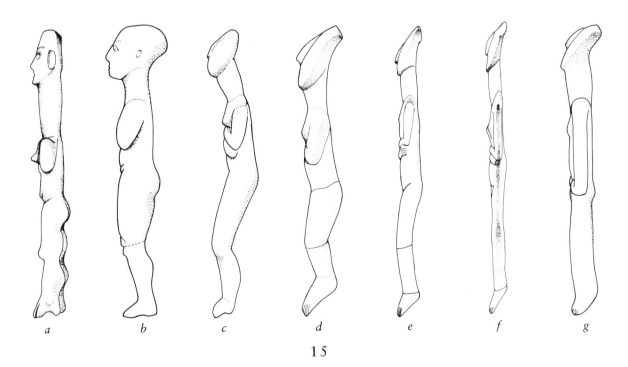

a b c d e f g

FIG. 8. Some figures with arm perforations.

a. Plastiras type. Athens, National Archaeological Museum 3919. H. 30.8 cm. "Amorgos." Athens Museum Master [2], pls. 18, 19, 20.

b. Plastiras type. London, British Museum 1890.9-21.5. H. 19.8 cm. "Grave D, Kapros, Amorgos." (*ACC*, no. 71.)

c. Dokathismata variety. Oxford, Ashmolean Museum 46.114. L. 18.8 cm. "Naxos." (Zervos, fig. 165.)

d. Dokathismata variety. Lund, Klassiska Institutionen och Antikmuseet 646 (ex Sam Wide Collection). Pres. L. 20 cm.

e. Dokathismata variety. New York, Metropolitan Museum of Art 1972.118.103 (bequest of Walter C. Baker). L. 35.9 cm. Provenance unknown. (PGP 1980, no. 33.)

f. Dokathismata variety. Athens, National Archaeological Museum 6174. L. 46 cm. "Syros." (*Aegean Islands*, no. 17.) (Fig. 17*b*.)

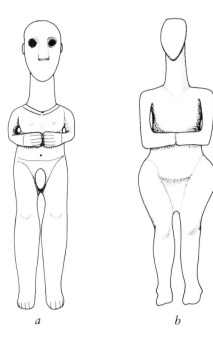

a   *b*

nearly so. A number of the figures in this group were carved in a type of marble whose surface becomes quite pitted during the process of weathering while the crystals seem to fuse in an uncharacteristic way, strongly suggesting that the figures carved in this particular stone were made on the same island – Naxos – and probably in the same locality. Kapsala figures were apparently not carved in large numbers. In some cases it is difficult to know whether to assign a piece to this variety or the next, its natural successor (see the discussion of the Israel Museum Master in chap. 5).

The Spedos variety is the most common and the most widely distributed form in Cycladic marble art and probably enjoyed the longest duration. It also shows the greatest variety in size, with figures ranging from 8 or 9 cm to nearly 150 cm. It seems possible to distinguish at least two general groups within this subtly diverse variety. To the "early" Spedos group belong both figures with a straight profile and a pubic region marked by raised thigh-tops (pls. X, 24–25) as well as figures with a strongly curving outline and accented profile axis, relatively narrow waist, and a curving abdominal line marking the pubic area (figs. 5*g*, 7*d*). The legs are divided normally by a perforated cleft. Beginning with them, all folded-arm figures (except a few very late ones) have feet that point downward and outward at an angle. The backward-tilting head, flexed knees, and angled feet represent a relaxed reclining position that is in marked contrast to the posture of the Plastiras figures. The latter are depicted as standing, though they do not do so unsupported, with their feet parallel to the ground. Again, as with the changes that occurred in the rendering of the arms, the new reclining posture was probably not prompted by a change in religious symbolism or in the function of the figures, nor by any external artistic influence. Rather, because it, too,

16

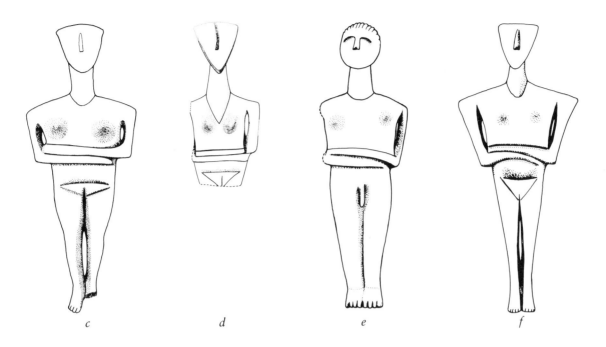

c   *d*   *e*   *f*

evolved gradually, it is probable that the reclining posture was introduced by the sculptors themselves. Since the figures were normally laid on their backs in the grave, it may have made sense to have them recline from the start.[10]

To the "late" Spedos group belong figures with a lyre-shaped head and an incised pubic V that forms a triangle with the center of the abdominal line. These figures have a straight profile and tend to be more elongated than the "earlier" ones, and the leg-cleft is most often unperforated (figs. 5*h*, 7*e*). Details tend to be rendered more by incision than by modeling.

The latest varieties of the classic folded-arm figure are flat, markedly angular, and highly stylized in their treatment of the human form (figs. 5*i*, *j*, 7*f*, *g*). Emphasis is placed on line rather than volume. Details are usually incised. The Dokathismata variety seems to have evolved from the Spedos since some figures combine elements of the two varieties (see the discussion of the Schuster Master in chap. 6). The attenuated, often very refined figures are occasionally quite large (the longest measures nearly 80 cm). The Chalandriani variety is a small, truncated version of the Dokathismata. The midsection is omitted altogether and the shoulders are consequently disproportionately broad. By now the legs are normally separated merely by a thin shallow incision and the feet are often rather rudimentary (figs. 5*j*, 7*g*). Only a few bold sculptors of Dokathismata-variety figures perforated the leg-cleft, although sculptors of both late classical angular varieties occasionally freed the upper arms from the sides of their figures in a hazardous effort to compensate for their extremely broad shoulders and in order to avoid making the upper arms excessively wide (fig. 8*c–f*).

By the beginning of the classical period of Cycladic sculpture, the folded arrangement of the arms had crystallized into a rigidly observed convention. Not only are the arms folded,

17

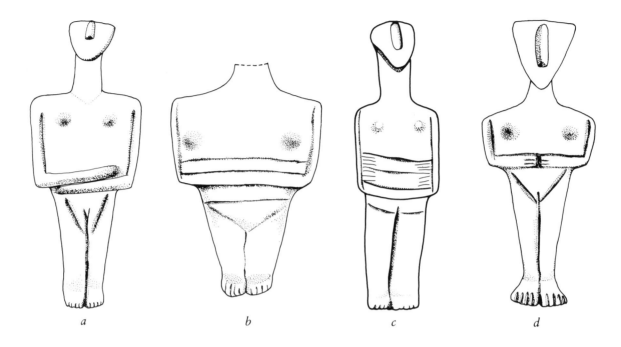

a   b   c   d

but for a long time and with very few exceptions, they are folded in one way only: the right arm is placed below the left. Once the eye has been trained by looking at a large number of these figures, the rare departure from the right-below-left formula will strike the viewer as decidedly odd (e.g., pl. *VA*).

Toward the end of the period of production, the canonical arrangement of the arms, possibly through hackneyed repetition or through a lack of caring, no longer prevailed exclusively. Although a limited revival of interest in the carving of facial detail and hair occurred among Chalandriani-variety sculptors, generally speaking they lavished less care on their works. The proportions were severely distorted for ease of execution and the traditional arm arrangement was often reversed or seemingly ignored or misunderstood (fig. 9). An extreme example is the clumsy figure said to come from Seriphos that appears to have no fewer than three arms and four sets of fingers. Angular figures with arms rendered in an unconventional manner have recently been called "postcanonical." However, at present there is no reason to believe that such figures, which conform to the late classical Chalandriani variety in all other respects, should be considered later than the more conventional figures of this variety.

This is perhaps the place to mention the *Koumasa* variety although it is not, strictly speaking, Cycladic. Named for the location of a communal tomb on Crete, this is an indigenous Cretan version of the folded-arm figure. Among these small, thin, flat statuettes that are found exclusively on the Cyclades' southern neighbor, at least two variations of the basic form can be recognized. One is angular in outline, its shape severely truncated, and is probably an imitation of the angular Cycladic varieties, particularly the Chalandriani. The other is

18

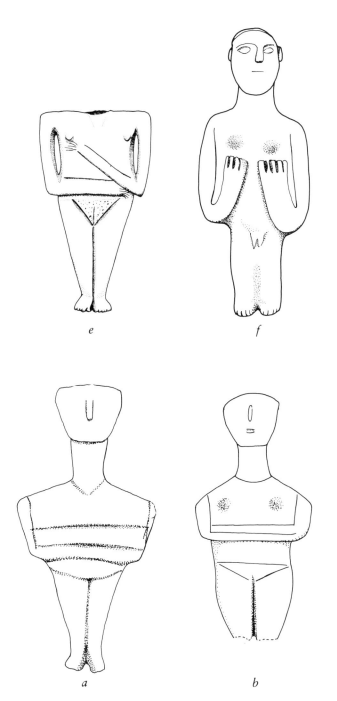

e   f

a   b

FIG. 9. Chalandriani-variety figures: departures from the canonical folded arrangement of the arms.

a. Athens, Goulandris Collection 102. L. 30.5 cm. Provenance unknown. (NG, no. 85.) (Fig. 7g.)

b. Private collection. Pres. L. ca. 13 cm. Provenance unknown. (Sotheby's [New York] 10–11 June 1983, lot 46 [with head of another figure].)

c. E. Berlin, Staatliche Museen, Antikensammlung MJ 8426. L. 22.2 cm. "Seriphos." (ACC, no. 244.)

d. Private collection. L. 30.2 cm. Provenance unknown. (ACC, no. 236.)

e. London, British Museum 1875.3-13.2 Pres. L. 23.6 cm. Provenance unknown. (ACC, no. 239.)

f. Private collection. L. 16.5 cm. Provenance unknown. Goulandris Hunter/Warrior Master. (Pls. 11B, 12B.)

FIG. 10. The Koumasa variety:

a) angular; *b)* rounded.

a. Oxford, Ashmolean Museum AE.172. L. 10.8 cm. "Siteia, Crete." (Renfrew 1969, p. 19, IVE.11 and pl. 6a.)

b. Herakleion, Archaeological Museum 123. Pres. L. 23.6 cm. Communal tomb, Koumasa. (ACC, fig. 138.)

less compressed and shows a more rounded outline, indicating a probable derivation from the Spedos variety (fig. 10). (A few examples of the Spedos variety itself have actually been unearthed on Crete; see discussion of the Fitzwilliam Master in chap. 5.) Koumasa figures, because of their extreme thinness, were prone to fracture and several of them show signs of having been mended.

19

Male Figures / Special Types

One standard representational type predominated in each phase of Cycladic sculpture: the standing female in the archaic phase and the reclining female in the classical phase. There was, however, a wide range of forms carved in the styles of these standard types.

The male figure was depicted in all phases of Cycladic sculpture and in a variety of postures and roles. Male representations occur with relative frequency in the first phase and account for about one-fifth of all the figures of the rather rare Plastiras type (pls. I*B*, 14[4], 18[2]). In keeping with the concern for anatomical structure and detail seen in the female figures of this type, the males are differentiated from the females both by clearly indicated primary sex distinctions as well as by the suggestion of secondary ones: the males tend to be somewhat narrower through the hips and broader through the waist than the females and breasts are either absent or less prominent (pl. I).

The attributes of the male Plastiras figures are also sex-related although not consistently so. Two of them have a belt incised across the front, while two others wear a conical ribbed cap (fig. 11). This was not an exclusively male form of headgear but the more usual headdress for female Plastiras figures is a cylindrical one.

One Louros-type figure wears the conical cap as well as a baldric running from the right shoulder to the left side and an elaborate belt, both in relief. In the absence of genitalia, the baldric and belt identify the figure as male. This is the only Louros figure that there is strong reason to believe represents a male. It is also the earliest figure depicted with a baldric, an attribute appropriate to the hunter/warrior which, after this single known instance, does not recur again until the end of the second phase (fig. 11*f–h*).

With the emergence of the folded-arm female figure as the canonical image of the islands at the beginning of the second or classical phase, there was a very marked increase in sculptural activity, reflecting a new need for marble objects due probably to an increase in both population and relative prosperity. The introduction of bronze tools may have been a contributing factor, but certainly the simpler, streamlined approach now taken by the Cycladic sculptor greatly facilitated the sudden surge in productivity. As already noted, not only was there a remarkable increase in the sheer quantity of ordinary female figures carved, but the standard figure was for the first time often carved on a more monumental scale. It was also a time of ambitious innovation: a whole array of special figure-types carved on a small scale now makes its appearance.

In contrast to the high percentage of male figures within the Plastiras type, there is, curiously, but a single male folded-arm figure from the first half or so of the classical phase rendered in the style of the Spedos-variety female figures.[11] Generally speaking, the male figure is more often shown filling a special role: he appears as a seated harp player, sometimes furnished with an elaborate chair; as a seated cupbearer seeming to propose a toast; as a wood-wind player standing on a rectangular base, syrinx or pipes held to his lips; and as part of a trio consisting of two similarly mounted figures supporting between them a sitting female

20

FIG. 11. Some male figures.

a. Plastiras type. Athens, National Archaeological Museum 3911. H. 25 cm. "Amorgos." (PGP 1980, no. 7.)

b. Plastiras type. Athens, National Archaeological Museum 3912. H. 20 cm. "Antiparos." (PGP 1980, no. 1.)

c. Louros type. Toronto, Royal Ontario Museum 930.80.2. H. 18.5 cm. "Crete." (PGP 1980, no. 8.)

d. Dokathismata variety. Oxford, Ashmolean Museum 1893.72. L. 30.6 cm. "Amorgos." (PGP 1980, no. 32.)

e. Chalandriani variety. Cincinnati, Cincinnati Art Museum 41.1976 (anonymous loan). L. 24.8 cm. "Ios." (PGP 1980, no. 34.)

f. Chalandriani variety. Dresden, Staatliche Kunstsammlungen, Skulpturensammlung ZV 2595. L. 22.8 cm. "Amorgos." Dresden Master [5], pls. 48, 49, 50.

g. Chalandriani variety. Athens, Goulandris Collection 308. L. 25 cm. "Naxos." Goulandris Hunter/Warrior Master. (Pls. 11*A*.1, 12*A*.1.)

h. Chalandriani variety. Seattle, Seattle Art Museum 46.200 (Norman and Amelia Davis Classic Collection). L. 19 cm. Provenance unknown. (PGP 1980, no. 30.)

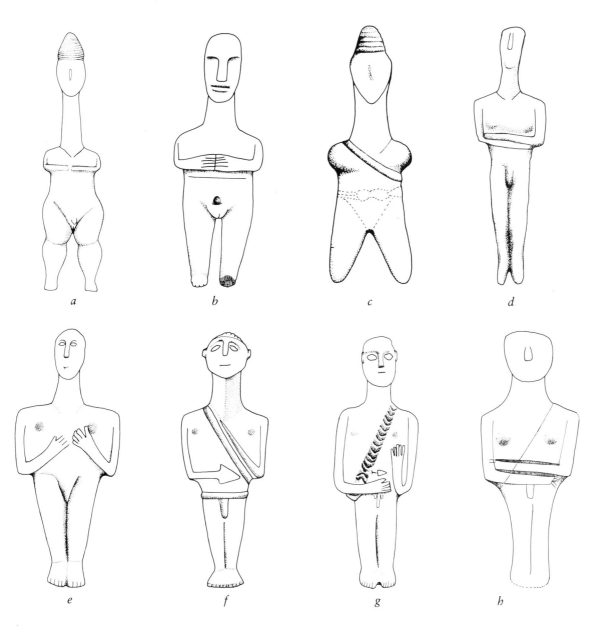

a   *b*   *c*   *d*

e   *f*   *g*   *h*

FIG. 12. Some fragmentary two-figure (and three-figure?) compositions.

a. Spedos-variety style. Athens, Goulandris Collection 339. Pres. L. 5.5 cm (feet of small figure and head with part of neck of larger figure only). Provenance unknown. (NG, no. 137.)

b. Spedos-variety style. Karlsruhe, Badisches Landesmuseum 82/6. Pres. L. 17 cm (right-hand figure missing except for left arm carved on back of left-hand figure, which is missing the head with most of neck, right arm, and legs from above knees). Provenance unknown. (J. Thimme, "Badisches Landesmuseum: Neuerwerbungen 1982," *Jahrbuch B-W* 20[1983]: 196–97.)

c. Spedos-variety style. London, British Museum 84.12-13.7. Pres. L. 16 cm (left-hand figure missing except for right arm carved on back of right-hand figure, which is missing the head with most of neck, most of left arm, lower torso, and legs). "Amorgos." (*ACC*, no. 259.)

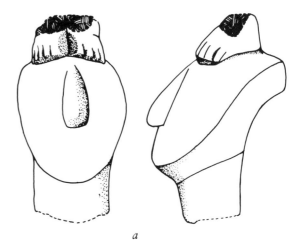

a

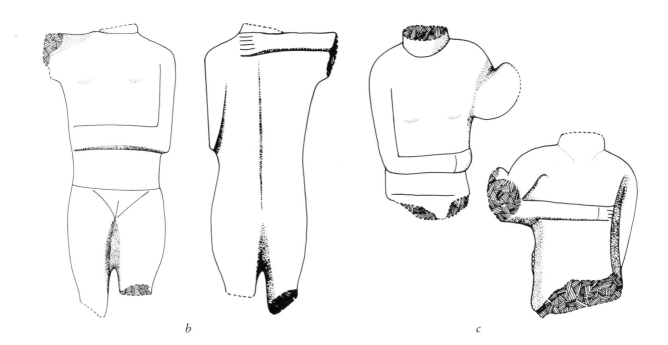

b   *c*

(pls. II*B, C*; III, VIII, 1*C*). The musical instruments and the wine cup are attributes that, like the baldric on the Louros hunter/warrior, identify the figures as male even though many examples of the seated types are devoid of sexual markings.

Unlike the special male figures that are all engaged in an active role, the special females of the early classical phase are all seemingly passive types. Prominent examples are the folded-arm female executed in a semisitting posture but without any stone seat or chair (pl. IIA). The same figure, in two examples seated with feet comfortably crossed (fig. 30), is more often seated on a simple stool like most of the harpers and cupbearers, though she can also be furnished with an elaborately backed chair. There is also the "tandem" two-figure composition in which a small folded-arm figure is carved on the head of a larger one (pl. 1A, B; fig. 12).[12] Another two- or possibly three-figure type (see pl. 1C) is known in which a pair of statuettes is set side by side, each one clasping the other about the shoulder while the free arm is held across the front in the usual position. No more than one of the figures (with the embracing arm of the other) survives in each case. Three of these are insufficiently well preserved to reveal the sex represented, while two others are clearly females. The sex of the missing figure(s) is of course not known.[13]

While the earlier part of the second phase was a time of exuberant self-confidence and virtuosity in Cycladic sculpture, toward the end of the period the spirit of the times seems to have changed, to judge by the radical differences of iconography and style now seen in the sculpture. After a gap of perhaps three centuries from which we have but the single male folded-arm figure mentioned earlier, the plain unaccoutred male returns in small numbers (fig. 11d, e). The hunter/warrior, after an unexplained hiatus of many centuries, also becomes a firmly established if rather rare addition to the sculptor's repertoire, perhaps reflecting some threat to the peace and security of the islands at this time (fig. 11f–h). These male figures are carved in the stylized, angular manner of the contemporaneous late classical Chalandriani- and Dokathismata-variety female figures.

On the hunter/warrior statuettes the most noticeable piece of equipment is always a baldric worn diagonally across the chest. A belt with penis sheath and a prominently displayed dagger are also sometimes present. Sculptors and their patrons alike seem not to have been very particular at this late date, for there are examples in which ordinary female folded-arm figures seem to have been perfunctorily transformed into males by the simple addition of a hastily carved penis and, more noticeably, an incised or merely scratched diagonal line on the chest and back to indicate the baldric. It seems not to have mattered that the baldric was added as an afterthought and cuts across the arms (fig. 11h).

Although some are carved with distinctive hairstyles apparently appropriate to males, in general, these late sculptors seem not to have thought or cared much about making sexual distinctions on their male figures. The breasts of these statuettes are usually similar in appearance to those of the female figures and the genitalia are in some cases only vaguely, even ambiguously, indicated. Structural differentiation of the sexes is altogether lacking in Cycladic sculpture after the Plastiras figures of the archaic phase. If anything, there seems to have been a curious, probably unconscious, tendency on the part of the sculptors of the classical phase to "masculinize" their female figures by giving them increasingly broader shoulders, waistless midsections, and narrow hips. Even the breasts that are either slight generalized swellings or knoblike protuberances on the chest are not particularly "feminine." As a result, the viewer might actually be inclined to call certain female figures males.

23

The Marble Vases

In a very real sense the term "Cycladic sculpture" should embrace both the figures and the often very beautiful stone vessels. The manufacture of stone vases, the majority of which are of marble, coincides chronologically with the production of the figures, and typological changes occur at roughly the same time in both classes of object (pls. IV, V). Moreover, while in the first Early Cycladic phase the range of basic recurring forms is very limited, by the early part of the second phase, there is a remarkable increase both in the number of vessels made and in the number and variety of new shapes. By contrast there seem to have been few, if any, new shapes introduced after this. These phenomena closely parallel the developments that took place in the figurative sculpture.

Stone vases greatly outnumber figures in both the archaic and the classical phases. This disparity is especially marked in the former from which a total of only about forty Plastiras figures survives as opposed to several hundred collared jars of marble. The parallel development of the two types of object in itself suggests that marble vases and figures were made by the same craftsmen, a supposition reinforced by the greater frequency of vessels. Although the craft of figure maker was a highly specialized one, with one possible exception – the Goulandris Master discussed in chapter 5 – there do not seem to be enough examples attributable to any one sculptor to indicate that they were kept busy making figures. If, however, we think of each master as having been responsible for both figures *and* vessels, the problem of seemingly insufficient workload becomes much less troublesome.

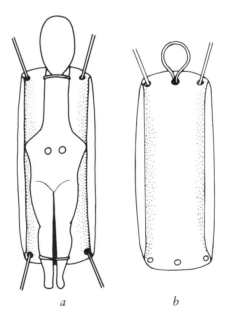

a *b*

FIG. 13. Figure with "cradle" showing the manner in which the figure may have been secured.

a. Louros type. Dresden, Staatliche Kunstsammlungen, Skulpturensammlung 43/446. H. 28.6 cm. "Naxos." (*ACC*, no. 87.)

a/*b*. Trough-shaped palette. Dresden, Staatliche Kunstsammlungen, Skulpturensammlung A.B.429. L. 22.2 cm. "Naxos." (*PGP* 1978, p. 9, *f* with figs. 13–16.)

Stone vases and figures tend to be found in the same cemeteries, occasionally in the same grave. Both probably represent more expensive versions of objects ordinarily made of less durable and more easily worked materials: wood for figures, clay for vases. If in fact there were wooden statuettes they would have been made by wood-carvers (or nonspecialist whittlers) rather than stoneworkers, just as the many surviving clay vases were undoubtedly made by potters, not marble workers. But marble figures and marble vases could easily have been fashioned by the same craft specialist even though different techniques would have been involved for certain steps in the production process in each case. Several more specific points further suggest that the vase maker and the figure maker were one.

From the archaic phase there are two marble beakers that have on one side a representation in relief of a female torso. The typical perforated suspension lugs of these vessels serve as the upper arms.[14] The depiction appears related to the contemporaneous Plastiras type. On these, as already noted, the bend of the elbows was in some examples perforated. In fact, the boring tool was used extensively not only on figures, but also on contemporaneous marble vases. Nearly all the vases of the archaic phase have perforations made with this tool. In addition, the borer was used on both figures and vases to make repairs. There is even one case (the name-grave of the Louros figure type) in which were found both a statuette and a bowl with mending holes. It seems likely that these holes were made by one person using the same implement and equally probable that this person also carved the two objects.

It is probably no coincidence that the horizontally perforated lug, the elbow perforations and indented details on figures, all made with this awl, went out of use at the same time. The new trend toward simplification and streamlining for ease and speed of production seems to have affected figure and vessel similarly. Even the conical or hourglass-shaped repair hole, made with a borer twisted in semirotary fashion, is seen only rarely after the transitional phase. This hand-rotated awl seems to have been largely replaced by a tubular drill that could produce smaller, more cylindrical holes. The new drill was used occasionally in the second or classical phase to make mending perforations and dowel holes (also for repairs) on figures as well as to make vertical perforations in the tubular or horizontal lugs now found on some stone vases. Such parallel developments suggest that the same craftsmen were involved in the manufacture of figures and vessels of marble.

In several cases a marble receptacle, known as a *palette* (and dating to the transitional or early classical phases) is said to have been found with a figure that it is thought to have served as a kind of cradle or pallet. In two examples there are three perforations at each end of the object that were presumably used to fasten the figure to it (fig. 13). Although no example comes from a documented source, it is nevertheless quite possible that figure and palette were carved by the same person who intended them for use in combination with each other. The two objects in each case fit well together in addition to being made of the same material and to being similarly preserved.

Zoomorphic vases are another engaging and varied group. These rare vessels depicting a pig, a sheep, a twin-headed bird, and perhaps a hedgehog are essentially figurative sculpture in the round with one or two bowllike hollows in their backs. There is also a spool-shaped pyxis whose lid has a central knob in the form of a freestanding dove, while a series of large circular trays have a row of thin, flat doves carved across their interiors, strongly resembling schematic figurines in their two-dimensionality.[15]

Finally, there is the charming group of three objects carved in the same scale that form a unified composition: two harp players seated on low stools and a closely similar stool or table surmounted by a miniature footed bowl with spout carved in one piece (pl. VIII*A*). This delightful assemblage vividly calls to mind the musicians who accompany dancing at religious festivals and weddings in Greece today. Set before them invariably is a table with refreshments. Here there can be little doubt that one master was responsible for all three objects. This singular group thus shows that one sculptor could and did carve both figures and vessels.[16]

Unfortunately, the current state of Cycladic excavation and scholarship makes it exceedingly difficult to differentiate individual hands among the many known vases or to identify particular vases as the works of specific sculptors of figures. It can only be surmised that when vases and figures are found in the same grave – especially if the grave contains but a single burial – they are likely to have been the work of one craftsman. However, as few as twenty systematically excavated and recorded graves are now known (published) that held both types of object. Among these the most common vessel is the plain bowl, while in several graves with more elaborate vessels, only examples of the simple schematic figure types were found. Needless to say, it would be extremely difficult, if not impossible, to isolate and compare stylistic nuances in the case of plain bowls and abstract figurines. Since the ultimate purpose of this book is to distinguish the hands of individual sculptors, a study of the marble vessels does not fall within its scope.

Discovery Contexts

The idea that some Cycladic objects at least were deposited in shrines or open air sanctuaries (perhaps closely associated with cemeteries) outside the settlements has yet to be tested through excavation since, with one possible exception (to be discussed in chap. 7), no such sites have yet been located.

With very few exceptions, then, Cycladic figures and stone vessels appear to have been found so far only in sepulchral contexts; the looted graves bear silent witness for the many objects that do not come from sanctioned excavations. In view of the large numbers of marble objects that have been recovered fortuitously in farmers' fields or through clandestine efforts, it is easy to overlook the fact that actually only a small percentage of Cycladic graves were furnished with marble objects. In fact, many hold no nonperishable furnishings at all, while others contain only a simple clay vessel or a few obsidian blades. The following is a brief review of some of the key points in the archaeological record.

26

Frequency of Occurrence of Marble Objects

Toward the end of the last century, Christos Tsountas explored some 233 unplundered graves of the archaic Grotta-Pelos culture in a number of cemeteries on Paros, Antiparos, and Despotiko (fig. 14).[17] In all, he found forty-eight figures, of which forty-six were schematic. Of the 233 graves, 102 were altogether unfurnished; 55 held one clay pot; 19 a few beads or obsidian blades, some with, others without a piece of pottery; 26 contained marble vessels, but only 12 yielded figures. Three of the graves were unusually rich in marble objects although the particular cemeteries to which they belonged were, in general, among the less elaborately furnished: grave 103 at Pyrgos on Paros held fourteen schematic figures (pl. 2*A*), five stone beads, seashells, and a clay jar; grave 117 at Krassades on Antiparos held thirteen similar figurines (pl. 2*B*), a small marble dish, and a marble beaker; and grave 129 at Leivadia on Despotiko held a marble beaker and a marble palette on which had been placed three schematic figures and two pebbles. Thus, these three marble-rich graves yielded a total of thirty of the forty-eight figures found in the 233 graves.

More recently, in the 1960s, Christos Doumas investigated three Grotta-Pelos cemeteries on Paros and Naxos, two of which had been heavily damaged and looted.[18] Only at the third, that of Akrotiri on Naxos, were most of the tombs undisturbed. Of the twenty-nine unplundered and two partially plundered graves excavated by Doumas in the three cemeteries, only two were completely unfurnished. These were small and very likely the graves of children. Eight graves held clay pots only, while nine others contained shell beads and/or blades of obsidian in addition to seashells. Five of the graves yielded eight marble vessels; six graves yielded twelve figures, of which half were of the Plastiras type, half schematic. Three of the graves held both figures and vessels of marble. A few of the graves stand out as being unusually rich in objects. For example, in grave 9 at Plastiras, Doumas recovered three marble vases, four figures (pl. 4*B*) of the type named after this cemetery, a whetstone, a bronze needle, and small fragments of obsidian; grave 5 at Akrotiri on Naxos yielded two pots, a marble jar and palette, one Plastiras-type figure (pl. 14[1]), one schematic figurine, twenty stone beads, and one of bronze.

Several large cemeteries on Naxos were explored around the turn of the century by Klon Stephanos: Aphendika consisting of 170 graves, Phyrroges with roughly 100, and Karvounolakkoi with 82, of which 22 unplundered ones were excavated.[19] Of the more than 300 graves, Stephanos described the contents of only 10. We can only assume that the rest did not yield any noteworthy furnishings – certainly not any marble objects. Only one figure from each of these cemeteries was recorded, while marble vessels numbering six are mentioned only for Karvounolakkoi. This cemetery and the one at Phyrroges seem to have been in use in both the first and second phases of the Early Cycladic period although the two folded-arm figures of the Spedos variety found in them belong to the second phase. The only finds recorded from the cemetery at Aphendika are a fragmentary harp player carved in the Spedos style and a stone axe, hardly enough to determine the date of this cemetery of 170 graves.

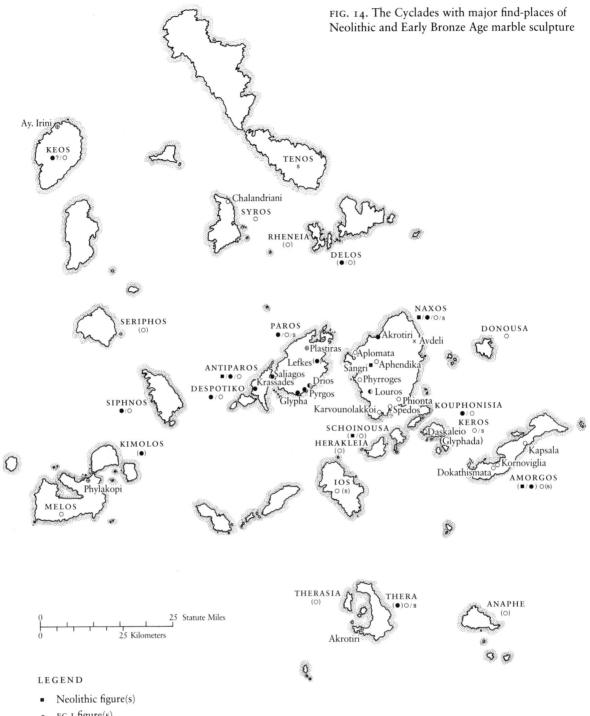

FIG. 14. The Cyclades with major find-places of
Neolithic and Early Bronze Age marble sculpture

Ay. Irini ⊕

KEOS
●?/○

TENOS
s

Chalandriani
SYROS
○

RHENEIA
(○)

DELOS
(●/○)

SERIPHOS
(○)

PAROS
●/○/s

Plastiras ⊕

Lefkes (●)

ANTIPAROS
■/●/○

Saliagos
Krassades
Drios
Pyrgos
Glypha

DESPOTIKO
●/○

SIPHNOS
●/○

NAXOS
■/●/○/s

Akrotiri × Avdeli

Aplomata ○
Aphendika ■
Sangri
Phyrroges ○
Louros ○
Phionta
Karvounolakkoi ○
Spedos

DONOUSA
○

KOUPHONISIA
●/○

KEROS

SCHOINOUSA
■/○
HERAKLEIA
(○)

Daskaleio ○/s
(Glyphada)

Kapsala
Kornoviglia
Dokathismata

AMORGOS
(■/●) ○(s)

KIMOLOS
(●)

Phylakopi

MELOS
○

IOS
○ (s)

THERASIA
(○)

THERA
(●)○/s

ANAPHE
(○)

Akrotiri

0 _____ 25 Statute Miles

0 _____ 25 Kilometers

LEGEND

■   Neolithic figure(s)

●   EC I figure(s)

◐   Transitional figure(s) (EC I / EC II)

○   EC II figure(s)

⊕   EC II figure(s) from post-EC-II contexts
    primarily if not exclusively

s   special type(s)

( ) reputed find-place

?   questionable

×   place mentioned in text (not necessarily
    source of figures)

Another cemetery on Naxos explored by Stephanos seems to have belonged primarily to the second phase. This cemetery, at Spedos, consisted of two groups of graves numbering twenty-five in all.[20] Only thirteen were described by their excavator. Again, it is presumed that the other twelve were either poorly furnished or without grave goods. One grave (no. 20) was furnished with pottery that may be dated around the end of the first phase; while another (no. 12), in which were found a Kapsala-variety figure and five marble vessels, is of mixed date – an all but unprecedented occurrence. Eight of the thirteen graves were furnished with marble objects: fourteen vases and eight figures, three of which are of the schematic Apeiranthos type.[21] The eight figures come from five graves, two of which also held marble vessels. One grave (no. 10) was particularly well endowed: besides a pair of figures of the variety named after this cemetery (pl. 6), it contained three marble vessels, a solid lamp model in marble, and seven clay vessels including an elaborate painted triple vase that may also have been intended as a lamp.

The richest Early Cycladic II cemetery explored to date is again on Naxos. The excavation of this graveyard, at Aplomata, was begun by Nikolaos Kontoleon and following his death has been completed by Vasilis Lambrinoudakis.[22] All told, some twenty-seven graves have been uncovered though many of them had been destroyed or disturbed through the later re-use of the site. Many of the finds were unearthed in the surrounding fill rather than in the graves themselves so that it was not always clear which objects belonged to which graves. Grave 13 appears to be the most lavishly furnished Cycladic grave ever excavated systematically. It contained thirteen figures (three of them seated females), four complete marble vases as well as fragments of others, and some poorly preserved silver(?) jewelry. At Aplomata the excavators have to date retrieved a total of some forty marble figures, including an astonishing seven complete and fragmentary seated females and a fragmentary male cupbearer, as well as some sixty marble vessels. Even in this unusually rich cemetery not every grave was furnished with figures, although very few of the undisturbed graves were without objects of marble: most contained one or more stone vases.

As might be expected from the evidence at Aplomata and from the proliferation of objects from undocumented sources, the Cycladic cemeteries richest in marble belong to the first half or so of the second phase, although not every cemetery from this period has yielded a wealth of goods. For example, at Kapsala on Amorgos Tsountas excavated a small cluster of eleven graves.[23] In two he found objects of bronze, but the only marble find from this cemetery was the figure that is the name-piece of the earliest variety of the female folded-arm type.

The largest cemetery with more than 600 graves, at Chalandriani on Syros, belongs near the end of the second phase. Few of the many graves described held marble objects.[24] From 20 graves Tsountas recorded a total of forty-one stone vases and six figures of the variety named for the site as well as examples of the Apeiranthos type. At Dokathismata on Amorgos he opened some 20 graves, but described only 2.[25] One (grave 13) held a single figure while the other (no. 14) was particularly well endowed. From it Tsountas recovered bronze weapons, marble and clay vessels as well as fragments of a silver bowl, and a pair of figures that give the Dokathismata variety its name. It is unclear whether the entire cemetery is, like the necropolis at Chalandriani, to be dated to the second part of the Early Cycladic II phase. Nevertheless, the archaeological record would seem to confirm the impression given by the unprovenanced finds, that the second half of Early Cycladic II saw a decline in the number of figures made and that, in general, graves furnished with marble goods were rarer than in the first half of the phase.

The Distribution of the Marble Objects

Vestiges of the Early Bronze Age culture have been found on most of the Cyclades, by chance if not by systematic site survey and exploration. Even today, in walking the time-worn country paths and goat tracks on any of the islands one is likely to find chips and broken blades of obsidian, sure signs of a prehistoric presence. Marble figures and vessels have been recovered on many of the Cyclades – and beyond – but certain islands are outstanding for the number of such objects unearthed in their fields. In the first phase Naxos and especially Paros with some of her smaller neighbors appear to have been the richest in marble products; by the first half of the second phase this distinction seems to have passed more definitively to Naxos along with some of the small islands to her southeast, notably Keros. For the latter part of the second phase the evidence is less clear. Excavated examples of the latest figures are known from Keos, Syros, Keros, and Amorgos but nowhere, with the possible exception of Keros, are these finds plentiful. Nevertheless, one would expect that as a rule it was the larger, more fertile, and centrally situated islands that were capable of supporting a population sufficiently large and prosperous to generate craft specialization on a significant scale.

The picture we have of the distribution of marble objects within the Cyclades has been badly blurred by extensive illicit digging and the corresponding paucity of documented finds. This situation is made all the more complex by the fact that, with one or two possible exceptions, it has not yet been possible to localize the marble sources of Cycladic objects. Cycladic marble is often misleadingly characterized as "Naxian" or "Parian," a differentiation that, however, is based on relative grain size as assessed by the naked eye. In actuality, both the coarser "Naxian" and the finer "Parian" types and many gradations between them are available on many of the marble islands.

One would especially like to be able to trace the origins of the stone because the island on which a marble object is found is not necessarily the island on which it was made, even though the two were doubtless often one and the same.[26] One case, for example, for which a distinction probably needs to be made between find-place and place of manufacture is the pair of harpers that, along with several marble vessels, was reputedly unearthed in a grave on Thera. Since Thera is one of the few Cyclades lacking good white marble – Melos is another – it is probable that it also lacked marble workshops (though of course raw marble could have been brought in from elsewhere – it would have made good ballast). Because of its light volcanic soil especially suited to viticulture, Thera was a fertile island by Cycladic standards and may well have had a number of prosperous inhabitants who could import marble goods from islands to the north.

The Meaning and Function of the Marble Objects

In discussing Cycladic sculpture the question most often asked is perhaps the most difficult one of all to answer in a more than very general way. This is the question of interpretation: what was the function of the marble figures and who or what beings did they represent? Although the archaeological record provides certain information that can and must be taken into account in any consideration of this subject, it is not the sort of question that prehistoric archaeology, in the absence of any written remains, can easily elucidate, for its answer lies in an understanding of beliefs and rituals that at best have left only an enigmatic mark in the form of nonperishable remains. One can only guess at what the Early Cycladic islanders believed about death and about supernatural powers, fortified here and there by clues from the way they furnished their graves. In doing so, we must acknowledge that as yet we know little about their dwellings and virtually nothing about their shrines and sanctuaries. It may be possible one day to show that the figures had more than one function, or even that the specific functions or rituals involving their use varied to some extent from place to place. For the time being, however, it would be wise to confine the discussion to their sepulchral use.

As shown earlier, marble sculptures are not found in every grave, not even in many, and some cemeteries are richer in figures than others. One major drawback in a determination of the function and identity of these figures is the fact that there is not a single case in which a figure was found with skeletal remains whose sex has been recorded. From the associated finds that include in some cases jewelry, somewhat simplistically thought to accompany the burial of women, and in a few cases weapons, probably belonging to the burials of men, it has been assumed, perhaps correctly, that the female representations at least were buried with people of both sexes and that they had the same meaning for both. Marble figures are in any case apparently confined to the graves of a small, prosperous, privileged segment of the population since they are normally found in "rich" graves furnished with other carefully crafted objects of stone and/or metal and delicate pottery. In fact, few elaborately endowed graves are without marble figures. It is, of course, possible, as has already been suggested, that the majority of the islanders went to their graves with wooden figures that have left no trace, and that in one way or another every person was similarly equipped for death.

From the discovery contexts it appears that the figures and marble vessels as well as the pottery constituted a special class of specifically sepulchral objects, though some scholars claim that the traces of mending found on a few of them show that these objects were first *used* by the living for some religious purpose. We have no way of knowing when or under what circumstances the damage to mended objects occurred, but it is quite possible that some of them at least broke and were repaired before they ever left the workshop. Yet even if they broke after completion, this need not be construed as evidence to deny their primary function as grave goods. Such objects would seem not to have been gifts made to the dead at the funeral but rather personal possessions acquired by the deceased person during his or her life for the express purpose of preparing for death. (Children's graves were apparently meagerly furnished, perhaps because children would not have had the means to acquire sepulchral goods of their own.) Such objects would have been kept and presumably displayed until their owner's demise. In the close quarters of an Early Bronze Age domestic setting they would have been subject to certain hazards, ranging from playful children to earthquakes. It should not be surprising, therefore, that in one or two instances (e.g., one at Ayia Irini on Keos and one on Daskaleio islet off Keros) figures have been found in dwellings. With the possible exception of the many images recovered on Keros, nearly all of the figures found in non-sepulchral contexts, however, were found in later Bronze Age settlements, not in their original contexts. The sculptures most often repaired, those of the archaic Plastiras type, are represented as standing. It is conceivable that the damage to these works, whose separately carved legs were particularly delicate, may have resulted from their being propped up in a niche or on a ledge either in the sculptor's workshop or in their owner's house. Unable to stand by themselves, they could easily have slipped and fallen. This may be the reason that the reclining posture – the posture they would assume in the grave – was adopted for most figures of the next phase, while those statuettes that because of their occupation had necessarily to stand were mounted on a base.

The picture is made all the more complex by the fact that the mended objects were not the only ones that broke before they were buried. On the contrary, it is a very puzzling fact that incomplete figures, small fragments of figures, stone vases without their lids, and even lids alone sometimes occur in Cycladic tombs. Even figures that had been repaired are in many cases missing the part that had been painstakingly reattached, or other parts, or both. The burial of incomplete objects has been viewed, like the traces of ancient repairs, as evidence of their active use before burial. But unless we look upon the figures as mere playthings or consider the Cycladic people of the Early Bronze Age to have been irresponsible in their handling of these objects, this notion seems untenable. Surely the marble and other goods must have been precious to their owners who doubtless had acquired them at some expense. It is unlikely that they would have treated them so carelessly as to lose parts of them, leaving in the end only a torso or pair of legs to take along to the grave. On the other hand, one cannot rule out the possibility that hatred, envy, or fear may in certain cases have motivated individuals to vandalize a dead person's property. Some sort of funeral custom may have existed, involving the intentional breaking of objects and even the deliberate discarding of parts of them (perhaps in the sea since the missing parts are never found). Doumas noted in his excavations of Cycladic cemeteries that the figures were not always accorded conventional respect at their interment with the dead: they were sometimes buried face down or weighted down by other objects.

There is at least one case of purposeful breaking of a figure. The largest completely pre-served piece known, a nearly life-size work (148.3 cm) from Amorgos now in Athens, had to be broken into several pieces in order to fit it into the grave in which it was reputedly found. (The very large figure [132 cm] illustrated in pl. X was broken in three places, presumably for the same reason.[27]) The Cycladic dead were buried in their small, confining tombs in a severely contracted, or fetal, position, wherefore such figures, though not quite life-size, would have been longer than the corpse.) The Procrustean act of fitting sculpture to grave has been taken as further evidence of a nonsepulchral function – in this case, because of the figure's great size, as a cult statue. However, its uncommon size may simply indicate that its owner was unusually wealthy or that its sculptor was unusually ambitious. Indeed, if it had been a cult statue of some importance to a community, one must wonder why it was put in a grave at all, let alone in one that was too small for it.

Several stone vessels are also known that have holes in their bottoms, apparently, if rather haphazardly, made intentionally. The holes, by rendering the vessels useless to the liv-ing, transfer them to the world of the dead, possibly after first being used at the funeral for libations over the dead. A deliberately broken sword was also uncovered in excavation on Ano Kouphonisi.[28] Similar rituals involving the deliberate breaking of figurines appear to have been practiced in the Early Bronze Age in Anatolia.[29]

Certain objects found in their graves indicate that the Cycladic islanders believed firmly in an afterlife. It would appear that they sought to prepare for this not necessarily with prac-tical, functional things, but rather with objects that would symbolize the renewal of life and light beyond the dark tomb and the journey to this other world: solid marble lamps and lead boat models; miniature bowls and goblets, mortars and pestles; pottery, much of it too deli-cate, and stone vessels, many too heavy and cumbersome to use in a literal sense. In this spirit the female figures fall naturally into place, not as dolls or concubines or nursemaids, not as self-images or revered idols or sacrosanct cult statues or priestly property, but simply as icons of a protective, watchful being – something on the order of a patron saint perhaps – at once spirit of death and symbol of eternal fertility. Characteristic of her nature as a nurturing, protective force, and emblem of her womb, is the vessel that was often substituted for her image.[30] The rare male figures may be viewed as symbols of virility and strength, protectors too, and in the case of the cupbearer and musician figures, comforting reminders that the senses that perceive the delights of wine and song would live on, too.

Cycladic Sculpture and the Sculpture of Other Lands

The practice of carving small-scale human figures in marble (as well as limestone and ala-baster) was widespread over the greater Mediterranean area and beyond during the third millennium and/or earlier. Particularly strong traditions, with numerous surviving examples, flourished around the same time as the Cycladic in Anatolia as well as Sardinia, while occa-sional pieces of marble or limestone sculpture have been unearthed in Cyprus, Persia, and the

Balkans, to name only a few places.[31] With rare exceptions, the female form is depicted, often in a schematic or highly stylized manner.

There is no concrete evidence that the Cycladic sculptural tradition was directly influenced by or that it exerted a direct influence upon the tradition of any of the contemporaneous nearby cultures except Early Minoan Crete and Early Helladic mainland Greece where it was imitated. Sculptors throughout this part of the world were simply seeking solutions to similar problems. That their solutions occasionally appear startlingly similar as a result should come as no surprise and should not require a diffusionist theory to explain them.

Cycladic sculpture probably differs from the contemporary sculpture of other lands less in meaning than in its sculptors' tenacity to certain principles of form and beauty. These are expressed both in a superb technical mastery of the marble and in a rigorous mathematical precision of design that, in the best examples of the classical phase, results in a harmony of proportion that is unique in prehistoric art. To many these qualities (discussed in detail in the next chapter) make Cycladic sculptures more appealing as a group than those of any other contemporary culture, and they inadvertently cause one to think ahead nearly two millennia to the achievements of archaic Greek sculptors whose basic ideals, again expressed in oft-repeated forms, were not so very different, after all, from those of their Early Cycladic precursors. Again, there is no evidence that Early Cycladic sculpture exerted any direct influence on either the later Bronze Age art of Greece or on archaic and classical Greek art even though Cycladic figures (or at least fragments of them) were sometimes found and used in later times.

Chapter Two

The Sculptural Tradition

In the first chapter we passed rather rapidly through a millennium of intense sculptural activity. The most important thing to bear in mind at this point is that virtually all the hundreds of extant pieces of Cycladic sculpture belong to established types or varieties. Cycladic sculpture is formulaic. There are no freely conceived pieces. Once formed, each type was repeated again and again with almost imperceptible change for centuries. In this respect Cycladic sculpture is probably no different from that of other preliterate societies well insulated by geographic position from constant commerce with the world at large. Cycladic sculpture does of course differ from that of many cultures in that it was made in considerable quantity and in a long-enduring medium, factors that, incidentally, greatly facilitate a close study of it. By no means, however, does the formulaic character of the figures render them monotonous in the sense that once one has seen a few examples of a type or variety one has "seen them all." On the contrary, within the constraints of the traditional craft there was room for a virtually infinite variety of subtle differences and a sculptor could easily stamp his works with his own "imprint." Nor are all Cycladic figures of equal quality. As one might expect, only a relatively small number can be considered masterpieces while not a few must be judged poor. The vast majority, however, fall between these extremes. Although Early Bronze Age standards of artistic excellence may have differed from those of the present day, it should be possible to assess the relative merits of a piece along lines with which the prehistoric islander might well have agreed.

Tools

The figures were made, laboriously, primarily by chipping and abrading the stone.[32] Pieces of emery from Naxos may have been used for these purposes; in the second phase chisels of bronze may also have been employed. Splinters of emery or obsidian from Melos were presumably used for incision work, while obsidian, flint, or emery awls were probably used for bored details. The final polishing of a figure would have been effected with sand and water and perhaps with pumice from Thera, whose volcanic eruptions send small pieces of this substance floating to the shores of other islands. One can easily imagine the sculptor's "studio" as being by the sea. There he could have found much of his raw material already worked for him by the action of the waves. He could have used the wet beach as his drawing pad and the sand and water to smooth his works. Nevertheless, at all times patience and diligence and a strong and steady hand must have been the sculptor's most valuable resources.

The Traditional Formula

The sheer labor involved in the production of any but the simplest small figure must have precluded a haphazard or a spontaneous approach in which the sculptor, however skilled, went about his work without a preconceived plan. Marble, which obviously lacks the malleability of clay or the tractable qualities of wood, requires a highly disciplined approach. Thus, in order to avoid time-consuming errors, formulae were developed that aided the sculptor in carefully composing his figure on the marble slab before he actually began to carve it. These formulae, which probably evolved out of necessity, may also have had a magico-religious component. No doubt they imbued the sculptor's craft with a certain mystique, which would have effectively discouraged others from fashioning their own images. The formulae, moreover, served as oral and visual vehicles for the transmission of the sculptural tradition from one generation to the next.

That such formulae were involved in the preliminary stages can be deduced by looking closely at a large number of figures. It is only by such means that one can explain the fact that beyond the uniform treatment of certain forms and details within each type and variety there is also a marked similarity in the proportions of many works. Although there was a progressive modification in the direction of more natural proportions during the transitional and the earlier part of the second phases, this similarity did not result from imitating the proportions of the human figure. And not only do the figures of each type and variety tend to have similar proportions, but the works of one artist, though they may vary considerably in size, will often resemble each other especially closely in this respect.

We would do well, then, to examine the rules that appear to have governed the design of the different figure types to see just what it is, besides the treatment of the arms or legs or face that makes one Cycladic figure closely resemble others of its kind. Although there are a few pieces that appear to be unfinished, work on these was stopped when they were near completion. No examples, with the exception of one or two schematic ones, have been found abandoned in the initial stages of block preparation or carving. Nor have any sculptors' tools or instruments been found. What one says about the procedures involved in the manufacture of Cycladic figures is therefore based solely on an observation of finished works and, as such, is necessarily a hypothetical reconstruction.

The Archaic Three-Part Canon

After selecting a piece of marble and trimming it to approximate the length, maximum width, and depth of the figure to be made, and smoothing the main surfaces sufficiently to draw on them, the sculptor would work out the outline and the position of the internal details. In the archaic phase, the human form appears to have been conceived in three equal parts – roughly one part for the head and neck, one for the torso, and one for the legs (fig. 15a). These divisions could have been made with a simple straight edge. But what seems to have been more important than the three divisions as just mentioned was the placement of certain key points near them on the outline – specifically the shoulders and the hips.[33] These were determined by means of arcs drawn with a primitive compass consisting of a bit of obsidian or even charcoal attached to a piece of string. Similarly, an arc passing through the midpoint of the figure often defined the position of the elbows.

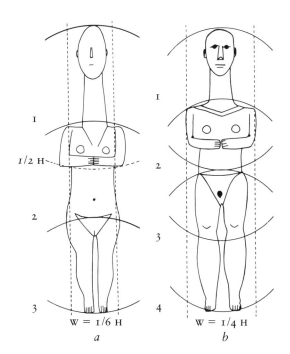
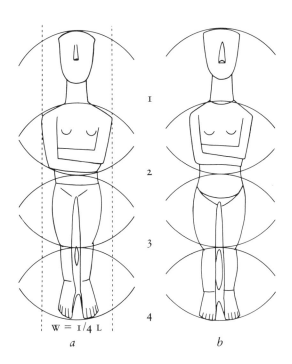

FIG. 15. The planning of archaic figures of the Plastiras type: *a*) the traditional three-part canon; *b*) an unusual early example of the four-part canon.

  a. Athens, National Archaeological Museum 4762. H. 31.5 cm. Grave 23, Glypha, Paros. Doumas Master [9], pls. 14, 15.

  b. Lugano, Paolo Morigi Collection. H. 29.6 cm. Provenance unknown. (PGP 1980, no. 4.) (Pl. I*B*.)

FIG. 16. The planning of classical figures of the Spedos variety: the four-part canon applied identically on figures carved by different sculptors.

  a. Cambridge, Fitzwilliam Museum GR.33.1901 (gift of R. C. Bosanquet). L. 25.6 cm. "Amorgos." Fitzwilliam Master [4], pls. 26, 27.

  b. E. Berlin, Staatliche Museen, Antikensammlung 8267. L. 25.5 cm. "Syros." (*ACC*, no. 165.)

37

The Classical Four-Part Canon

There are signs that already in the late archaic phase some sculptors had rejected the tripartite scheme with its exaggerated forms in favor of a new plan (fig. 15*b*). By the classical phase this new plan had become the canon according to which all varieties of the folded-arm figure, except the latest, appear to have been consistently designed. Out of a desire to decrease the fragility of their works by giving them more balanced proportions, the classical sculptor conceived his figure as divisible into four equal parts, with the maximum width (at the shoulders) often equivalent to one part (fig. 16). Compass-drawn arcs marked off the shoulders, the elbows or waist, and the knees. The top of the head and the ends of the feet were also curved, revealing further the influence of the hypothetical compass.

Within the basic divisions of each system proportions might vary – even in two works carved by one sculptor – and there was considerable flexibility in the placement of internal details. For example, in the four-part canon the location of the second division or midpoint

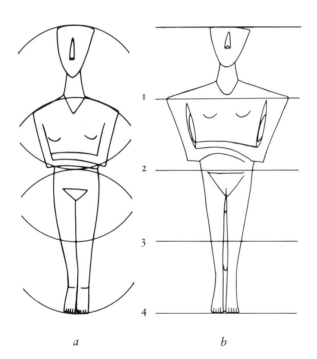

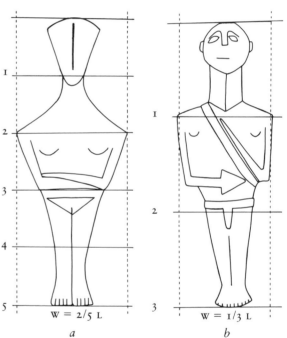

FIG. 17. The planning of late classical figures of the Dokathismata variety: the four-part canon applied by means of a compass (*a*) and by means of a straightedge (*b*).

a. Dominique de Menil Collection CA 6326. L. 36.7 cm. "Naxos." Ashmolean Master [2], pls. 42, 43.

b. Athens, National Archaeological Museum 6174. L. 46 cm. "Syros." (*Aegean Islands*, no. 17.) (Fig. 8*f*.)

FIG. 18. The planning of late classical figures of the Chalandriani variety: a) a five-part design; b) a three-part design.

a. Cambridge, Mass., Fogg Art Museum L. 63. 1984 (on loan from Frederick Stafford Collection). L. 27 cm. "Paros." Stafford Master [1], pls. 46, 47.

b. Dresden, Staatliche Kunstsammlungen, Skulpturensammlung ZV 2595. L. 22.8 cm. "Amorgos." Dresden Master [5], pls. 48, 49, 50.

of the figure can coincide with one of a number of different places on the torso although in the majority of the examples it comes either at the bottom of the right forearm, just below it, or at the middle of the abdomen. The basic number of divisions and the marking off of key points on the outline, however, remained constant and fixed for each canon.

Of the figures produced late in the second phase most give the impression of having been designed according to a purposefully applied formula. While some sculptors continued to use the canonical compass-drawn four-part plan (fig. 17a), others used elements of this system only, and many seem to have favored a straight edge over the compass (fig. 17b). A few sculptors evidently experimented with three- and five-part designs (fig. 18).

Among the angular figures, both those of the Chalandriani and those of the Dokathismata varieties, there seem to have been no preferred anatomical features used as pivotal points even when they are planned according to the four-part system. There is also no preferred ratio of maximum width to length and, except in certain statuettes designed in thirds and fifths, the maximum width bears no logical relation to the overall length. A number of Chalandriani-variety figures do, however, have a shoulder width that is equivalent to the length of the legs.

This is not to imply that the composition of *every* female figure except those just mentioned can be precisely divided into three or four components according to the canon appropriate to its type. In actuality, about half of the examples of each type seem to have been not only very carefully plotted but also executed in such a way that the initial design shows through in the finished work with considerable exactitude. Some of the remaining figures were probably laid out quite carefully according to the canon, but as finished works carved in differing planes they no longer reflect the precision of the preliminary drawing made on the raw flat slab. Other works show a conscious application of the canon but with modifications. For example, a folded-arm figure with typical first and second divisions might have unusually long thighs and correspondingly short calves, resulting in a failure of the third division to coincide with the knees. Such departures from the norm were probably made deliberately since they are often seen in the works of skilled sculptors – sometimes only on images assignable to a sculptor's maturity. From the craftsman's point of view, the traditional formula served him as a set of practical guidelines to safeguard his work against error and deformity. He was not a servant of the formula. On the contrary, once he had developed the skill born of experience, he could, without risk, adapt the formula to his own aesthetic sensibilities. This is quite different from the liberties taken by sculptors who seem not to have been trained in the proper use of the traditional canon. Their figures appear clumsy and disproportionate when compared to those based on time-honored precepts.

The Design of the Special Figure Types

The proportional formula played an important part in the design of the special figure types, especially the most complex ones. Only two or three complete examples of the "tandem"

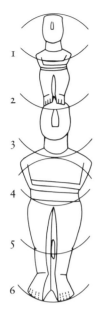

FIG. 19. The planning of a "tandem" two-figure composition. Karlsruhe, Badisches Landesmuseum B839 (ex Thiersch Collection). L. 21.6 cm. "Paros." (Pl. 1*B*.)

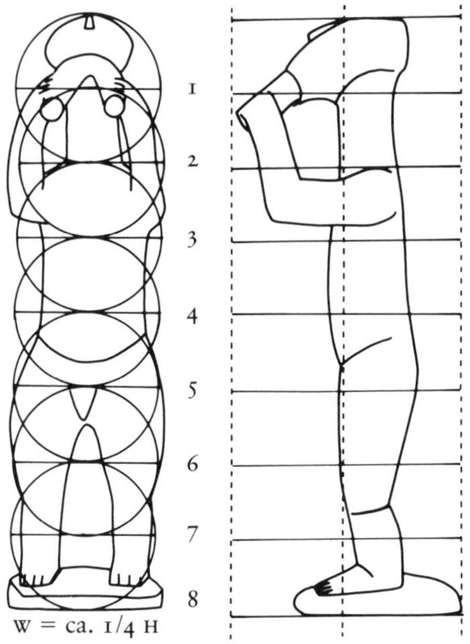

FIG. 20. The planning of a standing woodwind player. Athens, National Archaeological Museum 3910. H. 20 cm. Keros. (Pl. 10.1.)

W = ca. 1/4 H

two-figure compositions exist. These sculptures are interesting chiefly for their iconography, not for any outstanding sculptural qualities. There is, however, some indication that figures of this type were roughly planned according to an elaboration of the usual four-part scheme in which the overall length was divided into six parts of which slightly more than four were allotted to the larger figure and slightly less than two to the smaller one. (There is a short overlap where the two figures join since the feet of one rest on the forehead of the other [fig. 19]).

In the case of the standing woodwind player, a numerically small but consistent type, the height, including the base, can be divided into four parts that can be further subdivided to make a total of eight. The maximum width, as in many of the earlier folded-arm figures, tends to be equal to or only slightly greater than a quarter of the height (two units), as does also the depth of the original slab (fig. 20).[34]

For sheer virtuosity of technique, the most remarkable of the three seated-figure types is the harp player. Marble does not lend itself easily to this sort of composition with its delicate projecting and openwork elements and, indeed, time has not been kind to the survivors: only two of the eight known examples of this rare type are very well preserved. It is quite possible that such figures were more often carved in wood, a material better suited to the problems involved. The stool or chair on which the harper, as well as the cupbearer and seated female figure sit, was certainly based on wooden originals, as was also, of course, the harp.[35]

40

Although the few surviving harpers, which in two cases were fashioned as pairs, were probably carved at various points over a period of at least one hundred and perhaps as much as two or three hundred years, they form a remarkably uniform group in which certain conventions were adhered to very strictly. The musician sits straight, head high, seat well back on his chair or stool, feet parallel to the ground. On his right side he holds a triangular harp with a frontal ornament in the shape of a duck's bill.[36] His right arm, lower than his left, usually rests on or against the soundbox of the instrument. Wooden examples may have imparted a certain continuity to the type, but another reason that this essential uniformity exists, even though the harpers were carved only rarely and over an extended period of time, is that they were planned according to a specific formula. The variations that are observable among the better preserved figures – variations in relative harp size, arm position (particularly of the left arm), and type and degree of elaborateness of the seat – are probably the result of individual preference on the sculptor's part as was also the degree of naturalism attempted. Other differences may be due in part to the sculptors' varying levels of skill and experience since they were not in the habit of making harpers and in part to the fact that the harpers are carved in a number of styles ranging from the precanonical (pl. III*A*) through the Kapsala (pl. 7) and early Spedos (pls. IIC, 9, 10.2).

The harper, cupbearer, and seated female were treated more as four-sided works than as integrated sculptures in the round. Unlike the standard figures with their frontal emphasis, the most important view in these compositions is the profile, and in the case of the musician and cupbearer invariably the right profile – that is, the side on which the harp and cup are always held. In contrast, the other views in some examples seem awkward, while the front and the left side are sometimes lacking in detail (e.g., the genitalia) and a clear differentiation of planes.

It appears that the plan of these figures was worked out primarily on the right side of the marble block and that a grid was consistently applied to facilitate the carving process. The grid was based on a division of the height into the usual four primary units, while the width was made to closely approximate three of these units. The height and width were further subdivided to form a grid of eight by six "squares" (fig. 21). The lines of the grid tended to dictate the position of key points on the outline and certain internal divisions such as the chin, the top of the shoulder, the elbow, the cup, the top of the thighs, the top of the seat, and the apex of the harp. Although each sculptor used the grid somewhat differently, a substantial number of the same coincidences recur from piece to piece.[37] And, just as the compass seems to have affected the shape of the top of the head and the ends of the feet in the frontally oriented folded-arm figures, so the top boundary of the grid appears to have dictated the position of the head in the profile-oriented seated figures. This boundary often coincides with the forehead, giving the head a pronounced backward tilt that has been interpreted as describing a "heavenward glance" appropriate to a musician's rapt state. However, this head position is seen also on some of the passive seated figures, and may, therefore, be due rather to the influence of the grid frame.

41

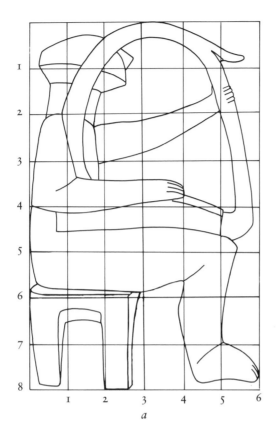

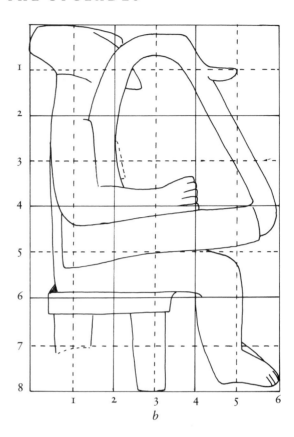

a

b

FIG. 21. The planning of two harp players.

a. Malibu, The J. Paul Getty Museum 85.AA.103. H. 60 cm. "Amorgos." (Pl. IIC.)

b. New York, Metropolitan Museum of Art L82.27.13. H. 24.1 cm. Provenance unknown. (*Ancient Art* [Robin Symes Gallery, London, 1971], no. 15.)

Before considering the planning of the remarkably intricate three-figure group, it is necessary to consider another controlling factor in the formulaic design of *all* types of Cycladic figures, and to add another instrument to the Cycladic sculptor's hypothetical tool kit.

The Harmonic System

It appears that Cycladic sculptors deliberately and consistently used specific angles based on the universal principle of the "golden triangle" to describe angular features of the outline of their figures, most notably the shoulder/upper arm angle, and details on the surface, the most important of which was the pubic V or triangle. The angles in question are derived from a triangle (or rectangle) with a height-to-base ratio of 5:8 (fig. 22*a*). Although not apparent to the naked eye, an astonishingly high percentage of the angular aspects of Cycladic sculpture can be described in terms of the two complementary angles obtained from

FIG. 22. The harmonic system: *a*) "golden triangle";
b) Minoan double axe sign; *c*) Minoan masons'
marks; *d*) suggested schema for an Early Bronze
Age protractor

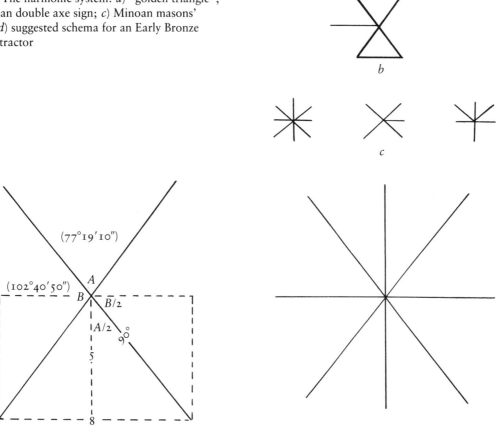

the 5 : 8, or "golden," triangle or in terms of simple fractions or combinations of these angles. Angle *B*, the larger of the two, occurs most often, while its complement, *A*, is found frequently also. The fractions and combinations of the two basic angles used by certain sculptors include:

$$A/2,\ B/2,\ (A + B)/2,\ A + (B/2),\ B + (A/2).$$

Angle *B* was preferred for the shoulders of all figure types and for the pubis of the classical folded-arm figure (fig. 23). Angle *A* appears to have been favored for the pubis on violin and Plastiras figures carved during the first phase, while it was used also for nearly a third of the pubic angles of Chalandriani- and Dokathismata-variety figures carved late in the second phase.

The formulaic use of specific angles was probably founded on a need for foolproof techniques to assure correct results. It would seem that many sculptors determined the shoulder

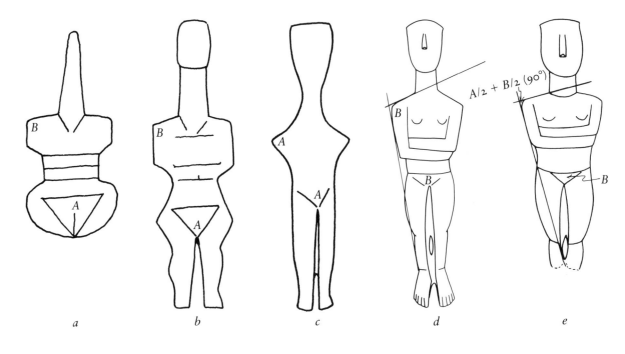

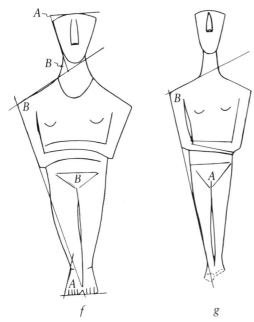

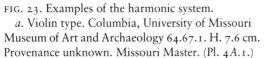

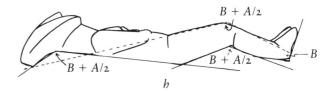

FIG. 23. Examples of the harmonic system.

a. Violin type. Columbia, University of Missouri Museum of Art and Archaeology 64.67.1. H. 7.6 cm. Provenance unknown. Missouri Master. (Pl. 4*A*.1.)

b. Plastiras type. Columbia, University of Missouri Museum of Art and Archaeology 64.67.3. H. 14.1 cm. Provenance unknown. Missouri Master. (Pl. 4*A*.2.)

c. Louros type. Athens, National Archaeological Museum 6140.10. H. 22 cm. Grave 26, Louros Athalassou, Naxos. (Pl. 3*A*.5.)

d. Early Spedos variety. Cambridge, Fitzwilliam Museum GR.33.1901 (gift of R. C. Bosanquet). L. 25.6 cm. Fitzwilliam Master [4], pls. 26, 27.

e. Early Spedos variety. Karlsruhe, Badisches Landesmuseum B 840 (ex Thiersch Collection). Pres. L. 16 cm (lower legs missing from mid-calves). Paros. (*ACC*, no. 164.)

f. Dokathismata variety. Hannover, Kestner Museum 1950.46 (ex von Bissing Collection). L. 17.3 cm. Provenance unknown. (*ACC*, no. 221.) (Fig. 26*b*.)

g. Dokathismata variety. Athens, National Archaeological Museum 4722. Pres. L. 20.5 cm (ends of feet missing). Grave 14, Dokathismata, Amorgos. Tsountas Master. (Pl. 13.2.)

h. Early Spedos variety. Oxford, Ashmolean Museum AE.178. L. 18.4 cm. "Amorgos." (Renfrew 1969, pl. 4*a*.)

angle with great accuracy only on one side – usually the right side. The ultimate result was not infrequently a rather pronounced asymmetry with one shoulder higher than the other. Whether this asymmetry should be attributed to carelessness on the part of the sculptor or whether it was intended as a way of avoiding the static, lifeless qualities of a mathematically precise pattern cannot, of course, be determined. One suspects, however, that it was often enough deliberate, for it is seen in the works of some of the most proficient sculptors.

Other features of the outline, such as the neck/shoulder and calf/foot angles, were also consistently affected by the use of the golden, or harmonic, angles and their derivatives (fig. 23f), as were also the V-shaped incisions made at the top of the chest and/or the top of the back of many figures. Also, despite their essentially frontal emphasis, a number of the earlier folded-arm figures exhibit a broken profile axis which appears to have been strongly influenced by the $B + (A/2)$ combination (fig. 23h). Most significantly, perhaps, the use of specific angles for elements of the outline not only determined those particular contours but tended to have a strong impact on the composition as a whole (fig. 23d–g), thus contributing to the essential homogeneity observable among figures of any given type or variety.

Except perhaps for the description of a right angle ($[A + B]/2$), it seems unlikely that such consistency and accuracy in the use of angles would have been achieved solely through simple visual means or an intuitive mathematical sensitivity. And yet, experiments conducted by the writer, just as this book was being readied for printing, do suggest that this may have been possible to a greater extent than originally thought.[38] Forty-one students lacking familiarity with Cycladic sculpture were asked to draw one or more isosceles triangles that they considered pleasing. No reference was made to particular anatomical features that could be described by means of angles. Of the forty-one individuals, thirty-eight drew – very often on the first attempt – at least one triangle that conformed to one of the harmonic angles, fractions, or combinations. Altogether eighty-five triangles were drawn. Of these, sixty-four (75 percent) conformed to the system, fifty-two of them with an astonishing degree of accuracy. The most popular angles were $A/2$, $B/2$, A, and $(A + B)/2$. The inevitable conclusion to be drawn here is that virtually anyone, without training or any practical aid, can reproduce harmonic angles. Less clear as a result is whether we are to believe that the Cycladic sculptor elevated this instinctual preference to a conscious level by using a specific device, made of wood presumably, something like the hypothetical model illustrated in figure 22d. The use of the principle of the golden triangle has been demonstrated in Aegean as well as Egyptian architectural design, and also in certain minor objects such as gaming boards, as early as the third millennium B.C. It has been suggested that the double-axe sign composed of two triangles set apex to apex that was commonly incised on the walls of Minoan palaces may be an ideogram of the golden triangle (fig. 22b).[39] Closer in form to the proposed model for a practical device are certain Minoan masons' marks, also incised on palace walls, that are related to the double-axe sign and that are themselves often drawn accurately according to the harmonic system (fig. 22c). Whatever its exact form, the primitive protractor may also have had a place alongside the compass and straight edge as an instrument of fundamental importance in the initial laying out procedure. In the discussion of the design of individual sculptors' works in subsequent chapters, the assumption is made that an actual device was employed, although in the light of the experiment just mentioned it seems at least conceivable that the traditional repetition of specific angles could have resulted from a habitual process of natural selection.

Although the carving process has altered the original proportions to some extent, there is some indication that the blocks used for certain of the seated figures were cut to conform to the basic proportions of the harmonic principle. The grid itself did not have these exact proportions, apparently because its boundaries did not extend all the way to the edges of the block.

Carved from a single slab of marble, the three-figure group was perhaps the most difficult of all the special works to fashion. Only one such composition exists today in its entirety, but several fragments suggest that, like the harpers and other seated types, it, too, belonged to a recurring though still rarer type. And, as one might expect, the surviving example reveals a greater complexity of design than any of the other special works (fig. 24). It seems that the maximum height and width of the composition were first determined by means of the angular system and that within the resulting harmonic rectangle the familiar grid of six by eight "squares" was constructed. Each of the three figures was allotted one-third (two squares) of the grid's width. The three figures appear to have been planned individually ac-

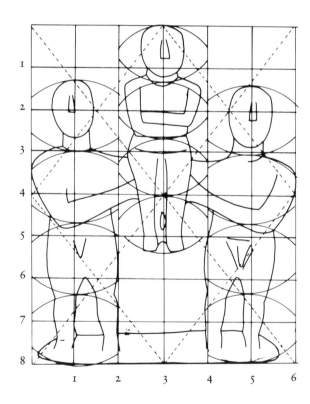

FIG. 24. The planning of the three-figure group. Karlsruhe, Badisches Landesmuseum 77/59. H. 19 cm. Provenance unknown. (Pl. 1C.)

cording to the standard four-part canon, but the cohesion of the composition as a whole depended on the geometric systems. In order to ensure accuracy in such complex, seldom attempted pieces, it thus appears that they were thoroughly plotted out according to a subtle interplay of protractor, ruler, and compass.

Following the preliminary planning and drawing of the outline and the pinpointing of important features on the surface, the excess marble was chipped and abraded away. The surface was then smoothed and the details were modeled in relief, again by abrasion (possibly with the aid of water) or incised with a sharp tool.

Sculptural Details

Like other aspects of the figures, the sculpturally indicated details were also standardized and many if not most tend to recur from piece to piece within each type or variety. A number of these details have been touched upon in other contexts; most speak for themselves in the photographs. Here the discussion will focus on several that have not been specifically mentioned before or that require further notice.

One of the most compelling hallmarks of Cycladic sculpture is a prominent nose raised in relief. After the archaic Plastiras figures this was usually the only facial feature treated plastically and it was given a clearly defined geometric shape. Only rarely were the ears, eyes, or mouth indicated in this way, and in only a single, possibly unique, case were the nostrils marked (pl. VII*B*).

After the Plastiras figures fingers were only sometimes incised, although toes were regularly indicated on figures of the more naturalistic types. Wrist lines are rare in contrast to knee and ankle grooves, which are common on figures of the classical phase. On the rear the juncture of neck and back is usually accented by incision, the spine is normally grooved, and the upper arms are indicated by incision or by a change in plane. On some of the folded-arm figures a horizontal buttock line was also incised; on others this line was indicated instead by a change of plane.

Of all the details carved on Cycladic figures, the treatment of the arms is perhaps the most arresting. The strict observance over several centuries of the convention of placing the right arm below the left has already been noted. Some might interpret this arrangement of the arms as having had a mystical or magical purpose. Yet, it is quite possible that the convention was established, unwittingly, by right-handed sculptors who found it easier to draw the forearms in this way. Having first established their lower boundary by drawing the right arm, the sculptor could then easily fill in the lines of the left arm above it, all the while leaving himself a clear view of the right one. (In much the same way right-handed artists when drawing their subjects in profile, if given a choice, will tend to show them facing left.)

Incision overruns are quite common, especially where forearm and upper arm meet (e.g., fig. 5*g*, pl. 26), though they also occur on other parts of the figure (e.g., pubic triangle,

47

FIG. 25. The folded-arm arrangement: asymmetrical (*a, b*) and symmetrical (*c, d*) renderings.

a. Spedos variety. New York, Paul and Marianne Steiner Collection. L. 49.5 cm. Provenance unknown. (Pls. VI*B*, VII*C*.)

b. Spedos variety. Fort Worth, Kimbell Art Museum AG70.2. Pres. L. 41.8 cm. (legs missing from knees). "Keros." Bastis Master [3], pls. 38, 39.

c. Spedos variety. Private collection. L. 27.4 cm. Provenance unknown.

d. Chalandriani variety. Athens, National Archaeological Museum 6164. L. 15.5 cm. Chalandriani, Syros. (Zervos, fig. 249.)

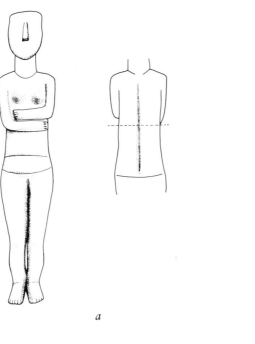

a

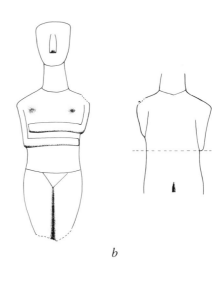

b

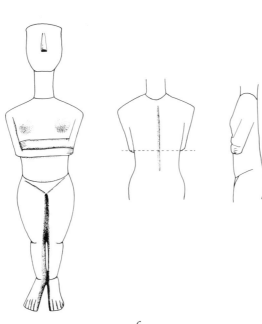

c

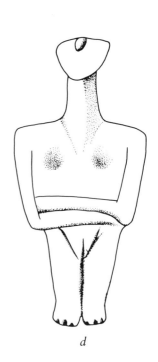

d

fig. 5*j*). Found in the work of some of the finest sculptors, such incision overruns probably resulted from the use of a straight edge as a guide in the engraving process, since it is much easier to start a straight incision on marble with one. When laid against the figure, this ruler would have obstructed the artist's view, causing him to go beyond the intended boundary of his incision. Curiously, Cycladic sculptors seem not to have minded such minor "inaccuracies" as incision overreaches or false starts, for if they had they could quite easily have erased them or at least made them less pronounced.

On some folded-arm figures whose arms extend beyond the sides of the torso there is a marked inequality in the level of the elbows (fig. 25*a*, *b*). (This is especially noticeable from the rear.) A number of sculptors – primarily carvers of Spedos-variety figures – sought a more symmetrical effect by extending the right hand beyond the torso as well, incising its fingers on what in back is the left elbow (fig. 25 *c*). Other sculptors – later ones mostly – often attempted a balanced effect by dropping the left elbow to a level approaching or equal to that of the right forearm (fig. 25 *d*).

The latter convention for attaining symmetry was used commonly on figures depicting the pregnant state (fig. 26). In order to accentuate the impression of a swollen belly, the forearms, particularly the lower one, were made to curve above it. In some cases the belly shows a marked contour; in others the effect is achieved primarily or even solely by means of the arched forearm(s). Pregnancy, or perhaps its aftereffects, was throughout the Early Cycladic period occasionally also indicated, especially on the flatter figure types (but never on Kapsala- or Spedos-variety ones), by a series of parallel grooves across the belly (fig. 27). These highly

FIG. 26. The folded-arm arrangement and the depiction of pregnancy.

a. Spedos variety. London, British Museum 1932.10-18.1 (ex. A. Evans Coll.). L. 20.7 cm. Provenance unknown. (*ACC*, no. 183.)

b. Dokathismata variety. Hannover, Kestner Museum 1950.46 (ex von Bissing Collection). L. 17.3 cm. Provenance unknown. (*ACC*, no. 221.) (Fig. 23*f*.)

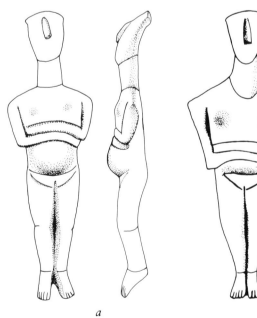
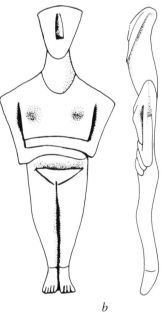

a   *b*

FIG. 27. Some figures with abdominal bands.

a. Violin type. Norwich, University of East Anglia, Sainsbury Centre for Visual Arts UEA 350. H. 25.4 cm. "Ios." (*ACC*, no. 40.)

b. Plastiras type. Private collection. Pres. H. 10.1 cm. Provenance unknown. Doumas Master [3], pls. 14, 15.

c. Plastiras type. Munich, Staatliche Antikensammlungen und Glyptothek 10.112. Pres. H. 9.9 cm. "Grave D, Kapros, Amorgos." (*ACC*, no. 105; Fellmann, no. 1, fig. 1.)

d. Louros type. Oxford, Ashmolean Museum 115.1889 (AE.150). Pres. H. 12.3 cm. "Amorgos."

e. Drios type. Dresden, Staatliche Antikensammlungen, Skulpturensammlungen ZV 1989. H. 13.5 cm. Provenance unknown. (*ACC*, no. 95.)

f. Dokathismata variety. Athens, Goulandris Collection 310. L. 30.7 cm. Provenance unknown. (*NG*, no. 73.)

g. Chalandriani variety. Basel, Erlenmeyer Collection. Pres. L. 16.1 cm. "Keros." Dresden Master [6], pls. 48, 50.

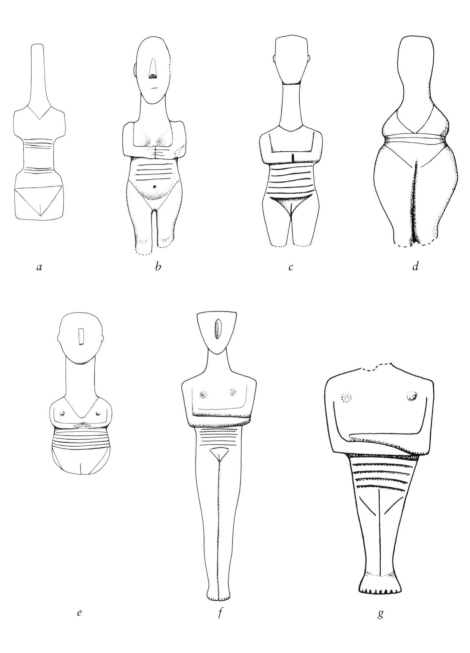

a b c d

e f g

decorative markings have been viewed as postpartum wrinkles or bindings. However, since they can occur in conjunction with a swollen abdomen,[40] one might well wonder if in fact they had any special significance of their own.

The Size Factor

The markings of the fingers on folded-arm figures was to some extent a matter of choice, to a greater extent a function of size. In assuming the folded-arm position the reader will notice that it is possible to conceal the fingers of the left hand under the right upper arm, while the fingers of the right hand lie against the side, more or less invisible from the front. Some sculptors may have taken the view that they should therefore not bother to incise the fingers. On the other hand, it is also quite easy to adopt the folded-arm position and still leave the fingers fully exposed.

Fingers were incised on many Plastiras figures, but in the classical phase they are found for the most part only on works of greater than average size – that is, figures measuring

FIG. 28. The depiction of fingers.

a. Plastiras type. Oxford, Ashmolean Museum 46.118. Pres. H. 20.8 cm (legs missing from knees). "Naxos." (ACC, no. 68; PGP 1981, no. 6.)

b. Precanonical type. Jerusalem, Israel Museum 74.61.213. H. 19 cm. Provenance unknown.

c. Spedos variety. Munich, Staatliche Antiken-sammlungen und Glyptothek 10.382 (gift of R. Becker). L. 47 cm. Provenance unknown. (Fellmann, no. 6, figs. 6–9.)

d. Chalandriani variety. Athens, Goulandris Collection no. 105. L. 13.7 cm. Provenance unknown. (NG, no. 110.)

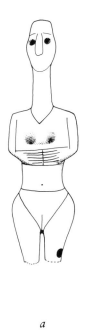
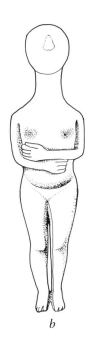
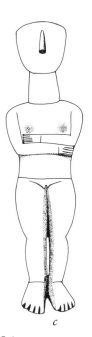
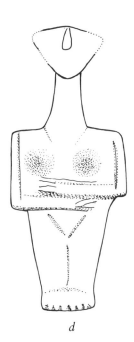

a   b   c   d

40 cm or more (fig. 28 c). On the much smaller Plastiras figures the hands were made considerably wider than the arms to allow sufficient room for the engraving of fingers, although the number indicated on each hand is often incorrect (fig. 28 a). (In the work of certain Plastiras sculptors the boldly delineated grooves have a pattern effect reminiscent more of abdominal creases than fingers.) A similar widening of the hands was tried in a more naturalistic fashion on a few of the experimental, precanonical figures with folded arms, but this approach did not take hold (fig. 28 b). Most sculptors of the classical phase, when fashioning small- or average-sized figures with their correspondingly narrow forearms, simply did not tackle the difficult problem of neatly incising the correct number of lines in a space of less than one centimeter, while a few sculptors went ahead and engraved too few and/or not very tidy ones (fig. 28 d). The feet of Cycladic figures are, by contrast, usually considerably wider than the arms, and toes – not always in the correct number, to be sure – were regularly incised even on quite small figures. The presence of toes, however, does not affect the appearance of a figure nearly as strongly as fingers whose central position makes them a focal point of the viewer's gaze.

One can only guess what factors prompted a sculptor to carve a figure in a particular size. Among the possible considerations might have been the wishes and relative wealth of the person commissioning the figure (if, in fact, figures were commissioned), the dimensions of the available raw material, the amount of time and energy the sculptor was willing to invest in the work, and the level of his proficiency. Generally speaking, a larger sculpture probably required more labor than a smaller one, but in terms of fragility the smaller sculpture was the more difficult to carve effectively to a high degree of refinement. Some sculptors may have felt more comfortable working in a particular scale, while others may have been able to work in different scales with equal ease. Most sculptors probably began with works of modest size. Some may have continued to work on a small scale throughout their careers, whereas others may have found a small scale too limiting once they had mastered the craft and may have preferred to work in a large or midrange scale where greater refinement was possible with less risk.

Large figures tend to be proportionately narrower than small ones, which suggests that the sculptor deliberately designed his figure in this way not only for the sake of elegance but also in order that it might fit his own palm comfortably during the carving process, enabling him to secure his grip on it for greater accuracy of execution. Another possible concern suggested by the proportions of the large figure was that it be sufficiently light and slender to be easily carried on the outstretched palms of a bearer (or bearers in the case of the nearly life-size works) for the procession to the gravesite.

It does not seem likely that there was in the Cycladic Early Bronze Age a standardized system of measurement used specifically by sculptors. If a single standard had been used, one would expect to find many figures carved in the same sizes. In fact, however, a great many different sizes are found. On the other hand, it is possible that some sculptors at least developed their own individual systems, guided perhaps by a measurement of their own hands or feet. In several cases the largest known work of a sculptor is in its length very nearly an exact multiple of his smallest surviving work, suggesting that modular units may have been used by these sculptors. Although we can only guess why a given figure is a particular size, it is clear that its size did have a direct influence on its appearance with respect both to its structure and the elaborateness of its surface markings.

Painted Details

The sculptor completed his figure by smoothing it, sometimes polishing it to a high luster (e.g., pls. VIA, X), after which, at least if he lived in the first half or so of the classical phase, he would have added certain details in red or blue paint. There is no evidence that the figures of the archaic phase *regularly* had specific details painted on them although one or two Plastiras pieces have a dab of red paint on the face or torso, and at least one late Plastiras figure has red stripes on the cheeks and neck (pls. IB, VIIA). But beginning with the pre-canonical figures, as the growing trend toward simplification began to reduce the amount of plastically treated surface detail, the idea of adding facial features and other details with paint evidently began to gain popularity. It is probably safe to say that by the time of the first true folded-arm figures at the beginning of the second phase, virtually all figures except the schematic ones received at least some painted detail. There is less evidence for the consistent use of paint on figures produced at the end of the second phase. The possible omission of painted details on the majority of these statuettes would be consistent with their stylized simplicity and their often summary execution.

The actual pigment is only rarely preserved, but many figures show paint "ghosts" – that is, once-painted areas that, because they were protected by paint, now appear lighter in color, smoother and/or slightly raised above the surrounding surface, which is often in poorer condition. In some cases the ghost lines are so pronounced that they have been mistaken for actual relief work.

Mostly the colored additions to the marble took the form of eyebrows and eyes with almond-shaped outlines and dotted pupils (though in some cases the entire eye was painted) and a solid band across the forehead that often merges with a solid area on the back and sides of the head, indicating hair. Less often curls were painted on the sides and back of the head, and there are one or two cases of painted ears and even nostrils (pls. VIA, VIIC). It appears that the mouth was not normally painted, a seemingly purposeful omission perhaps explained by the sepulchral symbolism of the figures.

The cheeks were frequently decorated with a "tattoo" of dots or stripes and the chin with dots, which may reflect the way the faces of the dead were painted for burial (pls. VIID, XI, fig. 42*f–h*). Occasionally stripes were painted on the neck or forearms (pls. VIID, IXA, figs. 42*h*, 45*a*), and sometimes grooves were highlighted with pigment (pls. VI, VIIC).

One magnificent figure stands out among all the others for its wealth of painted detail (pl. VIA, fig. 29). Carved in fine white marble, its surface highly polished, this masterpiece of the Kapsala variety exhibits, in addition to carved ears, dark (but originally blue) painted hair, eyebrows and eyes, red nostrils, and possibly, though by no means definitely, a red mouth. Red paint was used also for a tattoo of close-spaced rows of dots covering the face, for a delicate necklace whose loop motif is seen also at the sides of the head, and for a fringelike pattern at the top of the neck. Red is used again in the finger grooves and for a pair of vertical lines on each wrist. A faint dark line across the top of the pubic area suggests that this was painted blue originally. (A number of other Kapsala-variety figures seem to have had the pubic triangle similarly defined or painted as a solid area.)

Not all Kapsala- and Spedos-variety figures were as richly painted as this figure, but most if not all once had vividly colored eyes and forehead band (representing hair or possibly a diadem). The use of color in Cycladic sculpture may have a disturbing effect on the present-day viewer, accustomed as he or she is to the purity of white marble that has, like classical Greek sculpture and architecture, for the most part lost its color. But to the Early Bronze Age islander the color probably had a powerful magical meaning. The use of red ochre smeared on the dead to symbolize blood and hence the restoration of life beyond the grave is widespead among various peoples in different periods, and its use, largely for non-anatomical details, on Cycladic sculpture should probably be similarly interpreted.

Blue had a special significance also. In two graves at Aplomata on Naxos the excavator found that a blue dye had been poured over the body and the floor as part of the funeral rites. That both red (hematite and cinnabar) and blue (azurite) were prized by the Early Cycladic islanders as necessities for the afterlife is evident from the presence in many graves of lumps of coloring matter, mortars and pestles for grinding them, as well as palettes for mixing, bronze needles for applying, and pots and bone canisters for storing the pulverized pigments.

The Sculptor's Craft

In the light of the essential similarity of form, proportions, and details within each type or variety of Cycladic figure, and in view of the *relative* scarcity of figures of all types, it seems most unlikely that these sculptures would have been made during leisure time by ordinary farmers or seamen. On the contrary, it should by now be clear that the Cycladic sculptor's craft was highly specialized, governed, it seems, by simple yet sophisticated rules and requiring special tools and instruments. It was a craft, moreover, that was not apparently supported by ordinary islanders (who may have whittled themselves wooden figurines), but rather by a small minority of more prosperous souls. It cannot, therefore, have been practiced by many sculptors at any one time – a fact that was no doubt influential in solidifying and maintaining such a circumscribed tradition. The skills and techniques, the formulae and conventions for working marble were very likely handed down from father to son much

FIG. 29. Detail of a figure with elaborate painted detail. Kapsala variety. Possibly a work of the Kontoleon Master. Private collection. Pres. L. 69.4 cm (legs missing from knees). Provenance unknown. (Pl. VI*A*.)

as they still are on a few of the islands. In the mid-1960s, for example, a man known as Marmaroyánni (Marble John) was supplying the villagers of Apeiranthos on Naxos with crosses and gravestones: he had learned this craft from his father, Marmaroyórgo (Marble George).

Since the marble master's craft was practiced by individuals rather than by groups, with works of some of these individuals finding their way to other places – most often, probably, to coastal communities on neighboring islands – it seems that easily recognizable island "schools" did not develop. That is to say, one cannot look at a figure and, as some have tried to do, identify it as a Naxian or a Parian or an Amorgian product, even though it might well be possible to ascribe it to the hand of a sculptor who, it can be supposed from the archaeological evidence, lived on a particular island. At any given point, then, during the Early Cycladic period there seems to have been a more or less homogeneous style common to all the Cyclades that were producing marble objects in any quantity.

In this chapter we have examined the highly structured framework within which the Cycladic figure carver worked, and in doing so have touched on the sort of departures from the norm that were tolerated as well as on certain aspects of design and execution that were a matter of personal preference. As mentioned at the beginning of this chapter, within the basic format an almost limitless variety of form and detail was possible. This depended on a great many variables including the sculptor's innate ability, technical proficiency, training, experience, as well as his exposure to the works and criticism of others. The range of variety and nuance can only be understood against the background of the traditional precepts – the Pan-Cycladic style – and appreciated through a close examination of the personal styles of individual artists. It is time, then, to look beyond the strictures controlling the individual to the works of some of these masters. The next chapter will be devoted to the problems and considerations involved in isolating the works of particular sculptors.

Chapter Three

Isolating the Individual Hand

F R O M A N ultra-conservative standpoint it could be said that the only figures that can be attributed to the same sculptor unequivocally are those that are joined together, carved in a single piece of marble. Very few two- and three-figure compositions are well enough preserved to permit comparison of their component parts. But, as a preface to the subject of the present chapter, it might be useful to examine three of these groups that have survived in their entirety.

One-Piece Compositions

In the case of each of the two-figure compositions illustrated in plate 1, the "top" figure is in nearly every respect (except, necessarily, the feet), an almost exact replica in miniature of the "lower" figure. On the precanonical work (1 A), the only significant difference is one of iconography: the larger figure is represented as pregnant; the smaller one has almost no midsection at all. On the well-known Spedos-variety work in Karlsruhe (1 B), the only important difference has to do with precaution: the leg-cleft of the larger figure received the standard perforation; the smaller one, in order to keep its delicate legs as strong as possible, did not.[41]

The two males in the Karlsruhe three-figure group are, practically speaking, mirror images of one another (pl. 1 C). The only noticeable difference – a very minor one to be sure – may be seen in the treatment of the groin area. This difference could perhaps be attributed to a lack of familiarity on the part of their sculptor with the carving of male figures, with the result that he did not have a tried and true method or formula for depicting this part of the male anatomy. (Indeed, to judge from the awkward, albeit symmetrical, way in which the arms that support the female figure are indicated on the back of the composition, it would appear that this sculptor also was not accustomed to carving such trios.) The female figure sitting between the two males is similar to them in certain forms and details, such as the head and spine, that they have in common. On the other hand, those aspects of her image affected by differences of posture and arm position are treated quite differently. Most striking, of course, is the execution of the arms: whereas the female's are indicated in the standard fashion by means of grooves, the arms of the males which steady the female's legs are sculpted in the round. In general, the males have a more three-dimensional quality about them than the female. Indeed, if the female had been carved separately – such sitting figures without seats are known (pl. IIA) – and found in a different context from the males, it would not be possible to attribute this figure to the sculptor of the males, at least not without serious reservation.

The main point of interest here is that the figures in each of the three compositions were, of course, carved at the same time. This simultaneity of execution was of primary importance to the success of what was clearly a deliberate effort by each sculptor to make his figures of the same type be nearly exact duplicates of each other. On the other hand, an examination of the three-figure group has shown that figures of different types, even if executed at the same time as parts of one composition, do not necessarily resemble each other closely in style.

Variables

The extent to which Cycladic figures of one type carved by one artist, but not as part of a one-piece composition, resembled each other one would expect varied from artist to artist and even from piece to piece within the work of one artist. The variations would have been dependent upon a number of factors besides the very important one of the individual's disposition. Some of these variables might have been: (1) whether or not the sculptor had had previous experience carving examples of the particular type in question; (2) whether the type involved was simple or complex; (3) whether or not his figures were carved in close chronological proximity to one another; (4) whether or not he had any previously carved examples of his work on hand on which to model work in progress; (5) whether or not he worked on more than one piece at a time; (6) whether or not he was consistently meticulous, sloppy, or capricious in his workmanship; and (7) whether he was content to repeat himself or whether he was motivated to experiment and refine his style.

Although the precise circumstances involved in each case are obviously irretrievable, they are occasionally open to speculation of the sort just engaged in in the discussion of the Karlsruhe trio. One can surmise that two or more figures of the same type carved by one sculptor would resemble each other most closely if he carved them within a relatively short period of time and if he was a mature and meticulous craftsman thoroughly familiar with their type. One would expect, on the other hand, that the resemblance would have been less striking if the figures were carved during different developmental phases of the sculptor's career or by an erratic sculptor.

In the absence of written signatures or documents or the remains of abandoned work-shops, it would probably not be possible to identify the works of sculptors who out of a freer spirit, carelessness, or ineptitude did not develop an unmistakable style of their own. However, given the strength of the sculptural tradition and the limited number of artists who specialized in marble working, it is doubtful that there would have been many sculptors who could be characterized in these ways. Conscious deviation from established norms as well as conspicuous error were probably not easily tolerated and sculptors would not have wished to risk considerable investments of time and energy on objects whose reception was not guaranteed.

In any attempt to isolate the hands of individual sculptors working within a long-dead and highly conservative tradition, it must be assumed that an individual's works will resemble each other to a significant degree and that this similarity will be stronger than that to figures carved by any other individual. Even so, it is not certain that every work, even of the most conservative artist, will have been sufficiently similar to every other to enable one to recognize all of them as his. If, for example, a very early and a very late work, but no mid-career work, of a sculptor were preserved, it is quite likely that in the absence of this hypothetical "missing link" the early piece might be viewed as the work of one sculptor, the late piece as the work of another. This is the sort of limitation that besets a study of individual hands. However, the rewards of finding works that can be confidently attributed to particular sculptors, and even to specific stages of certain individual sculptors' careers, should far outweigh the limitations of this kind of endeavor.

Figures Found Together

Tsountas was the first Cycladic scholar to recognize the hand of a particular sculptor when he wrote of the two figures he found in the name-grave of the Dokathismata variety that they were "without a doubt" carved by the same person. He noted also that the two large series of schematic figurines found in grave 103 at Pyrgos on Paros and grave 117 at Krassades on Antiparos were most probably each made by one artisan. Tsountas's observations appear to be correct and therefore instructive, for in none of the three cases are all the figures similar in every respect to each other, a point to return to later.

If the safest place to look for figures carved by one sculptor was among the one-piece compositions, the next best place to look would be among those figures found together in the same grave, since the volume of demand in any community was probably never large enough to support more than one sculptor at a time even if, as suggested earlier, sculptors also carved marble vessels. That is not to say that one should expect all graves with more than one figure to contain the work of only one sculptor. Figures fashioned by sculptors in other communities could also have been acquired during travels to other islands or on trips to other parts of a person's own island, and it is also possible that some sculptors traveled about themselves. Indeed, it is likely that some communities had no sculptors of their own but acquired marble objects from outside sources (a subject touched on in chap. 1). Nevertheless, one should probably regard as exceptions rather than the rule all these possibilities, as well as the fact that a grave could contain more than one burial. Grave groups ought, then, to provide a good starting point in a search for individual sculptors and for an introduction to the criteria, problems, limitations, and the kinds of speculation involved in making attributions. Unfortunately, however, as the survey to follow will reveal, there is not an abundance of examples; among those that do exist some are not accessible for study or illustration.

The Archaeological Record

In the first Early Cycladic period schematic figures occasionally occur in quantity, as we have seen – as many as thirteen in grave 117 at Krassades, fourteen in grave 103 at Pyrgos (pl. 2). Usually, however, they occur singly, in pairs, or together with a Plastiras figure. There are two examples of the schematic/Plastiras combination from systematic excavation (Akrotiri, graves 5 and 20) and one group of two schematic figurines and a Plastiras statuette from an undocumented source that form a convincing group (pl. 4A). Few Plastiras figures have been found in excavation. Besides the examples just mentioned, there is one case of a single figure from a grave at Glypha on Paros (pls. 14–15[9]) and a series of four figures recovered from the name-grave of the type, also on Paros (pl. 4B).[42]

The name-grave of the Louros type, on Naxos, which held seven figures (of which five can still be identified with certainty), is the only systematically excavated and reported grave to contain figures of this transitional type (pl. 3A),[43] although another group said to be from Paros, consisting of six figurines, appears also to be a unified find (pl. 3B).

In the second phase figures of the folded-arm varieties tend to be found singly although there are isolated cases in which more than one has been found buried in the same grave. There is also a small number of these from undocumented sources whose reputed common find-contexts appear valid. For the Kapsala variety there are two figures said to be from a grave on Naxos (pl. 5), and a pair of figures from grave 13 at Aplomata on Naxos. For the Spedos variety there are two pairs of figures from excavated sites: grave 10 at Spedos on Naxos (pl. 6) and a deposit without skeletal remains (a cenotaph perhaps) on Ano Kouphonisi. Grave 13 at Aplomata held, besides the two Kapsala-variety figures just mentioned, several examples of the early Spedos variety, as well as three seated female figures, and two schematic, Apeiranthos-type figurines. The contents of this grave were found heaped together in a pit in the foundations of a late Roman building. The entire grave was not preserved and, indeed, the excavator thought it possible that the massing of the finds might have taken place in post-Cycladic times when other occupants of the area chanced upon the prehistoric grave in the course of their own building activities. It is, therefore, not clear whether or not grave 13 originally contained multiple burials. (Normally, tombs containing a number of burials were rather poorly furnished.) If it did, it is likely that the figures would have been the possessions of more than one owner and may represent the work of two or three generations of sculptors, a possibility suggested by the presence in the grave of at least two varieties of the standard type. Another grave at Aplomata (no. 23) held one complete figure and the head of another, while grave 27 yielded two folded-arm figures of the Spedos variety, a fragmentary double figure, as well as a schematic statuette. This last grave was, however, two-storied, which could mean that the figures found in it – it was badly damaged – belonged to different interments, possibly again to different generations of one family.[44]

The special sculptures carved in the style of the early folded-arm varieties tended to be buried by twos with some frequency: there are two harper pairs from undocumented excavations (pls. VIII*A*, 7, 8, 9)[45] and the harper and pipes player duo from a grave on Keros (pls. VIII*B*, 10) that also yielded two folded-arm females.[46] Besides the three seated females from grave 13 at Aplomata, a pair of small seated female figures was also found in grave 15 of this cemetery along with two reclining folded-arm figures (fig. 30). Sadly, all four pieces from this grave were stolen shortly after it was opened; only one of the seated figures has so far been recovered.

The Chalandriani variety is represented by one pair of figures found by Tsountas in grave 307 at the name-site of the variety on Syros, but it is not possible at present to identify both figures. Another pair of figures, one male and one female, is said to come from a single grave on Naxos, possibly with one or two other figures (pls. 11*A*, 12*A*). For the Dokathismata variety there is only the pair of sculptures from the name-grave of the variety mentioned above (pl. 13). Virtually all other examples were chance finds or the fruits of unauthorized digging. The Apeiranthos type contemporaneous with the folded-arm figures is represented by a trio of images from grave 16 at Spedos and by the pair found at Aplomata in grave 13.[47]

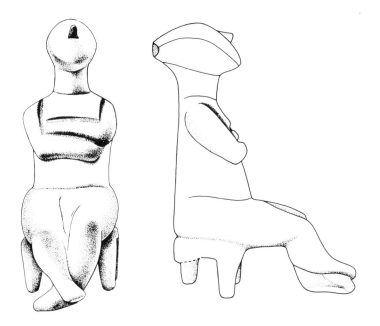

FIG. 30. One of two seated female figures from grave 15 at Aplomata. Early Spedos-variety style. Stolen from the Naxos Archaeological Museum: present location unknown. H. 12 cm. (Drawings based on photographs sent to author when piece surfaced briefly on European antiquities market in 1978. See PGP, *ECS*, fig. 28.)

Deciding whether two sculptures are the work of one sculptor is, admittedly, a somewhat subjective process. Yet, the styles of most Cycladic artists have left a distinctive mark of some sort on their works even though this "signature" cannot always be effectively described in words. It is precisely because subjective judgments are involved in making attributions to anonymous sculptors who worked more than four thousand years ago that it would be wise to look closely first at sculptures that were found together since the chances are good that they were carved by one artist.

Schematic Figurines

Beginning with the schematic images, it seems logical that here one should expect considerable diversity. These pieces are essentially modified beach pebbles (or in rare cases, shells) whose natural shape influenced the final form in their transformation into artifacts. Presumably the simplicity of these small works obviated the need for strict prescriptions (although even in many such figurines, as implausible as it may seem, specific harmonic angles appear to have been used). It should not be difficult to imagine one sculptor fashioning the fourteen figures found in grave 103 at Pyrgos (pl. 2A), for example, even though four different variants are represented. Nor should it be difficult to see that another sculptor made the thirteen figures found in grave 117 at Krassades (pl. 2B). This sculptor shows a fondness for indentations that is expressed on both some of his violin figures and on the tripartite piece (pl. 2B.13). In comparison to the first sculptor whose figurines have simple notched waists, this sculptor preferred to give his a well-defined midsection. Although it is possible to envision one sculptor at work in each grave group, this would have been impossible had the figures not been found in distinct groups. Both the differences observable from piece to piece in each case and the overriding simplicity of their forms are strong deterrents to any thought of assigning to the hands of these sculptors other pieces not found in association with the two groups, or at least not in the same cemeteries or localities, unless they are virtually identical to one of their members.

The Louros Type

The forms of the Louros type are a good deal more complicated than those of the various schematic types, and yet there is also considerable diversity of shape and detail from piece to piece in each of the surviving grave groups. Nevertheless, in the case of the figures from the name-grave, the similarity of their marble and workmanship and their similar, indeed, seemingly deliberately graduated sizes (ranging from ca. 13 cm to 22 cm, as compared to 6 cm to 28.7 cm for the type as a whole), strongly favor their ascription to a single sculptor (pl. 3A).[48] One might call him the Stephanos Master after their excavator.[49] (The term *master* is used throughout this book to denote a craftsman who was thoroughly competent in his profession although not necessarily highly skilled or capable of producing masterpieces.) The differences observable from piece to piece in the work of this sculptor appear to have been made intentionally, perhaps for the sake of variety within the group. These differences, however, are sufficiently great to make it difficult to attribute pieces from other sources to the hand of this talented sculptor unless they strongly resemble a particular piece in the group.[50]

The group of Louros figures in Cambridge (pl. 3B) is effectively unified by the fact that three of them are made of an unusual, though not unprecedented, material – shell (pl. 3B. 4– 6). The two smaller marble images are quite similar to the shell figures, while the largest marble piece, though more complex than the others, has elements found on other figures in the group. In short, it seems entirely safe to say that these six pieces represent the work of one sculptor, the Fitzwilliam Louros Master (not to be confused with the Fitzwilliam Master, a sculptor of Spedos-variety figures discussed in chap. 5).

The Plastiras / Schematic Combination

In two cases, at Akrotiri on Naxos (graves 5 and 20), a Plastiras statuette was found together with a violin figure, but aside from their common find context, nothing suggests that one sculptor carved both pieces though one should not rule out that possibility. Each of the violin figures is as large or larger than the Plastiras figure found with it, so that it is unlikely, in any case, that they were carved as companion pieces. The third instance in which both figure types occur is quite different. That the three small figurines in the Missouri group are the work of one sculptor, the Missouri Master, seems evident (pl. 4A). Carved in the same marble and in a more appropriate scale, the three works appear to have been fashioned as a group. Moreover, the proportions of the larger of the two violin figures are nearly identical to those of the Plastiras statuette if one thinks away its legs, while the proportions of the smaller violin figure, which is in other respects closely similar to the larger, do not differ appreciably. Finally, the outline contours of the shoulders and upper arms are virtually identical on all three pieces.[51]

The Plastiras Type

The situation appears to be somewhat different in the case of the four figures found together in grave 9 at Plastiras on Paros. Here it would seem that the hands of two different sculptors are represented, with one responsible for three figures (pl. 4B.1–3), another – a rather inept one – for the fourth (pl. 4B.4). All the figures are quite weathered, particularly 4B.3, whose outline is badly eroded, and it appears that the legs of 4B.1 were broken off at the knees in antiquity. The break surfaces have become so worn as to make it look as if the figure was originally made with truncated legs. Taking their state of preservation into account, figures 4B.1–3, while not replicas of each other by any means, are sufficiently similar to view them as the work of one artist whom one might call the Doumas Master after their excavator. Moreover, they share certain obvious qualities of form and contour, as well as such similarly executed details as the mouth, navel, and spine, all lacking on the fourth piece. One might speculate that this figure was the product of an untutored person (an apprentice perhaps) working alongside the sculptor of the other three and trying to copy him. Of the three figures by this sculptor, 4*B*.2 with its full oval face and somewhat more rounded contours is perhaps the most representative of his personal style. As will be shown in the next chapter, a number of other figures should be attributed to him. These tend to resemble 4*B*.2 more than 4*B*.1 or 3.

Folded-Arm Figures

Turning to groups of the second Early Cycladic phase, one might look first at the two Kapsala figures in Oxford said to have been found together in a grave on Naxos that apparently also contained a third figure and four lead boat models (pl. 5).[52] The two figures are carved in the same marble (mentioned in chap. 1) that has weathered in the distinctive manner typical of a number of other Kapsala-variety figures. There are many noteworthy differences among the two images: the larger one has a more sharply broken profile axis, its forearms do not taper, the hips are fuller, and in general its forms are more rounded. Nevertheless, both figures are not only typical examples of the Kapsala variety but are also similar enough to each other to warrant an attribution to a single hand. It is possible that they were carved at somewhat different points during the sculptor's career.

With the exception of one seated figure (fig. 30), it is not possible to illustrate the finds from Aplomata, and since only some of the many figures found at this site have received preliminary publication to which the reader can refer, remarks made here must necessarily be brief and limited. The contents of grave 13 of this cemetery in particular cannot be ignored, however, for it is the largest and, with at least four different sculptural types or varieties, the most complex grave group discovered to date.

While the two schematic statuettes of shell are so similar to each other as to leave little doubt that they were fashioned by one person, there is no way of telling whether the same person carved any of the other sculptures found with them.

The unearthing of three seated female figures in one grave was an extraordinary event in Early Cycladic archaeology, and one might expect that such a trio would have been the work of a single hand. This is by no means obvious, however. Seated figures were popular at Aplomata and evidently a number of sculptors carved them.[53] Nevertheless, a case could be made for the attribution to one sculptor of the three works despite substantial differences of form and detail if one thinks of them as representing three distinct phases in an ongoing learning process as experienced by that one artist.

Of the eight other members of the unique assemblage of figures from grave 13, I am at present unable to identify two. Of the remaining six, all of which are similar in size, four belong to the early Spedos variety, while two are well-developed examples of the Kapsala variety. At least three different Spedos-variety sculptors seem to be represented, whereas the

Kapsala-variety figures are apparently the work of one gifted sculptor whom one might call the Kontoleon Master after the first excavator of the cemetery.[54] This artist is discussed in chapter 5. It is unclear at this point whether any of the sculptors of the Spedos-variety figures found in the grave were responsible for the seated figures found with them.

All one can say at present in summarizing the figurative finds from this group is that they seem to represent an assortment of sculptors and styles. If, in fact, one person was the owner of all these works – something that is far from clear – he or she would have the distinction of being the first true collector of Early Cycladic art.

The two figures found in grave 10 at Spedos differ in so many obvious points of form, outline contour, and detail that it is not easy to ascribe them to the same artist (pl. 6). On the other hand, they have a similar structure and share the same basic approach to the human form, factors that cannot be overlooked. In a case like this where two figures share certain features but not enough, it would seem on first appraisal, to attribute them with confidence to a single hand, there are two possible explanations. One is that they were carved by two different sculptors who were closely associated: one figure would have been fashioned by a master, the other presumably by his apprentice, the limited demand for marble objects making it unwise to postulate anything more complicated than a master/apprentice or father/son relationship. The idea of a workshop in which a group of sculptors worked side by side, mutually influencing one another, while attractive in the abstract as a way of accounting for differences observable among somewhat similar works, simply does not fit the available archaeological evidence.

The second explanation is that the two works are indeed the productions of a single hand, but that they were carved at different times. As mentioned earlier, it is likely that two figures carved in close chronological proximity will resemble each other more closely than two figures by the same sculptor carved some years apart. This may have been the case even after the personal style of a young master was fully developed. The two figures from grave 10 at Spedos, which differ in size by 14.5 cm, do not seem to have been carved as companion pieces, but were probably acquired at different points during their owner's lifetime.

For the two figures in question, the second explanation seems preferable, with the smaller, less well balanced work viewed as the earlier one. Two features deserve close attention here: the presence on one figure but not on the other of a perforated leg-cleft and the presence on only one figure of incised fingers. It is true that most sculptors seem to have adopted one method of treating the leg-cleft for all their works. Usually the earlier Spedos-variety sculptors perforated it, while the later ones did not. A few sculptors used both methods (pls. 38, 44); in the case of the tandem two-figure compositions, the two methods were even used on the same sculpture (pl. 1B). In the last chapter the size of a piece was seen as an important consideration influencing the depiction of fingers. It is no coincidence that the larger of the two figures is the one that has carefully incised fingers: its modeled forearms are twice as wide as the flatter, grooved arms of the smaller work.

The presence of the perforated leg-cleft and of fingers on only one of the two figures in each case does much to accentuate the impression of their dissimilarity. However, the presence or absence of such details ought not to have any bearing on whether or not two pieces are attributable to the same or to different hands. And, as we shall see in the work of the Goulandris Master, for example, relief modeling of the arms can be an indication of a sculptor's full maturation (see chap. 6).

In contrast to the sculptures from grave 10 at Spedos, the pair of excellently preserved early Spedos-variety figures found together by Photeini Zapheiropoulou on Ano Kouphonisi are both quite small. They differ to a considerable degree in overall appearance, particularly in their head and leg forms, although they share certain features such as the brief midsection recessed below the arms. It is unclear whether the two figures, which are apparently carved in the same marble, were made by two different sculptors in contact with each other or by a single artist, a rather mediocre one, who may not have had a discrete style of his own and who may have made them at different times.[55]

Special Figures

Each of the three pairs of seated figures found together appears to be the work of one individual. In each case the two compositions are very close to each other in size and appear to have been deliberately made for use as a pair. Yet in each case one work appears more competently fashioned than the other. The two seated figures from grave 15 at Aplomata vividly call to mind a pair of plump little ladies, such as one might see in the Cyclades today, sitting on low stools with their arms and feet crossed, enjoying a bit of leisure and gossip in front of their houses. The two pieces are, in some respects, nearly duplicates of each other, a fact that should become clear once both are published. The crossing of the feet is at present unparalleled in the work of other sculptors (fig. 30).

In the case of the two pairs of harp players significant differences of form and detail are observable from one piece to the next. Even so, the two members of each pair resemble one another in planning as well as in form and detail far more closely than they do any of the other figures of their type. The sculptors of such rare pieces must ordinarily have carved reclining folded-arm females: the sculptor of the privately owned pair (pls. VIIIA, 7, 8) would have carved Kapsala-variety figures, while the sculptor of the Karlsruhe pair (pl. 9) would have carved his females in the style of the early Spedos variety. Thus, they were accustomed to working with an essentially two-dimensional planklike slab of marble rather than with a rectangular solid. The harper type with its unprecedented intricacies provided the sculptor with problems different from any he encountered while making standard pieces. And in the absence of sketchbooks and models in other materials, each of these rare works must have stood not only as a finished piece but in a sense also as a trial piece. The differences of form and detail and even of the position of certain parts such as the arms can perhaps be attributed to a conscious desire on the part of the sculptor not merely to copy himself but, within the guidelines of the canon, to improve his work from one piece to the next as he gained confidence and experience with an unfamiliar and difficult type. As with the seated ladies of Aplomata, it is clear that one member of each harper pair is more competently executed, better balanced, and freer and more relaxed in attitude than the other, indicating that in carving it the sculptor had learned from the "mistakes" made when he fashioned the other member. Thus, for example, in the case of the Karlsruhe harpers, the problems encountered by the sculptor in carving the figure in plate 9.1 – largely in the area of the right shoulder and arm – were corrected by him when he went on to make the figure in plate 9.2.[56]

Every sculptor of special figure types no doubt carved many standard female figures during the course of his career. Indeed, sculptors probably did not even attempt exceptional works until they had become thoroughly proficient at making standard ones. And yet, because of the typological differences, it is very difficult to attribute to these artists any of the many known reclining figures. As in the three-figure composition discussed in chapter 2, it would appear that the sculptor had to alter his personal style quite drastically when fashioning figures that are iconographically different.

The grave group from Keros, besides two folded-arm figures,[57] contained the harper and pipes player in Athens (pls. VIIIB, 10). Here, too, because of typological and iconographic differences (and perhaps also because the hands and feet of the harper are missing, the latter inaccurately restored in plaster), it is not possible to tell if the two musician figures were made by the same person. Not only does the piper have a somewhat stockier structure than the harper but the two works are carved in a different scale, which probably means that they were not originally conceived as companion pieces.

Late Classical Figures

Turning now to grave groups of the second half of the Early Cycladic II phase, there is, first of all, the assemblage in the Goulandris Collection said to have come from a grave on Naxos (both Spedos and Phionta have been mentioned as the find-place, as has Keros also). The group is alleged to have contained four figures, but its integrity is not entirely convincing (pls. 11A, 12A). Two of the figures, a male and a female of the Chalandriani variety – called "king" and "queen" by the islander who found them – certainly belong together and were undoubtedly carved by one sculptor. A third figure, a pregnant female of the Spedos variety, could not have been made by this sculptor and in fact was probably carved several generations before his time. The fourth figure is a curious, seemingly unfinished, limp-limbed work of poor quality that, in some of its forms and contours (but not in the depiction of the forearms), bears a slight resemblance to the "king" and "queen." It is rather similar to another figure in the same collection, presumably from the same source, which bears a somewhat closer resemblance to the "royal" pair (C). These poor pieces appear to be uninformed renderings of the standard folded-arm figure – note the uncanonical reversal of the arms – although they conform to the specific conventions of no particular variety of the type. It is conceivable that they were immature works of a sculptor who went on to develop the rather unorthodox Chalandriani-variety style seen in the "king" and "queen" and in a second female figure whose provenance is unknown (pls. 11B, 12B). This sculptor is called the Goulandris Hunter/Warrior Master to distinguish him from a superior sculptor of late Spedos-variety figures known simply as the Goulandris Master (see chap. 6).

The Goulandris Hunter/Warrior Master is one of a very small number of sculptors from whose hand survive figures representing both sexes. His are, however, the only extant male and female figures of the same type thought to have been found together in one grave.[58] This artist's works lack the crisp angular lines normally associated with the Chalandriani variety. But while the basic structure of his figures is rather amorphous and slack, they display an attention to detail that is quite uncommon at this late date in the manufacture of Cycladic sculpture. Despite an indifferent execution, their strangely sensitive fingers and stern tight-lipped expressions are, therefore, all the more arresting. One or two details seem to be unique to this sculptor's work: his is the only male figure of the second phase with testicles, while his female figures are unusual in that the apex of their pubic triangles is open to indicate the vulva; his "queen" also has superficially incised eyelashes. Unlike the other figures with a carefully depicted baldric, indicated by a simple strap in relief crossing over the right shoulder, the baldric of the Goulandris hunter/warrior is worn over the left shoulder and is elaborately worked in a different pattern for each surface. This figure also has a hair "roll" at the nape of the neck that is not present on the female images carved by him although all three have a curious caplike headdress or hairdo at the top of the head. The hair roll is seen on two other male figures made by different sculptors and seems to have been an exclusively male coiffure (fig. 11d, e). Differences of gender and iconography aside, the three works attributable with confidence to the hand of the Goulandris Hunter/Warrior Master are remarkably similar in virtually every respect except the position of the forearms, which differs slightly in each case.

The last grave group to consider is the pair of angular figures found by Tsountas in grave 14 at Dokathismata on Amorgos and identified by him as the work of one sculptor (pl. 13). These sculptures are interesting because although on the front they are very much alike from the waist up, below this point they are markedly different from each other. So different, in fact, is the treatment of their legs and pubic areas that if this were the only part of the figures preserved, no one would think of attributing them to the same hand. And yet the similarity of their upper halves is so strong – note especially the treatment of the forearms – as to leave no doubt that they were carved by a single person one might call the Tsountas Master.[59]

This is perhaps the only pair of figures representing females found together whose differences could conceivably be viewed as deliberately intended to reflect a difference of identity. Scholars who interpret the Cycladic folded-arm female as an image of a goddess look upon the two-figure compositions as well as such figure pairs as representing the goddess as a mother accompanied by her daughter – a prehistoric Demeter and Kore, if you will. Indeed, the larger of the two sculptures from Dokathismata with its ample, clearly incised pubic triangle might be interpreted as a mature woman, the smaller one with its simple forked pubis (and smaller breasts) as the image of a young girl. However, the occurrence of two folded-arm female figures in the same context – at least among systematically excavated and credibly reported cases – is, as has been shown, exceedingly rare, even rarer than two-figure compositions. The only difference regularly observed among such works is that one is smaller than the other, but as already noted, the size of a piece could have been determined by a number of factors other than the relative ages of the being(s) depicted.

Criteria for Identifying Individual Sculptors

Perhaps the most important point to be gleaned from the foregoing survey of sculptures found in the same contexts is that the considerations involved in attributing pieces to a particular hand are in no two cases exactly alike. The degree of similarity observable among figures ultimately assignable to one sculptor can vary considerably. In some cases, it is easy to isolate the works of an artist on the basis of the most casual visual inspection because in all major respects they seem to be recreations of one another. Sometimes the figures of one sculptor are very similar to each other in overall appearance even though in size, and in certain details associated with size, they might differ markedly. Other sculptors' figures may differ in many respects but show resemblances in certain areas that are so strong as to rule out the possibility of coincidence. Still other sculptors' works may be sufficiently dissimilar to make ascriptions less reliable.

In the absence of any really compelling similarities among figures of the same type or in the face of figures of different types, it is much easier to make attributions to a single hand if they share the same find-context than if they had not been found together. In the next three chapters we abandon the safe haven of the grave groups for the most part to choose from among the many figures scattered in Far Eastern, European, and North American museums and private collections in an effort to isolate several works by a number of different sculptors, many of them in their maturity consummate practitioners of their craft.

In striking out in these uncharted waters, it has been necessary to adopt a somewhat more conservative approach than was possible with the known grave groups. In each case only figures of the standard complex (that is, representational) types have been chosen for discussion, although it is not unlikely that some or all of their sculptors produced simple schematic figurines (not to mention marble vessels) as well, while some may also have fashioned figures belonging to the special types.

What one must look for in making attributions is a recurring complex of characteristics that define a sculptor's style within the framework of the tradition. As with the figures buried together, this might involve aspects of the outline contours, the treatment of specific forms, an unusual use of the angular system, an adaptation of the canonical plan, and/or the manner in which certain details were executed. In all likelihood no single feature will be startlingly unique to one sculptor's work. Originality – or, more accurately, individuality – in such a tradition-bound art form lies not in the adoption of new elements so much as in the particular choice or combination of familiar ones. Individual excellence, moreover, would have depended not at all on an innovative rendering but rather on the harmony of a well-balanced, skillfully executed design utilizing traditional formulaic elements. (The quality of the marble and the surface finish and painting would also have been considered.) Given the obvious fact that the sculptures were made by hand with handcrafted tools, the execution of these traditional elements, regardless whatever other factors might have been involved, would naturally, not deliberately, have varied from sculptor to sculptor and even, to some extent, from piece to piece within a sculptor's work.

It has not been my intention in speaking about the Cycladic sculptural tradition to give the impression that it was some sort of all-powerful deity before which the artist humbled himself, restraining his urge to create freely as it constrained him to obey its laws. On the contrary, the time-tested ways of producing a piece of sculpture must have been a comfort to the sculptor, allowing him to control his material and exercise his skills in the knowledge that after considerable effort the final outcome would be successful, which is to say that it would be fully accepted. The tradition was, after all, the creation of sculptors, not an impersonal force manipulating them, and while in impact it transcended the work of any one individual or any generation of individuals, it was itself the sum of all the personal styles of many individuals working over many generations. Each sculptor's approach to the human figure contributed to and participated in the general, traditional style. This tradition changed, to be sure, but over a period of time as sculptors gradually introduced new ways, for example, of positioning the arms, or reducing the risks of fracture or the amount of labor required to produce a finished work. Because stylistic innovations were introduced slowly and not for their own sake, one would not expect to be able to define any particular individual's contribution to the shaping of the tradition. By the same token, it would probably be impossible to single out those unusually inventive sculptors who, in response to some cultural need, first introduced the special figures. These novel forms were easily integrated into the traditional repertoire, becoming established as conventional, albeit rarely used types through their repetition by other artists.

The primary concern of the next three chapters, then, is to identify the works and discuss the personal styles of individual sculptors. In doing this, we will define the ways in which each sculptor's works resemble each other and the ways in which they differ. Each artist's work will be set against the background of the tradition and any apparent idiosyncracies will be identified. The quality of each sculptor's work will be assessed, and where there is a sufficiently large body of material, we will speculate about the development of his style. And finally, note will be taken of the geographic distribution of his work.

In the final chapter, the question of distribution will be considered more comprehensively and the thorny problem of the relation of find-place to place of manufacture will be addressed in an effort to discover the island home of at least some of the sculptors of the classical phase introduced in chapters 5 and 6.

Chapter Four

Three Archaic Sculptors

I<small>N</small> <small>T H I S</small> and the two following chapters, the work of sixteen sculptors is discussed. At least some of the pieces attributed to each of these artists are illustrated, while a checklist of each artist's oeuvre is included in Appendix 1. The entries in the checklists are identified in the text by bracketed numbers. The illustrations also carry these checklist numbers. The reader is urged to study the plates devoted to the works ascribed to each master before reading the discussion.

T H E   D O U M A S   M A S T E R
[Pls. 4B, 14, 15; Checklist, p. 155]

We begin with a sculptor whose three name-pieces from grave 9 at Plastiras were discussed in the last chapter (pl. 4B). It seems possible to attribute several additional works to his hand, including two male figures [4, 5], one of which has an incised belt [5], and four female figures [1, 2, 3, 9], of which one has four incised creases on her abdomen [3]. One of the figures [6] from grave 9 has three similar grooves that are not visible on the photograph (pl. 4B.1).

With one exception, the figures are all closely similar in style and small in size, ranging in height from about 11 cm to 15.3 cm. The exception [9], which comes from a grave at Glypha on Paros, is slightly more than twice the size of the largest of these and is, incidentally, rather large for the Plastiras type as a whole.

Exacerbated to some extent by their present weathered surfaces, the workmanship of eight of the nine statuettes seems uniformly rather rough, the modeling somewhat amorphous. As a result, certain features such as the nose, neckline, and arms are not clearly distinguished; the incised details, moreover, are only very superficially drawn. The fingers, absent altogether on some figures, are crudely scratched on the others. The piece from Glypha,

71

on the other hand, was carved with greater care and interest in the definition of individual forms and in neatness, particularly in the execution of the fingers and also the toes, which are not indicated on the three other completely preserved figures in the group. The greater size of the Glypha figure allowed the sculptor a better opportunity to make the requisite number of fingers and toes with tidy, closely spaced parallel incisions.

The outline contours of the nine works show a strong resemblance to each other. This resemblance is especially marked in the line of the shoulders, which are slightly higher at their widest point, and in the line of the upper arms, which shows a slight convexity. With the exception of the male figures, whose broader waist and unaccentuated hips are more appropriate to their sex, the outlines of the midsection and the strongly curving hips are also very much alike. (The hips of the largest member of the group from grave 9 appear to be angular in outline [8], but this is perhaps an illusion caused by encrustation that has formed where the hips are widest.) In profile the figures all show the same straight axis, with the back exhibiting little contour except for a slight bulge at the buttocks.

The proportions of the nine figures do not differ appreciably though some are notice-ably stockier than others. All appear to have been planned more or less accurately according to the standard Plastiras canon in which the height is divided into three equal parts (fig. 15a). Moreover, the angular aspects of the figures seem to have benefited from the system of har-monic angles: the shoulder/upper arm angle conforms very well to the larger of the two com-plementary angles, while the pubic triangle corresponds to the smaller one. As one might expect, the Glypha figure is the most carefully designed of the nine works.

Also strikingly similar from piece to piece is the rendering of individual forms and de-tails such as the almost straight-topped oval face with knob ears (partially worn away on some examples), short slit mouth, and on the female figures the small round navel and the bikinilike pubic triangle depressed between the thighs, which has a small section cut out of its apex to indicate the vulva (though on the Glypha figure the vulva is rendered by incision). Along with the upturned shoulders, narrow waist, and the particular way the hips curve on the females, these constitute the recurring elements that make the Doumas Master's style readily recognizable even though there is nothing about his works that is in any way atypical.

The Doumas Master was the most prolific sculptor of Plastiras figures now known. Of the approximately forty sculptures of this type that are preserved in their entirety or in part, roughly 25 percent can be attributed to his hand. He was a sculptor primarily of modest works on which he did not lavish a great deal of care, but he was capable of some icono-graphic range and did carve at least one very carefully conceived work in a larger scale. It is tempting to look upon the Glypha figure, which is clearly his best effort, as the product of the sculptor's maturity and to view his other works as belonging to an earlier phase of his career.

There is good reason to believe that the Doumas Master was a Parian. Four of his works have been found in the course of systematic excavation on Paros: three in grave 9 at Plastiras, one in grave 23 at Glypha. A fifth statuette [2], now in Oxford, was acquired at Lefkes and is

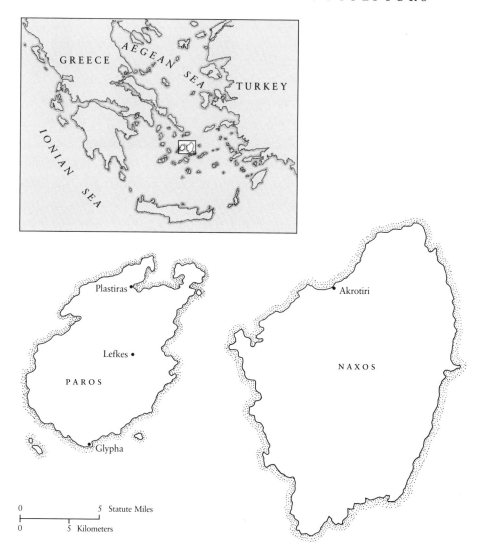

FIG. 31. Find-places of figures attributed to the Doumas Master

presumed to have been found in a grave in the vicinity of that village. A sixth work was recovered, along with a violin figure that may or may not be by the Doumas Master's hand, in grave 5 at Akrotiri on Naxos [1]. This, then, is the earliest known case in which figures attributable to one sculptor have been found not only at more than one site on one island, but also on more than one island. The find-spots, located on the north and south coasts and the east side of Paros, on the one hand, and on the west coast of Naxos, on the other, are accessible to each other by sea, especially in good weather (fig. 31). It was perhaps no less difficult for the people who lived in these places to maintain contacts with each other than it was for them to interact with the inhabitants of their own islands who lived further inland. It is, of course, possible that the Doumas Master himself wandered from community to com-

73

munity, satisfying the need for marble objects as he went. The find-spots of the male figures now in Geneva and Dresden [4, 5] and the female figure with bands [3] are not known.

It is likely that the Doumas Master, whether at home or in his travels, also made marble vessels, especially collared jars or *kandiles*, and that this type of marble carving may even have formed the major part of his workload. A small kandila that was found with one of his figurines in grave 5 at Akrotiri is quite similar in form to the kandiles found at Plastiras in grave 6, and with three of his figurines in grave 9.[60] The finding of similar marble vessels in graves on two different islands containing the figures of one sculptor suggests, at least, that the same sculptor was responsible for making them as well. (It is possible, too, that this sculptor also made the marble palette found in grave 5 at Akrotiri and the bowl with vertical lug found in grave 9 at Plastiras.)[61] It is also conceivable that the lugs of these vessels were perforated with the same implement used to make the repair holes on either side of the break in the left thigh of the male figure in Geneva [4].

THE METROPOLITAN MUSEUM MASTER
[Pls. IA, 16, 17; Checklist, p. 156]

The three well-preserved works in New York, Geneva, and East Berlin, assignable to a second sculptor of Plastiras figures, all represent a female wearing a plain cylindrical headdress, or *polos*. All three are carved in roughly the same scale, their sizes ranging from 18.3 cm [1] to 23.5 cm [3] – that is, about average for the Plastiras type as a whole. The workmanship of the figures is exceptionally fine, and they display a richness of sculpted, incised, and bored detail as well as a surface finish that exemplify the Plastiras type at its best. And despite their strange long ears and empty circular eye sockets, originally inlaid with obsidian or dark pebbles, these bizarre figures show a degree of facial expressiveness not often seen in Cycladic sculpture.

Allowing for certain differences of proportion, as well as for some minor damage (e.g., to the ears of the Berlin figure) that creates an illusion of dissimilarity, their contours as viewed from the front are, with the exception of the shoulder line and elbows, nearly identical. Particularly noteworthy is the strong undulating line of the hips, legs, and ankles. Viewed in profile, the figures all exhibit the same straight axis along which their outlines are punctuated with frequent changes of contour. Though closely similar in pattern on all three, the outline is particularly bold in execution on the name-piece with its jutting nose and chin, pointed breasts, and prominent abdominal bulge and kneecaps. All three figures show the same individualistic treatment of the back line with the small, deeply undercut buttocks, curving thighs and calves, and the small feet with exaggerated arches. On the strength of the similarity in the outline contours alone, it should be possible to attribute the three images to a single hand.

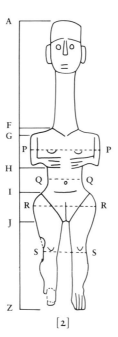

Proportion	[2]	[1]	[3]	Maximum margin of difference
AF : AZ	38%	34%	30%	8%
GH : AZ	12%	10.5%	15%	4.5%
FJ : AZ	31%	32%	41%	10%
HI : AZ	9%	12%	13%	4%
IZ : AZ	40%	44%	51%	11%
PP : AZ	25%	23%	28%	5%
QQ : AZ	12%	16%	15%	4%
RR : AZ	23%	23.5%	24%	1%
SS : AZ	15%	15%	13%	2%

FIG. 32. Comparison of the proportions of the three figures attributed to the Metropolitan Museum Master

[2]

The degree of resemblance of the proportions of the three figures can perhaps be most easily appreciated by studying figure 32. Contrary to what one might expect from a visual appraisal alone, the figures in New York and Geneva resemble each other quite closely, while the figure in Berlin is in most of its proportions closer to the latter. All three are, however, very similar to each other in the ratio to their heights of their widths at various points.

The discrepancies in the apportionment of the vertical elements of the three compositions can be explained in large measure by the particular way in which each one was planned. The Metropolitan Museum Master knew and used the tripartite canon appropriate to the Plastiras type, but his application of it varies from piece to piece. For his name-piece [2], the polos was *added* to the three-part schema, whereas it is an integral part of the design of the other figures (fig. 33). One can appreciate the diversity permitted within the canonical unit, for in each case one-third of the height was allotted to the head (with or without polos) and neck (to the shoulder line). Yet, on the New York figure, the head with polos is equal in length to the neck; on the Berlin figure the head with polos is somewhat longer than the neck; while the piece in Geneva has a very long head, a high polos, and a correspondingly short neck.

The second division of the design was also treated in two different ways by this sculptor. On the Berlin figure the two-thirds mark occurs at the hips, while on the two other figures it falls at the crotch. As a result of these differences, the Berlin figure has a proportionally longer torso and shorter legs than either of the other two. And again, within the space allotted to the middle unit of the composition, there is considerable variety: the New York figure has an ampler upper torso and a shorter midsection than the Geneva piece, while the two areas are more evenly balanced on the Berlin figure.

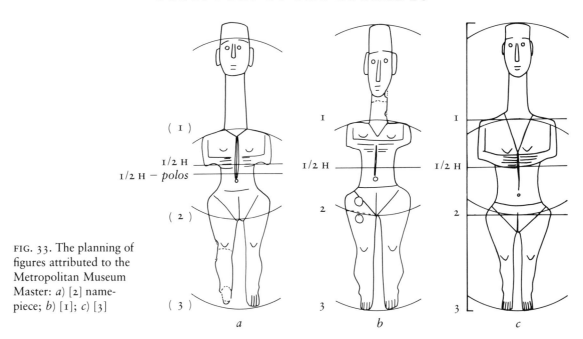

FIG. 33. The planning of figures attributed to the Metropolitan Museum Master: *a)* [2] name-piece; *b)* [1]; *c)* [3]

From the drawings it can also be seen that the Metropolitan Museum Master did not rely as heavily as some sculptors on the compass to define important points on the outline. In the case of the Berlin figure, one could actually say that the important planning device was a straight edge and not a compass.

It would seem that in the hands of this especially skillful and self-assured sculptor the traditional canon was something with which to experiment, something to modify and adapt to his own particular concept of the female form as it developed and changed from piece to piece.

This same spirit may also be seen in the sculptor's use of the harmonic system. Although he employed its angles throughout his pieces, he did not always consistently choose the same ones for the same angular feature on each figure. Whereas, for example, the outline of the shoulder/upper arm conforms to angle B on all three figures, the pubic V on the Geneva and Berlin figures is a right angle $(A + B)/2$; that of the New York piece conforms to angle A. The incised neck V shows three different angles: B on the name-piece, A on the Geneva figure, and $A/2$ on the Berlin piece. Differences in the choice of angles, of course, also contribute to the slightly different appearances of the three images.

Similarities and differences in the treatment of details on the three works can be easily appraised through an examination of the photographs. A few details are of special interest because, along with the boldly conceived outline contours of his pieces, they help to define the Metropolitan Museum Master's unmistakable signature. The unusually long and prominent oblong ears – those of the Berlin figure were originally similar to the ears of the other two – can be considered one of the features peculiar to this sculptor's style. Another mannerism found at present only in his work is the vertical groove that bisects the torso from sternum to navel on all three figures. The angular grooves that converge at the top of the spine, marking the shoulder blades on the New York and Geneva pieces, are also unparalleled at present.

The execution of the details on the three figures is for the most part precise and clear, though again the name-piece stands out as the most carefully made in this respect. Compare, for example, the sharply defined breasts of this figure with the rather amorphous ones of the Berlin piece. In the treatment of one detail only does the Metropolitan Museum Master seem to have wavered. This was the incision of the fingers. The reason for his difficulty had to do with the small size of his figures. The piece on which the fingers are most successfully treated – the one in Berlin – is also the largest of the three, but on none of the works was the minimum of 1 cm required to incise five fingers allotted to the hands and, consequently, even on the Berlin piece, whose fingers are neatly incised, only four could be accommodated on each hand. Despite the fact that the sculptor carved small feet, he had less trouble incising the toes. This was perhaps because the front of the feet curve slightly, giving them a larger surface area than is apparent to the eye. Still, only on the largest figure was he able to incise the correct number of toes.

It is quite likely that the same awl of emery or flint was used to bore the eye sockets, navels, and iliac dimples on the three figures as well as the repair holes in the right leg of the name-piece and in the right thigh and the neck of the Geneva figure. Because of the tool's shape and because of the "wobble" effect resulting from the fact that it was rotated by hand, the path of the hole made by it is conical: the deeper the hole, the larger the opening at its point of entry. Thus, the mending perforations are much larger than the shallow borings of the anatomical details. The size of the latter also varied according to their depths: the eyes, uniform in diameter on the three figures, are slightly larger than the navels, which are shallower.

On the Geneva figure the repair holes were bored from both directions (giving them a distinct hourglass shape), but on the name-piece, because of the site of the fracture, the sculptor had no choice but to bore the top hole from the outside only, while, to minimize the size of the hole on the more visible surface of the calf, he made this lower hole entirely from the inside. The diameter of the hole at the point where the awl completed its perforation of the calf is closely similar to that of the eyes, indicating that the same tool was probably used for both. The obvious conclusion to be drawn from this is that the same craftsman was responsible for both the fashioning and the restoration of the figures. It is, of course, not possible to know whether the New York and Geneva pieces broke while they were being made or if they were returned to their maker for repairs later on.

All three of the figures ought probably to be assigned to the Metropolitan Museum Master's mature phase, but beyond this it is not possible to determine or even to guess at the order in which they were carved, or at what interval.

It is also not possible to hazard a guess as to the island home of this very talented sculptor. None of the three works was found in systematic excavation. The find-places of the name-piece and the figure in Geneva are altogether unknown, while the Berlin figure is supposed to have been found on Delos where it was acquired in 1860. Although the possibility that this figure at least was made and/or found on Delos (or Rheneia) cannot be ignored, one should probably not accept this provenance too readily. For although there is good evidence that Delos was inhabited at least as early as the second Early Cycladic phase, as yet no graves of the Early Bronze Age have been uncovered and no prehistoric marble objects have appeared in sanctioned excavations on this well-explored island. Moreover, Thucydides' description (1.8.1) of the purification of Delos in 426 B.C. and the removal of tomb contents to Rheneia does not seem to refer to such graves. A number of nineteenth-century travelers reported that Early Cycladic objects had been found on Rheneia and Delos, including four Early Cycladic I marble vases in Leiden acquired on Delos in 1825. But, inasmuch as Delos was then, as now, a very popular site for foreign visitors to the Cyclades, it is also possible that finds from nearby islands might have been brought to Delos to be sold, and that the sacred isle of Artemis and Apollo would have been mentioned to unsuspecting foreigners as the provenance of such objects, their interest – the figures were considered quite ugly at the time – heightened by the divine associations. In favor of the Delian find-place perhaps is the apparent fact that to date marble objects of the first Early Cycladic phase have not been found on any of the nearby islands (Tenos, Syros, Mykonos). On the other hand, one would expect that an artist whose works epitomized the Plastiras type at its finest would have lived on an island more in the mainstream of sculptural activity than Delos and her neighbors seem to have been at the time.

It is doubtful that the three surviving figures, which are clearly the works of a very experienced sculptor, would have been the only ones carved by him. There is good reason to hope, therefore, that other examples from his hand will eventually turn up. It is likely that the Metropolitan Museum Master also carved marble vases, for the heads of his figures are rather reminiscent of their forms: the polos seems equivalent to the collar, the face to the body, and the neck corresponds to the base or foot of the jars (kandiles), though the long face of the Geneva piece is perhaps more reminiscent of the beaker shape; the ears of all his figures strongly suggest the vertical lugs found on both jars and beakers – both types, incidentally, having been acquired on Delos (pl. IVC, D).

THE ATHENS MUSEUM MASTER
[Pls. 18, 19, 20; Checklist, p. 156]

To the hand of a third sculptor of Plastiras-type figures, four works can be attributed at present. Only one of these, a male figure in Athens [2], is preserved in its entirety.[62] The broken pieces include a privately owned female whose legs are missing from just above the knees [1], a head in Geneva [4], and the lower torso and thighs of a female with abdominal bands in Oxford [3].

The iconographic range seen in the four works can best be compared to that of the Doumas Master. The quality of their workmanship, skill in modeling, and attention to detail, on the other hand, are much closer to the work of the Metropolitan Museum Master. Like both these sculptors, the Athens Museum Master may have been the mender of his own figures: the fragment in Oxford has repair holes in both thighs.

The four works, despite the very fragmentary state of two of them, should be immediately recognizable as the products of a single hand. In their outline contours and proportions (insofar as comparison is possible) they are strikingly similar even though both sexes and two very different scales are represented. In those areas where there is some slight discrepancy, sex distinction may be the controlling factor. Thus, in order to accommodate the fuller breasts of the female, her chest was made larger than that of the male, and her upper arms are as a result longer than his. Similarly, the difference in width between the waist and hips is more pronounced on the female figures than on the male, and the abdominal area is proportionally longer on the females.

The Athens Museum Master's outline contours are much softer and more rounded than those of the Metropolitan Museum Master, but equally distinctive. Especially noteworthy on the profile is the manner in which the thighs are brought forward as if the knees were meant to be slightly bent.

Because the proportions are essentially consistent from piece to piece, it is possible to estimate the original heights of the three fragmentary figures with some expectation of accuracy on the basis of a comparison with the name-piece, which measures 30.8 cm. The better preserved female was probably slightly smaller than this, while the figure in Oxford would have been about the same size or slightly larger than the male. The head, however, belonged to a

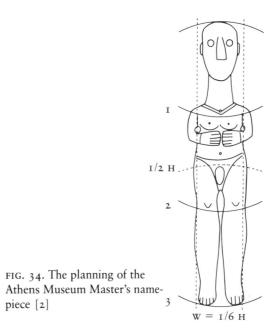

FIG. 34. The planning of the Athens Museum Master's name-piece [2]

figure that was twice the size of the other three. The smaller works of the Athens Museum Master, which may have been of average size for him, were somewhat larger than the normal Plastiras figure (e.g., the work of the Metropolitan Museum Master), while the fourth, by the standards of the type, was monumental. It is, in fact, the largest Plastiras figure of which we have any knowledge.

An analysis of his one complete figure reveals that the Athens Museum Master used a carefully conceived plan in which the height was divided into three equal parts with a sixth part used to control the width at various points (fig. 34). (The width is one-sixth of the height at the waist.) The three vertical divisions were used by this sculptor in a novel and presumably idiosyncratic way. The first occurs somewhat lower than usual – the shoulders are described by an arc drawn from the two-thirds mark rather than from the top of the head – so that the elongation of the head and neck is not as extreme as on some Plastiras figures such as those of the Metropolitan Museum Master. The second division, or two-thirds mark, falls at the knees rather than at the pubic area (from which point arcs normally describe the position of the hips).

This unusual application of the canon resulted in a curious telescoping of the thighs so that when viewed in profile the buttocks reach nearly to the level of the knees. The lower legs, on the other hand, are unnaturally long. Taken together with the large head and hands, these unusual proportions give the composition as a whole a decidedly ungainly appearance. Since the proportions of the fragmentary figures are similar to those of his name-piece, it is likely that the Athens Museum Master used the same modification of the conventional plan for all his works. This rendering of the canon should, therefore, be regarded as a distinguishing feature of his approach to the human form.

Angularity is not a salient characteristic of the Athens Museum Master's style, yet, where called for, he appears to have used the harmonic system. The pubic triangles of the two female figures, for example, conform to angle B.

Apart from the obvious differences of sex, there are very few variations in form and detail among the four works as they are preserved. A few minor points of difference may be noted, some of which are not readily apparent on the photographs. The mouth is indicated, by a straight line, on the large head and the better preserved female, but not on the male; superficial wrist grooves are present only on the male as is also the navel; and shoulder blades are incised on the back of the female but not the male.

The Athens Master, despite his preference for strange proportions, displayed an interest in anatomical verisimilitude that was especially keen, even though it does not extend to every detail of his works. In the execution of individual forms and details his style appears somewhat less mannered than that of the Metropolitan Museum Master, for example. A number of details are particularly noteworthy for the degree of their naturalism: the shape of the head and prominent nose; the bi-grooved collarbones with shallow center depression (sternal notch); the breasts with raised nipples; the separation of the upper arms from the torso; the forearms which bend back at the elbows, set at a slightly oblique angle to the torso; the cupped hands whose large rounded surfaces provided space for the sculptor to incise five fingers with neat parallel lines; the plastic treatment of the back as two distinct sections bisected by a deeply furrowed spine, and with gently curving buttocks; and, finally, the modeling of the knees and calves, particularly when viewed from the front or back.

While most of the carefully treated details seen in the work of the Athens Museum Master are found on one or more Plastiras figures by different sculptors, the naturalistic breasts with raised nipples, the incised shoulder blades, and the separation of the arms from the body by means of bored holes are, at present, found only in his work. More important than the apparent uniqueness of any single detail as a hallmark of the sculptor's style is the idiosyncratic combination of elements – a few unparalleled, some rare, some familiar – that he chose to include on his figures.

One of the most striking features of the Athens Museum Master's style is the frequent and varied use of the boring tool. On his name-piece there are no fewer than ten cavities made with this implement. Most probably the same implement was used to make all of them. The deeper cavities, those of the ears and eye sockets, and the arm perforations, are, because of the shape and/or wobble effect of the tool, also the largest. Small shallow depressions for the navel, sternal notch, and iliac dimples are present also, but these are barely visible on the photographs. The Athens Museum Master is the only Cycladic sculptor now known who made the eye sockets sufficiently deep and fitted the inlays tightly enough to enable some of them to survive in situ to the present. Coincidentally, one dark pebble is (or, in the case of [1], was until at least 1968) preserved on each of the three heads.

It is probably no coincidence that the Athens Museum Master chose to separate the arms from his figures' sides by means of bored holes, for he was most probably proficient at perforating the suspension lugs of marble vessels, which the arms of his figures resemble. Nor as a stone vase maker would he have had any trouble making the repair holes in the thighs of the Oxford fragment.

From their present state of preservation, the four works of the Athens Museum Master resemble each other so strongly in virtually every respect as to suggest that they represent a single, mature phase of the sculptor's development and that they were probably carved in close chronological proximity to one another. The very large head that shows particularly careful workmanship, for example in the hollowing out of the ears, and sensitivity in the intense tight-lipped expression may well have belonged to his finest, most ambitiously conceived piece.

The name-piece and the Oxford fragment are said to have been found on Amorgos; there is no information regarding the find-place of the other two works. Although Amorgos has yielded remains of the first Early Cycladic phase, to date Plastiras-type figures have been found in systematic excavations only on Paros and Naxos (and nearly all of these are the work of the Doumas Master). Others are reported to have been found on Antiparos, Amorgos, and, as we saw in the case of the Metropolitan Museum Master's Berlin piece, also on Delos. The Athens Museum Master may well have been from Amorgos, but at present there is insufficient evidence to make a firm judgment. It is also possible that he was an itinerant craftsman or that his works were imported or brought back to marble-poor Amorgos by travelers. If the work of the Athens Museum Master should turn up in excavations on another island or islands, the tentative suggestion that he was a native of Amorgos would have to be reassessed.

The three sculptors discussed in this chapter were, together with the Missouri Master (see pl. 4A),[63] responsible for about half the Plastiras-type figures known at present. Although clearly the accidents of preservation and recovery must be taken into account, it would appear that these four sculptors were among the most active of their period in fashioning such images. Of the remaining Plastiras figures, there are one or two cases in which two might be assignable to the same artist, but for the most part each was carved by a different artist.

Chapter Five

Eight Classical Sculptors

THE KONTOLEON MASTER
[Pls. 21, 22; Checklist, p. 156]

A T L E A S T eight figures can be viewed as the work of one sculptor, named after the archaeologist who in grave 13 at Aplomata uncovered the two examples mentioned in chapter 3. Ironically, it is not possible at this time to illustrate the Kontoleon Master's namepieces, nor have good photographs of them been included in the preliminary publication of the Aplomata finds in Greek journals.[64]

A talented sculptor of folded-arm female figures of the Kapsala variety, the Kontoleon Master worked the marble with care and sensitivity in sizes ranging from 17.5 cm to 36 cm or more — that is, about average to somewhat larger than average for the Kapsala variety as a whole.

Although the surviving works of the Kontoleon Master represent perhaps three separate phases of his career and show a number of dissimilar features, many traits are, with one or two exceptions, shared by all of them. These include a characteristically long, broad-cheeked, oval face with a delicate nose well above the prominent chin; a rather long neck; softly rounded shoulders; pointed breasts set just above the tapered forearms. The thighs are exaggeratedly long, the naturalistically modeled calves by contrast short. The knees are indicated plastically; the feet, with lightly arched soles, are small. Neither toes nor fingers are incised and, in fact, the only incised detail common to all the figures is a spine. The back is flat, with the upper arms rendered in a lower plane.

From the front, the outline contours of these slender figures curve subtly and there are few straight lines. The profile axis is sharply broken along the legs and the head exhibits a marked backward tilt toward the top.

All the figures, moreover, appear to have been designed in the same way, strongly suggesting that their sculptor used a preconceived plan. This was essentially a modification of the four-part canon, adapted to fit his preference for long-bodied, long-thighed figures (fig.

35). In his work the first division, or quarter, defines the shoulders by means of an arc drawn from the top of the head rather than from the figure's midpoint, as is more common, resulting in a lengthening of the space normally allotted to the upper body. The midpoint of the Kontoleon Master's figure occurs at the top of the pubic area. This, too, is lower than usual. And the third division tends to fall short of the knees on the smaller works. The greatest width of his figures is consistently about one-fifth of their length. Such narrowness is not unusual on Kapsala-variety figures, which, as a result, were particularly vulnerable at the narrowest points: neck and ankles.

Although the emphasis in his figures is on rounded contours rather than angularity, there is some indication that the Kontoleon Master used the harmonic system to determine the shoulder angle. This consistently conforms to angle B.

The differences observable among the sculptor's works may be explained largely on the grounds that they belong to different stages of the sculptor's development and as such express varying levels of skill and experience. To an early stage one might assign the smallest works – a figure in Athens [1] and one in the de Menil Collection [2] measuring 17.5 and 18.9 cm, respectively. These pieces are generally less refined than the others in their outline contours, which exhibit less curvature; in their proportions and planning, which are less well balanced; and in their surface workmanship. The arms are very thick and, with the elbows indicated on the body, the figures appear to be tightly clasping themselves as if in discomfort. The midsection is abbreviated, the waist obscured by the forearms, and the pubic area is indicated simply by a horizontal depression just above the beginning of the leg-cleft. The leg-cleft is perforated from knee to ankle. Finally, on the back of the de Menil figure the spine is rather ineptly skewed.[65]

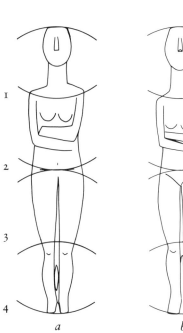

FIG. 35. The planning of figures attributed to the Kontoleon Master: a) [2]; b) [6]

To a more developed phase belong the two name-pieces from grave 13 at Aplomata ([3, 4] as well as the torso in the Erlenmeyer Collection in Basel [7]). Nearly identical in size and only slightly larger than the works just discussed – they measure 21.4 and 21.7 cm, respectively – these figures are also better balanced and more carefully worked, and they appear more relaxed in attitude, their contours more confidently curved. The arms are more skillfully modeled and the elbows protrude very slightly from the body that now has a proper midsection with an indented, feminine waist. The abdomen is slightly swollen as if to indicate an early stage of pregnancy. The pubic area of the smaller name-piece [3] is rendered as a triangular depression between slightly slanted thigh-tops, while that of the larger [4] is not marked sculpturally at all, probably because it was painted originally. The leg-cleft has a wider perforation that imbues the figures with a quality of lightness. The spine is drawn straight. On the smaller figure it continues into the leg-cleft and the buttocks are subtly marked with short superficial horizontal grooves.

To a slightly more advanced stage of the Kontoleon Master's career one should assign the figures in the Metropolitan Museum of Art [5] and a private collection [6]. These works are larger – 30 and 31 cm, respectively – and still more carefully executed. The figure in Heidelberg [8] that belongs to this stage also may have been as large as 36 cm originally. On the privately owned figure the curves and countercurves of the outline contours are particularly sensuous, while those of the Metropolitan Museum figure are by contrast rather understated. The elbows now stand out more from the body and the arms are slightly narrower. The pubic area is defined by obliquely slanted, raised thigh-tops. On the Metropolitan Museum piece, the ghosts of a large solid-painted triangle are also visible as a smooth area. It is likely that the other figure was similarly painted.

The legs of these figures were carved separately from the knees downward in the manner of the earlier precanonical images. Having gained complete mastery of his material, the Kontoleon Master perhaps felt sufficiently confident now to attempt such a risky procedure, abandoning the safety device of the membrane joining the ankles seen in his earlier works. (It is noteworthy that both with and without this "connective tissue," at least one foot of five of the six well-preserved figures discussed here sustained a fracture – normally just above the ankle – presumably some time following their completion.)

On the Metropolitan Museum figure the spine continues into the leg-cleft, without any special marking of the buttocks. On the privately owned figure the buttocks are indicated plastically and accented with a delicate curving incision. Differences such as this or in the rendering of the arms and pubic areas of the name-pieces might have been due to the flexibility of the sculptor's approach, or they may indicate that within each stage the surviving works were carved at some chronological remove from each other, and that the sculptor probably did not "copy" other examples of his own work. In no way, in any case, are any of the figures markedly atypical in their design or execution. The use of three repair holes for reattachment of the head of the Metropolitan Museum figure is at present unique to the Kontoleon Master.[66]

It is tempting, finally, to view the largest and finest of all surviving Kapsala-variety figures as a product of the Kontoleon Master's hand – as a work that might represent the very
pinnacle of his artistic development (pl. VIA). This masterpiece of Cycladic sculpture, which
originally measured more than 80 cm, resembles the works we have been considering in its
outline contours and attenuated proportions, but the head, with carved ears, is of a different
shape. The separated forearms, the incised fingers, and the exceptionally bold modeling of
the breasts and arms are, on the other hand, features one might expect to find on an unusually large figure carved by a highly skilled artist during his best period.

At present there are no pieces that might represent a phase or phases intermediary between the most developed of the works discussed above and this remarkable figure, which
makes a reasonably assured attribution of it to the Kontoleon Master problematical. It should
be pointed out, however, that such a masterwork could not have sprung fully formed, as it
were, from the hand of its creator. Surely, more modest works of the sort ascribed to the hand
of the Kontoleon Master here must have preceded it.

The Naxian provenance of the name-pieces is certain, but no such precise information is
available for any of the other figures of the Kontoleon Master illustrated here. The figure in
Athens was found on Naxos, perhaps in Stephanos' excavations at Spedos.[67] The de Menil
figure is said to be from Paros. The figure in the Metropolitan Museum has no find-place
attached to it, but a Naxian origin is suggested by the fact that it is carved in a marble (mentioned earlier) apparently peculiar to Naxos, which weathers in an unusual manner.

THE ISRAEL MUSEUM MASTER
[Pl. 23; Checklist, p. 157]

The three figures in Washington [2], Athens [3], and Jerusalem [4] illustrated here can be
ascribed to a single sculptor, named after the museum that houses one of them. In addition,
at least two or three unpublished figures in the Naxos Museum [1, 5] can be attributed to
his hand.

An accomplished sculptor of folded-arm female figures that share features of both the
Kapsala and early Spedos varieties, the Israel Museum Master's style is quite similar to that
of the Kontoleon Master although generally speaking his figures exhibit less pronounced
round modeling, a characteristic more appropriate to the early Spedos style, in which greater
emphasis is placed on incision work.

The Israel Museum Master carved figures in sizes ranging from about 17 or 18 cm to
45.5 cm. Most of his surviving works are of average length, while the largest is unusually
large for figures of the Kapsala, though not for figures of the early Spedos variety.

The three works illustrated here, together with the largest piece, form an entirely homogeneous group, suggesting that they were produced during a single period of the sculptor's

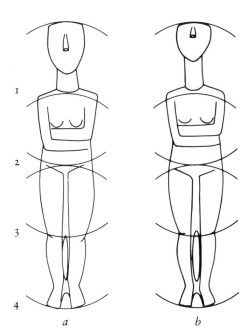

FIG. 36. The planning of figures attributed to the Israel Museum Master: *a*) [2]; *b*) [4] name-piece

artistic life. Like the earlier works of the Kontoleon Master, the figures of the Israel Museum Master have their elbows indicated on the body and the waistline is obscured when one views them from the front. Like the Kontoleon Master, he had a fondness for rather slender, long-limbed figures. All his images have a (once painted ?) pubic area bounded by oblique, raised thigh-tops, and the leg-cleft is perforated, like that of the Kontoleon Master's name-pieces, with a long, broad cutting.

Unlike the figures of the Kontoleon Master, those of the Israel Museum Master have straight arms of equal thickness as opposed to tapered ones and, although toes and fingers are not incised, the knees are marked with light incisions visible on the front, sides, and rear. (This detail becomes common practice by the time of the early Spedos-variety figures.)

The outline contours of the four figures are closely similar to each other, and resemble those of the Kontoleon Master's works as well, though their shoulders are somewhat more angular and their profile axes are rather less sharply broken.

In design these figures also resemble the Kontoleon Master's, particularly those of his more developed phase, being for the most part – the largest is less accurately planned – harmoniously proportioned (fig. 36). The complete figures of the Israel Museum Master all have a maximum shoulder width that is 21 percent of the length. This sculptor was also consistent in his use of angle B for the shoulder.

The provenances of the name-piece and the figure in the Hirshhorn Museum are not known, but the other works attributable to the Israel Museum Master come from Naxos. While the find-place of the figure in Athens may have been Spedos,[68] the figures in the Naxos Museum were definitely recovered there in (unpublished) excavations conducted by Kontoleon in 1948. In view of the similarities visible in their styles, it should not be difficult to imagine that the Kontoleon and Israel masters were both compatriots and contemporaries, the latter perhaps somewhat the younger of the two.

THE COPENHAGEN MASTER
[Pls. 24, 25; Checklist, p. 157]

Six works, of which three are only partially preserved, should, despite significant but partly explicable differences, probably be attributed to a single sculptor, named after the location of the museum housing the first of the figures to come to light.

An excellent craftsman, the Copenhagen Master carved early Spedos-variety female figures of unusual size and in a wide range of sizes. Even his smallest known work, of which only the head survives [5], was, at ca. 53 cm, about twice average length. The smallest of the complete works are nearly identical in length and slightly larger than this. The largest, in the Goulandris Collection, measures 70.7 cm [4] although, if it had been completed according to the sculptor's original design, this figure would have been as much as 86 cm long. The name-piece [3], which is preserved to just above the knees, had an original length of approximately 63 cm, while the second head [6] belonged to a work of 70–75 cm. Finally, an unpublished, privately owned head, measuring 20.2 cm to the chin, belonged to an outsize figure with a length of 105–10 cm or more.

Although the outline contours, proportions, and relative thinness of the four most fully preserved works differ from one another to a considerable degree, they share with the two fragments a quite distinctive head shape. From the front the face is pear-shaped and carries a high-placed nose that varies in width from piece to piece. The straight line of the chin continues on the sides and back of the head on all except the name-piece, which shows more typical slanting lines. In profile the head is unusually straight and free of contour, except for the backward bend at the very top. The nose is flat, the toruslike chin shallow. Also unusual is the slightly convex profile of the front of the neck of several of the works [1, 3, 4, 5].

Other characteristics that may be considered distinguishing features of the Copenhagen Master's style are shared by the four better preserved works. These include careful modeling of the breasts and arms that contrasts sharply with an extremely slender profile almost without contour at least as far as the knees. The missing calves and feet and the bend at the knees of the name-piece may have originally resembled [2] more than [1], to judge from the profile of the buttocks and thighs, while the nearly complete absence of flexion in the knees of [1], as well as its exaggerated thinness and small feet, may have been influenced by the gray- and cream-colored, alabasterlike, layered marble chosen for the figure. Possibly the sculptor considered it prudent not to cut across the layers and risk a fracture, or he may also have considered it aesthetically desirable to let the form of the figure follow these naturally occurring bands.

The awkward, truncated appearance of the legs of the Goulandris figure [4], on the other hand, as well as their absolute straightness are, it appears, the result of an accident, incurred probably during the carving process. A fracture sustained at a point originally intended to mark the knees, just below the beginning of the perforation of the leg-cleft, forced the sculptor to telescope the legs, virtually omitting differentiated calves and feet. If one thinks away the calves and feet of the smallest figure, the remainder is remarkably similar. The somewhat different proportions of the larger image are due primarily to attenuation – a characteristic common among figures conceived on a very large scale. Indeed, it was the Copenhagen Master's fondness for elongated thighs, seen in less exaggerated form on [2] and [3], that enabled him to salvage the work in this way although, because the other parts are elegantly elongated, the legs appear all the more peculiar by contrast. Of particular importance here is the fact that adjustments prompted by such factors as the character of the material in the case of [1] or necessitated by its fragility in the case of [4] do much to foster an impression of dissimilarity among the figures ascribed to this rather ingenious sculptor.

Another feature of the Copenhagen Master's work is the unusual way in which the pubic area is treated – slightly differently on each piece – as a roughly triangular space articulated across the top by a straight incision and bounded on the sides by slightly raised, arching, and slightly asymmetrical thigh-tops. (In the work of the Kontoleon and Israel Museum masters we saw how the thighs of the Kapsala and early Spedos figures are often raised above the pubic area, though not normally with the distinctive arc seen in the work of the Copenhagen Master or in combination with a straight top groove.)

The rendering of the arms on the front and back of the four images as well as the placement of incisions is also closely similar, although there is some variation (reinforced to some extent by differing states of surface preservation) in the definition of the engraved detail that ranges from superficial (e.g., the spine of [1]) to quite strong (e.g., the spine of [2]). Curiously, on the largest figure – just where one would most expect to find them – fingers were not incised, though these are present on the other works, and the "small" figure [2], whose incision work is especially fine, even shows wrist grooves.

Other features such as the broad sloping shoulders and the low-placed breasts are shared by the three complete figures, but not the name-piece, though one can sense a logical progression in the rendering of the shoulders on the four works: 3-2-1-4. Moreover, whereas the name-piece may have been planned according to the traditional four-part canon, the complete figures with their exaggeratedly long thighs were not.

All the surviving works attributed to the Copenhagen Master represent a talented sculptor in his prime. It is likely that [1] and [4], which are closer to each other than either [2] or [3] in proportions, outline contours, and relative thinness, were made fairly close together in time. Since their proportions are also more extreme and were apparently made so deliberately, it is possible that they were also carved somewhat later in the sculptor's career than [2] or [3], especially since [4] was conceived on a more monumental scale. Figure [2] to some extent resembles [1] and [4] in its upper body contours, while it shares with the name-piece

[3] a short midsection whose outlines merge more fluidly into those of the thighs, which are also more rounded. The two figures [2, 3] would appear not to have been made at a short interval either in relation to each other or to either of the other figures. Based on these observations, the order of execution of the four figures, spaced over several years perhaps, might have been 3/2/1, 4 – that is, the same order suggested for the changing form of the shoulders. If, on the basis of size, form, and relative thinness, one were to add the two heads attributed to the Copenhagen Master that are illustrated here, the following would result: 3/2, 5/1, 4, 6.

None of the Copenhagen Master's works was found in the course of systematic excavation. The name-piece is said to have been found on Amorgos, the Goulandris figure on Naxos, while the two heads belong to the "Keros hoard," a huge assemblage of objects that will be mentioned frequently in this chapter and the next and will be discussed in some detail in the final chapter. Nothing is known of the origins of the two smaller privately owned figures, but the curious layered marble (known from several other, unpublished pieces without provenance) of which [1] is made is so distinctive that one might reasonably expect its source will one day be identified.

THE FITZWILLIAM MASTER

[Pls. 26, 27; Checklist, p. 158]

Four figures, in Stockholm [1], the Bastis Collection in New York [2], Herakleion [3], and Cambridge [4], can be attributed to one sculptor named after the museum that houses the largest of the four.

A sculptor of classic early Spedos-variety female figures, the Fitzwilliam Master worked the marble in the modest scale normal for the great majority of the earlier folded-arm figures. The four works range in length from 19.6 cm for the piece in Stockholm to 25.8 cm for the name-piece.

The Fitzwilliam Master's figures resemble each other quite closely in almost every respect. The single major discrepancy is the fact that the Cretan figure is represented in an advanced stage of pregnancy, with the result that her midsection, which is conspicuous and rounded in profile, had much more space allotted to it than did the midsections of the other figures.

Characteristic features of the Fitzwilliam Master's style include a classic lyre-shaped face with prominent high-placed nose and well-defined chin; broad, sloping shoulders; wide upper arms and thick flat forearms without fingers. The midsection, as noted, is normally abbreviated and the pubic area is marked by a broad shallow triangle formed by an abdominal line that continues onto the sides of the figures and by slanting inguinal lines that are bisected for a short space by the top of the wide leg-cleft. The leg-cleft is perforated for only a short distance between the disproportionately short calves. The angled feet, with long grooved toes, are by contrast unusually long and are carved separately for much of their length. On the back the spine is lightly incised and the tapered upper arms, carved in a lower plane, are further defined by oblique grooves.

The outline contours of the four figures are marked by strong contrasting curved and slanted lines. The profiles exhibit a broken axis with pronounced flexion at the knees and feet.

The Fitzwilliam Master used the traditional four-part plan in the classic manner and with considerable precision (figs. 16*b*, 37). Of particular interest is the apportionment of parts in the fourth quarter of the design, which demonstrates the essential flexibility of the canon. The formula "specified" that the third division coincide with the knees, but just how the sculptor treated the limbs from this point was his decision entirely. Thus, he might choose to make the calves rather long and terminate his figures with short small feet, as many if not most sculptors did, or, as the Fitzwilliam Master elected to do (on all but the Stockholm figure, which is more duly proportioned), he might significantly curtail the calves and carve elongated feet. (This mannered approach is seen also on the larger member of the two-figure composition in Karlsruhe [pl. 1*B*].)

The Fitzwilliam Master consistently chose angle B for the shoulders, but he was less constant in his choice of angles for the pubic area: this conforms in two cases to angle B, in the other two to the combination $A + (B/2)$.

One might suppose that the four figures were fashioned within a relatively short time-span and that they belong to the same phase of the sculptor's development. They do, however, exhibit varying degrees of care and attention to detail. The Bastis figure [2], for ex-

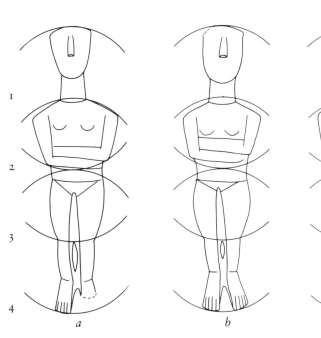

FIG. 37. The planning of figures attributed to the Fitzwilliam Master: *a*) [1]; *b*) [2]; *c*) [3]

91

ample, has two prominent incision overruns on the forearms; the Cretan figure [3] shows one. (That on the Stockholm figure is less pronounced.) The treatment of the arms and upper torso is in general neater and better balanced on the Stockholm figure and the name-piece, which is also somewhat less wide through the shoulders. These two pieces also show more incision work than the other figures: a buttock line on the former and carefully drawn knee and ankle grooves on the latter. In the unevenness of the ends of the feet of the name-piece one can perhaps observe an unusual interest in the depiction of individual toes of different lengths.

Nothing is known of the find-places of the Bastis and Stockholm figures. The piece in Herakleion (which has weathered quite differently from the other three and seems to have been carved in a more porous kind of marble) was found in the excavations, conducted early in the century by Stephanos Xanthoudides, of a communal round tomb at Koumasa in the Mesara region of southern Crete. The piece was recovered along with several figurines of the local variety named after this site (e.g., fig. 10*b*). There can be little doubt, however, that the Fitzwilliam Master's work was imported to Crete from one of the Cyclades. The name-piece was acquired on Amorgos at the turn of the century by Richard Bosanquet who gave it in 1901 to the Fitzwilliam Museum.

THE STEINER MASTER
[Pls. 28, 29, 30; Checklist, p. 158]

At least five complete figures and one partially preserved figure are recognizable as the work of one sculptor, named after the collection that houses the largest and finest of them. In addition, there are a number of smaller fragments that are evidently by the same hand.

The Steiner Master carved standard female figures of the late Spedos variety in sizes ranging from at least 34.5 cm, and probably as little as 21.5 cm, to 60.2 cm.[69] Although the six works represent different levels of proficiency and although they give the impression of having been carved at some remove from one another in time, they nevertheless share characteristics that form the basis of their sculptor's style.

The almost U-shaped head of the Steiner Master's figures is typically large and broad-cheeked, with a rather slender nose placed well above the chin. The neck is correspondingly short though similarly broad, the upper torso, with rounded shoulders and breasts in the form of generalized swellings, rather statuesque. Except on the small figure in Tokyo [1] (and perhaps [2]), the bulkiness of the upper part both frontally and in profile contrasts strongly with the lower part, which is quite slender through the midsection, hips, and legs. (Because of this narrowing, the figures were particularly vulnerable at the knees, breaks at this point having been sustained by four of the six examples.) The leg-cleft, as on most works of the late Spedos variety, is unperforated.

Allowing for certain differences of proportion, the outline contours are similar throughout and are noteworthy for the absence of any marked angularity. In profile the axis is very straight, and the figures exhibit little contour though they are thicker through the upper torso. Even the back of the head is without the usual arching contour. The rear is flat with the upper arms set off at an oblique angle.

The details are for the most part similar in concept although they vary in execution. Fingers are crudely incised with short uneven strokes and not always in the correct number; the toes are likewise short. The right forearm extends as far as the left elbow, slightly beyond the side of the figure, although only on the figure in the Goulandris Collection [4] is the right hand carved on what in back is the left elbow. On the larger figures the abdominal area is marked by a broad curving line below, but not attached to which are oblique groin lines. (The pubic area of the small figure in Tokyo is treated somewhat differently, while that of the small image in Naxos [2] is only vaguely indicated and might have been painted originally.) Knee grooves appear on the sides and rear only, ankle grooves on the front and sides where they are unusually strongly slanted toward the soles of the feet. All the figures have an incised spine and a low-placed horizontal buttock line. In general, the incision work is quite superficial.

The Steiner Master seems to have planned his figures quite carefully according to the standard four-part canon, although he used the first division and the midpoint slightly dif-

FIG. 38. The planning of figures attributed to the Steiner Master: *a*) [2]; *b*) [4]; *c*) [5]; *d*) [6] name-piece

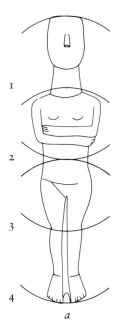
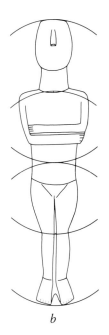

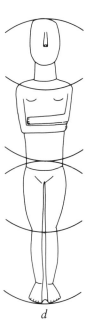

a   *b*   *c*   *d*

ferently on his name-piece than on the others (fig. 38). Their greatest width averages one quarter of the length for the three smaller complete figures, while that of the name-piece, which is considerably larger and somewhat less conventionally planned than the others, is only one-fifth of its length.

Such narrowing of unusually large figures and the consequent elongation of their individual parts are quite typical. As explained in chapter 2, the narrowing may have been effected for purely aesthetic reasons, although one suspects there were practical considerations, too: a narrower figure would have fit the hand of the sculptor during the carving process as well as the hands of a bearer if it was carried during a funeral procession, and it would also have considerably reduced its weight.[70] Moreover, on figures of exceptional size (60 cm or more) the risk of fracture at the least substantial points (neck, knees, and ankles) would have been less great than on smaller ones.[71]

The Steiner Master seems to have used the harmonic system occasionally but even then not consistently. This is not surprising in view of the fact that his figures are lacking in angular contours. What is more, he seems not to have invested a great deal of time or interest in incision work: the pubic incisions, for example, tend to be so lightly incised as to go almost unnoticed. On the figure in the Goulandris Collection, for example, only one inguinal line is visible.

The works attributable to the Steiner Master at present appear to belong to several phases of his development. The earliest is represented by the piece from the Naxos Museum [2]. This is one of the smallest of the works and, in terms of workmanship, it is the least accomplished. Notice particularly the lack of clear differentiation of the arms from the chest, the unevenness of the forearm groove, and the untidy fingers and toes; on the back the spine begins well above the neckline, the perfunctory buttock line is straight rather than curved, and the leg-cleft is irregular. Although structurally the figure is well balanced and shows evidence of having been carefully planned, the execution of the finer points reveals a relatively inexperienced sculptor. To a slightly later phase one might assign the small figure in Tokyo. This sculpture is much more competently crafted than the one from Naxos, yet in its small size and thick profile, as well as the similar treatment of such details as the spine and buttock line, the work can be recognized as another product of the Steiner Master's immaturity.

A more advanced stage of the sculptor's development may be seen in the three mid-sized works [3, 4, 5]. It is probably not possible to place these figures in proper sequence, for each one resembles his masterwork, his name-piece, in some respects though not in others, and they resemble each other in certain ways only. For example, the figure in the Goulandris Collection [4] in its planning and proportions is closer to the name-piece than any of the others although its surface workmanship is still rather unrefined. A much higher level of craftsmanship may be seen on the largest of the three figures. Here the forearms are separated from each other by means of a clear space rather than a wide groove, and the left forearm does not continue all the way to meet the upper right arm, details found also on the name-piece, on which they are, however, more precisely executed. The Erlenmeyer figure [3], which resembles this work in its proportions, alone of this mid-sized group had a curving buttock line (now largely obliterated by a fracture), foreshadowing the graceful articulation of this detail on the name-piece.

With his name-piece the Steiner Master reveals a new mastery and skill no doubt born of years spent fashioning smaller works. The integration of the various parts of this figure shows a rare harmony of conception and gives the work a refinement of line and a monumental presence that is little affected by the fact that even here the sculptor's incision work lacks boldness and, in the execution of the fingers, meticulousness.

Of the figures discussed here none was found in a systematic excavation, and nothing at all is known about the find-places of four of them, including the name-piece. The early image [2] was confiscated in 1964 along with a number of other sculptures from a Naxian smuggler. It is assumed but not certain that the figure was found on Naxos. The Erlenmeyer piece and the head of a large figure [7], as well as two or three smaller fragments that appear to be from the Steiner Master's hand, belong to the "Keros hoard."

THE NAXOS MUSEUM MASTER
[Pls. 31, 32, 33; Checklist, p. 158]

One of the best documented of Early Cycladic sculptors is the Naxos Museum Master. Named for the collection that houses five full figures and the legs of a sixth, at least eighteen pieces can at present be confidently assigned to his hand. Of these, ten are complete or very nearly so, and it is therefore possible to form a clear idea both of his style and, because several phases of his career are distinguishable, of his artistic development as well. Regrettably, I am unable to illustrate most of the sculptor's name-pieces here, with the result that the earliest and middle phases are not represented in the plates or figures.

The Naxos Museum Master carved standard female figures of the late Spedos variety in a wide range of sizes. His smallest work [1], in Naxos, is only 18 cm long, while his largest, in the Goulandris Collection [11], measures 72 cm.[72] Because this large work is exactly four times as long as the smallest, one might well wonder if the sculptor used a modular ruler to determine the size of his figures. Supposing that he was guided by a foot of 18 cm, his smallest figure would have been one "foot" long, his largest four. Unfortunately, however, the lengths of the other figures from his hand do not conform to such a system. For example, none of these figures is one and one half feet long or two feet or two and a half feet long. If one supposes that he used a foot of 24 cm, the smallest figure would be three quarters of a foot, another figure in Naxos [8] with a length of 48 cm would be two feet long, and the Goulandris figure would be three feet long. However, again none of the other figures fits the system. Only if one divides the hypothetical 18 cm or the 24 cm foot into twelve and ten "inches," respectively, does one find more coincidences, although they are not the ones one would expect. Moreover, no two of the Naxos Museum Master's surviving figures are, or were, the same length.[73] Without a larger sample one cannot draw definite conclusions, but one might suspect that this sculptor did not as a rule carve his figures according to accurate predetermined measurements. The difficult question of the use of units of measurement by Cycladic sculptors will be taken up again and in greater detail in the next section, on the Goulandris Master.

Although the Naxos Museum Master's figures belong to perhaps as many as five different periods of his development, and although they vary in the quality of their workmanship from very crude to quite fine, each one bears the unmistakable stamp of his particular approach to the female form.

Among the salient features of his style, found in each case on the majority of his figures, are a long, broad-cheeked face with a narrow nose placed well above the chin; sloping shoulders; generalized breasts beginning nearly at the shoulders; wide upper arms only partially differentiated from the chest; and thick forearms with incised fingers of unequal length. The elbows are set close to the body and the right hand extends as far as the left elbow, with the result that the left elbow, being carved on the back of the right hand, is lower in back than in front. Whereas the Steiner Master used this convention on only one of his surviving figures, the Naxos Museum Master used it on all except his two largest works.

One of the most unusual features of the Naxos Museum Master's style – something one sees normally only on Chalandriani-variety figures – is the absence, on all but his largest figure, of a midsection: the pubic area is defined either by a broad, shallow incised triangle set just below the right forearm (and not always centered) or the forearm itself forms the top of the pubic triangle. The legs are set close together; the cleft, which continues nearly to the end of the feet, is unperforated; the stubby feet, with short grooved toes, are rounded at the ends. Knee and ankle incisions (not always at the same level) encircle the limbs like constricting bonds. The back is flat and the spine is indicated as a broad shallow depression. The backs of the arms are rendered in an oblique plane, while the buttocks form a shelflike lower boundary of the back.

The outlines of the figures are similar throughout: with the exception of the small figure in Athens [2], there is a notable absence both of pronounced curves as well as marked changes in contour. The profile axis is normally straight and there are few changes of plane. The back of the head and neck has a distinctive outline, with the head set off at an angle to the slightly bulging neck.

The Naxos Museum Master was apparently guided in the design of his figures by the standard four-part canon although, because he normally omitted the midsection, he used it somewhat differently from other sculptors: the midpoint of the design in his work tends to occur at the bottom of the arms or higher rather than on the abdomen (fig. 39). This sculptor also seems to have used the harmonic system for the angular aspects of his figures, although he was not altogether consistent in his choice of angles nor always meticulous in following

96

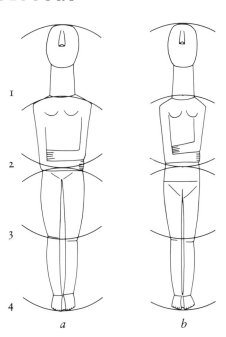

FIG. 39. The planning of figures attributed to mature phases of the Naxos Museum Master's career: *a*) [10] name-piece; *b*) [11]

the particular angle chosen. For the shoulder (which tends to be more crisp and angular on his larger figures) he preferred angle B, for the pubic area the angle combination $A + (B/2)$, and in some cases the taper of the figure and even the position of the right forearm seem to have been influenced by the use of the harmonic system.

One of the most interesting aspects of the body of work attributable to the Naxos Museum Master is that one can discern in it the pattern of his growth from raw novice to accomplished craftsman.[74] To the earliest, most immature phase of his artistic development belongs the smallest figure, which is in every respect except its faithful adherence to the four-part canon a coarse and clumsy piece of work. Nevertheless, within its lumpy, undifferentiated forms and slack outlines one can recognize the untried hand of the individual who went on to carve much more carefully formed and finished images. Considerably less crude, but also an early attempt, probably, is the somewhat larger figure in Munich [4].

To a somewhat more advanced stage of the Naxos Museum Master's career belong ten works, including several unpublished fragments and a figure, also unpublished, from Aplomata [3]. This stage is represented here by a work in Athens [2] and three privately owned pieces [5, 6, 9]. Small- to medium-sized – only one [9] exceeds 40 cm – and still stocky and thick in profile, these figures are obviously the products of a more confident hand. Of the three, the small figure in Athens [2] is perhaps the latest, showing as it does more developed contours. In this stage the sculptor introduces incised fingers and toes, but he has trouble fitting in the correct number of the former: each of the figures has five fingers on the left hand – that is, on the hand that is most exposed to view – but (with the exception of [9]) not on the right one. However, on two of the three works [2, 6] the sculptor, in order to compensate for an injudicious allotment of space, simply scratched the "thumb" of the left hand directly on the chest, while on the third work [5] he slanted the hand slightly upward to accommodate five fingers.

To a third stage of the sculptor's development belong two very similar figures in Naxos that were presumably found together [7, 8]. These works are somewhat larger (ca. 43 cm originally and 48 cm) than the ones just discussed and much more refined in overall appearance even though the incision work is not more advanced. One can see in these images the beginning of a tendency toward attenuation, achieved through a lengthening and narrowing of the head/neck and the legs and feet. This is developed in the next stage, which is represented by a somewhat larger figure in Naxos [10]. On this carefully planned piece the width is significantly reduced. For example, the shoulders are 21 percent of the length as compared to 25 percent to as much as 28 percent in the earlier works. The fingers now finally number five on each hand.

The fifth and perhaps final stage of the Naxos Museum Master's artistic evolution is represented by the outsize figure in the Goulandris Collection [11]. In this work attenuation is carried to its logical extreme: all parts are significantly narrowed. The shoulder width is now only 17 percent of the length. As part of the elongation process this one alone of all the figures is endowed with a proper midsection and a deeper pubic triangle. The figure is also half as thick in profile as the sculptor's earliest works, and quite a bit thinner than the figures of the third and fourth stages. Only the arms retain their former thickness. In such a slender format they appear disproportionate and uncomfortably stiff. One might suppose that this was one of the first very large figures attempted by the Naxos Museum Master.

If the smallest and largest figures were the only ones of the group to have survived, we might not easily recognize the two images as the works of the same sculptor. This is not surprising since they were probably carved at least ten or fifteen years apart. But, with the aid of a relatively large number of intermediary works representing different phases through which the sculptor passed as he gained experience and mastered his craft, the connection between what appear to be his earliest and latest works becomes evident.

Of the eighteen pieces attributable to the Naxos Museum Master's hand at present, four have been unearthed in cemeteries on Naxos. The figure in Athens was found in grave 28 at Phyrroges, excavated in 1904 by Stephanos; one of the name-pieces [1] was found in 1948 by grave robbers at Phionta; while another, [3], and a pair of legs were found at Aplomata in 1951 and 1972, respectively. Indeed, the Naxos Museum Master is the only sculptor whose works have been found at as many as three different documented sites on one island.

Two other name-pieces [7, 8] were found twenty-five or more years ago by a Naxian farmer while plowing his fields and given to the Naxos Museum. The fifth name-piece [10] belonged to the group of illicitly obtained objects confiscated in 1965 (mentioned in connection with the Steiner Master), which is thought to have been Naxian in origin. The figure in the Goulandris Collection is also said to have been found on Naxos. Several fragmentary pieces, including one illustrated here [5], belong to the "Keros hoard."

THE GOULANDRIS MASTER
[Pls. VIID, IX, 34, 35, 36, 37; Checklist, p. 159]

The sculptor named after the Greek private collection that contains at least two complete figures and a head from his hand was not only one of the finest sculptors of his time, but he was apparently the most prolific of all Cycladic figure-makers, to judge from the many works attributable to him – a number that greatly exceeds that of any other sculptor known. (In this respect, the Naxos Museum Master takes a distant second place to him.) And from our remote vantage point four and a half thousand years after he lived, it would seem that this man may well have been the single most important artist of his time. Certainly his many works must have given him wide exposure over what was, one suspects, an unusually long career, with the result that other sculptors may have benefited from contact with this master carver and his work.

At present count nearly one hundred pieces, representing at the very least, fifty-two different works, can be attributed with assurance to the Goulandris Master's hand. Although it is possible to trace his development through different phases, he was one of the most consistent sculptors throughout. His many works are stamped with the imprint of his particular style, making even small fragments easy to recognize and enabling one to estimate the original lengths of these broken works within a reasonable margin of error.

Thirteen of the Goulandris Master's figures are complete or very nearly so [1, 2, 4, 6, 7, 8, 10, 13, 15, 21, 25, 26, 27]. From these pieces, in particular, especially the larger ones, one can appreciate the harmony of proportion, the elegant understatement of line, and the careful workmanship that must have contributed to the unprecedented popularity he enjoyed in his own day. Indeed, it is with the Goulandris Master's style that one might best compare our own perception of aesthetic perfection in classic Cycladic sculpture to that of the Early Bronze Age islanders. Although, as we shall see, his works are not all imposing in size or impressive in the same degree in their design and execution, one might agree that those who had images carved by him did well to choose him as their sculptor.

The Goulandris Master appears to have carved standard females exclusively. Since his figurative output was so enormous compared to that of other sculptors, one might well wonder if, besides having had a long career, he may have been one sculptor who did not carve marble vessels in appreciable numbers.

It would, of course, be very useful to know just how long it took a skilled sculptor using handmade and hand-operated tools to fashion a folded-arm figure of average size from the initial selection and hewing of the marble to the final polishing and painting. (It would be useful, too, to know how long it took to fashion the common vessel types.) To date, little research has been done in this area,[75] and one can only imagine that it must have taken many days if not weeks for one man to produce a carefully finished piece of some size.

Our ignorance of the role of time in the manufacture of Cycladic sculpture is due in part to the fact that we do not know how much time on the average sculptors spent practicing their profession. They may well have devoted some or much of their day to other pursuits such as fishing, farming, or stock raising. The amount of time spent in marble working doubtless varied from sculptor to sculptor. While the demand for the Goulandris Master's figures may have been greater than that for most sculptors' works, one suspects that, in general, the marble carver was forced to supplement his livelihood through other means, much as craftsmen and other specialists still do in small communities on the islands. This would necessarily have limited the number of pieces a sculptor would have produced during the course of his career. Our lack of knowledge in these areas, however, makes it impossible to give even rough estimates of the number of figures and/or vessels a sculptor might have fashioned in his lifetime, although the numbers of surviving works attributable to individuals lead one to suspect that most sculptors made fewer than fifty folded-arm figures.

The Goulandris Master carved the standard late Spedos-variety figure in an unprecedentedly wide range of sizes (see Appendix 2), and, as we shall see, scale evidently played an important role in the development of his style. The smallest work attributable to him without reservation at present, a badly weathered but intact figure in Norwich [1], is a veritable miniature at 16.5 cm, while his largest figure, of which only the head and neck remain, in Copenhagen [36], was, at about 98 cm, conceived on an unusually grand scale.

It is very tempting to think that the Goulandris Master determined the length of each of his figures with the aid of a specific unit of measurement. Certainly it seems significant that his largest known work was six times the size of his smallest, while the next largest ([28] and a privately owned figure preserved to the knees [46]) appear to have been about four times the size of the smallest. We may thus be talking about a "foot" of 33 cm, according to which the smallest figure would measure a half foot and the largest would have had a length of three feet. Whether or not this hypothetical foot was further subdivided into "inches" (and if so, how many inches) is a matter for debate. Two factors need to be taken into account. The first is that a finished work might not have exactly the dimensions originally intended: one might expect that it would be slightly smaller. Secondly, as explained in the discussion of the Naxos Museum Master, the available measurements of Cycladic figures are not always, if often, absolutely accurate. This is largely due to the fact that their extremities lie in different planes – that is, if a figure is placed on its back on a flat surface, the top of the head will rest very near that surface while the ends of the feet will rise above it, making it necessary to drop a vertical line from them to the surface in order to take a precise measurement.[76] For this reason, it is not unusual for two people to come up with two slightly different measurements for the same piece, unless, of course, they are each extremely careful. Moreover, because of modern restorations, it is impossible in some cases (e.g., [21, 26]) to be certain that an accurate measurement of a figure in its present state represents the exact dimension of the original. Bearing in mind, then, that all of the dimensions may not be accurate to the nearest millimeter, and considering that even if they are they may not represent exactly the measurement the sculptor had in mind when he first trimmed his marble slab and laid out the design of his figure upon it, it may be interesting to compare the lengths of some of the Goulandris Master's best preserved works with absolute measurements based on different subdivisions of a foot of 33 cm.

Length in cm	Foot of 10 in	Foot of 12 in	Foot of 13 in
[1] 16.5	16.5 = 5″	16.5 = 6″	17.76 = 7″
[2] 33	33 = 1′	33 = 1′	33 = 1′
[7] 35.2	36.3 = 1′1″	35.75 = 1′1″	35.54 = 1′1″
[8] 38.2		38.5 = 1′2″	38.07 = 1′2″
[10] 39	39.6 = 1′2″		40.62 = 1′3″
[13] 42	42.9 = 1′3″	41.25 = 1′3″	43.15 = 1′4″
[21] 54 (estimated)	56.1 = 1′7″	55 = 1′8″	55.85 = 1′9″
[27] 63.4	62.7 = 1′9″	63.25 = 1′11″	63.49 = 1′12″

Each of the three is appealing in part.[77] Yet, it is quite possible that the correspondences are all fortuitous, for if the foot had been subdivided in a consistent way, one would expect that such lengths as a foot and a half or a foot and a quarter would be standard, recurring sizes. But they are apparently not. Although the margin of error for the estimated lengths of the Goulandris Master's many broken figures is too great to allow them to be of much use for precise determinations, it is nevertheless important to note that, taken together with the complete figures, all but the smallest and the largest works fall in the one-to-two-foot range and that within this range nearly every measurement (to the nearest centimeter) seems to be represented (see Appendix 2, on which I include estimated original lengths only for the better preserved fragments that definitely belonged to different figures).

One might conclude tentatively that while it is possible that the Goulandris Master used a ruler of about 33 cm – the length of the foot having probably been determined by him – the subdivision of the foot into smaller units would have been made visually. This would account for the great variety in figure length within the one-to-two-foot range. That is to say, it is doubtful that the sculptor said to himself: "I think I shall make a figure one foot and three inches long," but rather something like, "Out of this piece of marble I will be able to make a figure that is a bit longer than one foot." Very likely the size of the available marble slab had a great deal to do with whether a particular figure was a few centimeters longer or shorter than another carved by the same sculptor. Moreover, the purchaser of a piece probably neither commissioned it to conform to a precise measurement nor would he have paid for it "by the centimeter," a method of pricing rumored to have been in use among grave robbers in recent years.

Certain characteristic features are present in the Goulandris Master's works (insofar as they are preserved) virtually without fail, regardless of their size or the phase of the sculptor's development to which they might belong. As such they may be regarded as hallmarks of his style.

The works are sturdy in appearance, exhibiting soft, subtle contours, punctuated at regular intervals by neatly incised, parallel lines marking the horizontal divisions of the chin, neckline, abdomen, knees, and ankles. The head is of the classic lyre shape with a shallow chin and a prominent long semiconical nose often extending rather low on the face. The arms are narrow; the small breasts spaced wide apart. The abdominal area is defined by a broad line which forms the top of a small pubic triangle. The knee and ankle grooves continue around the figure, interrupted only by the leg-cleft. This is treated as a deep unperforated groove.

While the torso is conceived as a relatively flat surface in front, the back normally has a distinct curvature that is unusual. Whether intended or not, this rounding of the back imbues the figures with a strong tactile appeal while at the same time rendering them somewhat unstable when placed on a flat surface. The Goulandris Master may have curved the backs of his figures for a practical purpose: the convex form must have fit the contour of his palm more comfortably than a flat one, affording him a securer grip and greater control for the execution on the front of incised details. (And if, as suggested earlier, such images were carried in a funeral procession, their rounded backs would also have made them easier and more comfortable to hold on upturned palms.) The sculptor normally elected not to incise

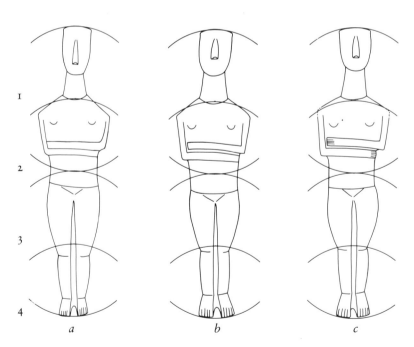

FIG. 40. The planning of figures attributed to the Goulandris Master: *a*) [13]; *b*) [25]; *c*) [27] name-piece

a *b* *c*

102

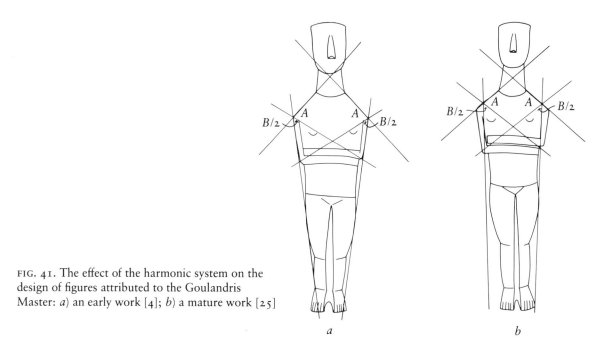

FIG. 41. The effect of the harmonic system on the design of figures attributed to the Goulandris Master: *a*) an early work [4]; *b*) a mature work [25]

a   *b*

the spine, a feature found on most late Spedos-variety figures, perhaps because it would have been difficult to make the long groove straight on the curving surface.

The Goulandris Master consistently used the four-part, compass-drawn plan in laying out his works although on some examples he failed, at least on the finished sculpture, to make the third division coincide with the knees (fig. 40). The compass, incidentally, being nothing more elaborate presumably than a bit of obsidian or charcoal attached to a string, would have been adjustable to any size figure. Within the four-part design the proportions vary to a certain extent, although certain ones such as the ratio of the head/neck or shoulder width to the length remain constant at about 25 percent.

The Goulandris Master also employed the harmonic system to determine important angles on the outline and surface and perhaps as a compositional aid as well. He was quite consistent in choosing the same angles for the same features. The most significant of these choices was the angle combination $A + (B/2)$ that he applied to the shoulder/upper arm contour in one of two ways (fig. 41). While this angle, which gives the shoulders a very pronounced slope, is not unique to this sculptor's work, it is seen infrequently elsewhere. It is, indeed, one of the distinguishing characteristics of the Goulandris Master's style. Like most sculptors, the Goulandris Master carefully defined the right shoulder only. His figures as a result often show an asymmetry that is accentuated by the great length and slope of the shoulders.

A number of features are found on only a relatively small number of the sculptor's figures. These include relief modeling of the forearms and their separation by means of a clear space rather than a simple groove, meticulously incised fingers, and a straight spinal groove.

Some figures exhibit all three of these features [16, 26, 28]; some exhibit arm separation and fingers but no spine (e.g., [21, 27]); others exhibit arm separation only [14, 22, 25]; and several have only a spine (e.g., [1, 40]). With the exception of the backbone that can occur on smaller figures, and with the exception of one fairly small torso in Athens on which the fingers of the right hand only appear to be incised [42],[78] the unusual embellishments are found exclusively on larger figures, the majority of which exceed 50 cm in length.

Whereas the spine would have been just as easy or difficult to incise and just as appropriate on a small figure as a large one, the careful cutting of five parallel fingers of uniform width required a space of at least one centimeter and are therefore generally found only on figures of 40 cm or more. The separation of well-modeled forearms, which occurs rather rarely and usually in conjunction with incised fingers on large figures carved by skilled sculptors (e.g., pl. VIA), appears to be an aesthetic device designed to allow the eye to focus on the arm region, and in so doing to relieve the monotony of long plain surfaces. The separation of the forearms, in combination with incised fingers, alters the appearance of a figure significantly. The Goulandris Master used these details with particular effect.

The figures carved by the Goulandris Master that exhibit unusual embellishments tend also to be more refined in other respects than the smaller, plainer ones. Their profiles are generally thinner, their outline contours, when viewed from the front or rear, also tend to show more pronounced curves and the elbows stand out further from the body. Such figures are for the most part more harmoniously conceived and more accurately executed according to the four-part system, and in general they give the impression of having had greater care lavished upon them. These differences can be best appreciated by comparing the smallest and the largest complete works attributable to the Goulandris Master at present [1, 2, 27].

It would seem that the smaller, less elaborate, thicker figures of the Goulandris Master [1 through 11] represent an early phase of his development,[79] while the larger, thinner, more detailed, more carefully planned and modeled works (e.g., [14, 21, 22, 24 through 28]) represent the master's highest attainments. In between these two groups are a number of midsize works that are quite refined in their lines but do not exhibit special features (e.g., [13, 15, 18, 19, 20, 23]). These perhaps preceded the master's most mature and finest work.

The Goulandris Master may not have carved smaller figures exclusively during his formative years, but he no doubt first mastered his craft by producing rather modest works, only attempting more ambitiously conceived ones later on. Indeed, numerous attempts on a smaller scale and even several executed in a large size (e.g., [23, 45]) must have led to such masterpieces as the larger of the name-pieces [27], the figure in Canberra [21], and the fragmentary privately owned piece [28]. Having fashioned such figures, whose size provided greater opportunity for him to exercise his considerable skill and talent, one might think the Goulandris Master would have preferred to continue making figures on an ampler scale.

The sculptures of the Goulandris Master took on an individual appearance through the addition of painted detail. Actual pigment and clear paint ghosts survive on a number of his works and it may be assumed that all his figures from the smallest to the largest once carried

104

FIG. 42. Variations in the use of paint for hair and for decorative patterns on the face of figures attributed to the Goulandris Master. (The eyes of all the master's works were originally painted as in *d*.

Schematic drawings: the outlines are not individualized.) *a*) not listed; *b*) [26]; *c* [27] name-piece; *d*) not listed; *e*) [31]; *f*) [32]; *g*) [29]; *h*) [36]

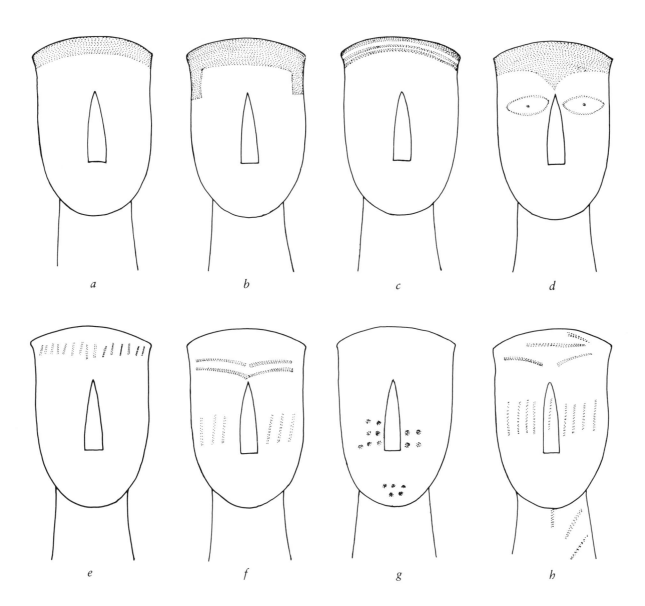

a *b* *c* *d*

e *f* *g* *h*

some color. It is, in fact, in the work of this sculptor that we have the best evidence for the varied use of paint by Cycladic sculptors of the second phase.[80]

The Goulandris Master painted eyes and some sort of headdress or hair as a matter of course in finishing his figures (fig. 42). The eyes were almond-shaped outlines with dotted pupils. The forehead received a solid band of color, a band that arches over the eyes like brows or possibly a "widow's peak," a band of horizontal lines, short vertical strokes, double

FIG. 43. Painted details on the sides and/or backs of the heads of figures attributed to the Goulandris Master. (Schematic drawings: the outlines are not individualized.) *a*) [26]; *b*) [29]; *c*) [45].

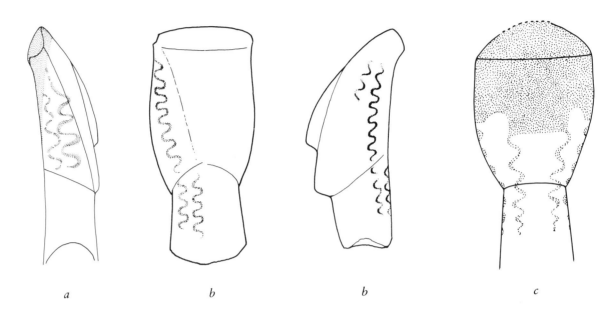

a   *b*   *b*   *c*

arching lines, or a combination of straight and arching lines. In some cases there seems to be a continuation of the hairline on the sides of the face. The cheeks may be decorated with a pattern of dots or with vertical strokes. The chin in at least one example is also dotted, and in several cases the nose carries a streak of paint [25, 31, 36].

On the back of the head paint ghosts take the form of a solid area of varying shape (fig. 43). In several examples paint ghosts for strands of curled hair are visible at the side and back of the head and neck [e.g., 24, 26, 29, 35] as well as on the front of the neck [46, 48]. The larger name-piece [27] shows a different design apparently: the back of the head is treated in the usual manner, but in addition it appears that the neck may also have been painted as a solid area from the base of which on either side originate ribbonlike lines that seem to continue down the back (fig. 44*a*). It is not really clear whether these lines and the arching parallel lines that run from the right shoulder onto the forearms (fig. 44*b*) are, in fact, paint ghosts, or even actual paint stains, or whether the marble at these points contains darker striations.

One or two figures by the Goulandris Master had painted lines on the neck [36], while at least two others show traces of pigment in the upper neck groove [29, 31]. The large figure in Bloomington [25] has painted bangles on the forearms (fig. 45). It is possible that the Goulandris Master and other sculptors used paint to show nonanatomical details (tattooing and body ornamentation) more often than we are aware because in general details in the form of dots and narrow lines are not easily recognized unless actual pigment is present.

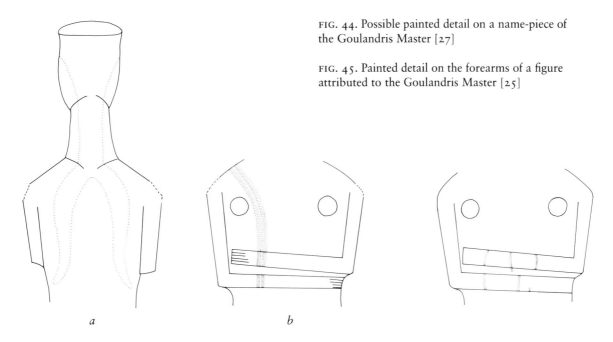

FIG. 44. Possible painted detail on a name-piece of the Goulandris Master [27]

FIG. 45. Painted detail on the forearms of a figure attributed to the Goulandris Master [25]

a

b

The patterns in which the painted details were executed by the Goulandris Master are probably not unique to his work. What they do show is an unprecedented variety. It is tempting to think that the skin of the deceased owner of a figure (and perhaps of his mourners as well) would have been painted with the same patterns as part of the funeral preparations.

It is rather a sad commentary on the state of Cycladic archaeology that of the dozen complete (or nearly complete) works and more than eighty fragments from the hand of the Goulandris Master only one complete figure and some half dozen fragmentary ones were found in sanctioned investigations. With the possible exception of some fragments that may have been chance finds made by farmers while cultivating their fields, most are apparently the fruits of unauthorized digging. A number of fragments, said to come from Panormos on Naxos, have been donated to the local museum of Apeiranthos (e.g., [40, 43, 44]).[81] Quite a few have no provenance attached to them and the alleged find-places of those that do (including donated pieces) must, of course, be treated with extreme caution. While in some cases one can probably trust the island named as the source of a figure, except in the case of very early acquisitions, one should probably discount the specific site mentioned – information that is supplied only rarely anyway. Consequently, the provenance given for figures that do not come from documented excavations are of but limited use in a close study of the geographical distribution of a sculptor's work. This is particularly frustrating in the case of the Goulandris Master, so many of whose works survive, because one would like to know just how widely his figures were dispersed.

The excavated pieces by the Goulandris Master include a small figure from grave 23 at Aplomata [7], an unusually rich tomb that also contained the badly weathered head of a large figure perhaps carved by our sculptor as well,[82] and the torso of a figure with separated forearms [14] and four or five smaller fragments recovered at the site on Keros opposite the islet of Daskaleio. The fact that the Goulandris Master's figures were found at these sites is of some significance since he is one of only two sculptors (the other being the Doumas Master) whose work is indisputably documented on two different islands (fig. 48).

In addition, more than a dozen works carved by the Goulandris Master, including the name-pieces, are said to have been found on Naxos, while a large number of mostly fragmentary ones belong to the Keros hoard (e.g., [4, 8, 17 through 20, 22, 24, 28, 29, 31, 34, 37, 41, 43, 44, 46, 47, 49]). Naxos may actually have been the source also of six well-preserved unprovenanced works [6, 13, 15, 21, 23, 25] as well as a large figure said to have been found relatively recently on Paros [26]. On the other hand, Keros could have been the find-place of some of these and probably yielded at least some of the fragmentary works that are now without any alleged provenance (e.g., [3, 5, 9, 11]).

A torso fragment in the British Museum [16] as well as the painted head in Copenhagen [36] are said to have been found on Amorgos at the end of the last century, although it is conceivable that one or both actually came from Keros. A head in the Louvre [48], also acquired in the late nineteenth century, has a somewhat firmer association with Amorgos, since it is said to have been found at Kornovelge [sic], a site identified by Lila Marangou as Kornoviglia, not far from Dokathismata (see fig. 14), where she has found abundant traces of Early Cycladic occupation.

In sum, it is conceivable that as many as a third of the known works of the Goulandris Master could have been found on Naxos, while nearly two-thirds could have come from Keros. The possible importance, if any, of Paros (and of other islands not yet mentioned) as well as the extent of the importance of Amorgos in this distribution picture will have to be demonstrated through further excavation.[83]

THE BASTIS MASTER
[Pls. 38, 39; Checklist, p. 162]

In distinct contrast to the Goulandris Master, the Bastis Master is known at present from only four works. Named for the collector who donated to the Metropolitan Museum of Art the largest and finest of these, the Bastis Master carved late Spedos-variety figures in at least three different sizes. His smallest known work, in Naxos, has a length of only 22.5 cm, while his largest, at 63.5 cm, is nearly three times as large. The other two works – a second figure in Naxos [2] and one in Fort Worth whose legs are missing from the knees [3] – are (or in the case of the latter, was) 50 and ca. 54 cm long, respectively. Two of this sculptor's works – his name-piece and the larger of the Naxian figures [2] are depicted in a pregnant state. These were fashioned with great delicacy and skill.

Even though the figures can be assigned to three different stages of their sculptor's development, and are therefore different from each other in important ways, all four are nevertheless stamped with his distinctive signature. All four have a long, angular head – this is somewhat less severe on the Fort Worth figure – with a prominent arching nose and a rounded chin. Allowing for certain differences of proportion, the outline contours, which combine straight lines in the upper part with long subtle curves in the lower part, are markedly similar. All four pieces have similarly executed curving horizontal incisions at the neck, abdomen, knees, and ankles. Those at the knees and ankles "wrap" around the figure, interrupted only by the leg-cleft. The breasts are small and wide-spaced and the abdominal area is defined by a broad horizontal line that forms the top of the pubic triangle. The feet are long and unusually slender and are carved separately for most of their length.

In profile the axis of the figures is straight and exhibits little contour, especially on the smallest. Particularly noteworthy is the absence of the usual curvature along the back of the head toward the top. The rear of the figures shows a distinct convexity, one of the characteristics of the Bastis Master's work that is strongly reminiscent of the Goulandris Master's style.

Another unifying element within the Bastis Master's works is his evident use of the four-part canon in their design (fig. 46). The name-piece and the larger Naxian figure were planned in nearly identical fashion, with the first division occurring rather low, while the small work

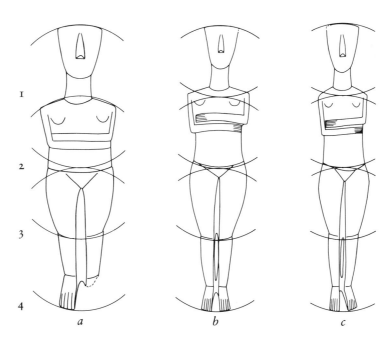

FIG. 46. The planning of figures attributed to the Bastis Master: *a)* [1]; *b)* [2]; *c)* [4] name-piece

109

was designed more conventionally. The Bastis Master was also quite consistent in his use of harmonic angles. He favored angle B for the shoulders, a right angle ([A + B]/2) for the pubis.

Although they are not plentiful, the Bastis Master's figures reveal a pattern of stylistic development that in a number of ways is strikingly similar to that of the Goulandris Master. Like him, the Bastis Master seems to have begun by making small, sturdy, but rather clumsy figures that still seem to partake of the shape of the original block, which was in this case perhaps roughly cylindrical [1]. As he gained experience and confidence he increased the size of his figure, balancing the longitudinal proportions, accentuating the contours, and modeling the forearms between which he left a clear space [3]. This resulted in a marked disparity in the level of the elbows, a characteristic that is particularly noticeable from the rear (fig. 25b). Eventually he combined the separation of the arms, which was now less exaggerated, with long, delicately incised fingers [2, 4].

Clearly we lack a substantial number of works from the Bastis Master's hand. Particularly noticeable perhaps is the absence of works intermediate between the small figure in Naxos and the Fort Worth piece. However, those figures by this sculptor that have survived show an even greater range of development in certain areas than do those of the Goulandris Master. While the Bastis Master's earliest piece is thicker than the earliest known works of the Goulandris Master, the degree of refinement attained in his largest (latest) works may be thought to surpass that of the largest well-preserved works of the Goulandris Master. He added to the lightness and elegance of his finest figures by perforating the leg-cleft along the calves and by making them more slender. (The Goulandris Master adhered to a width-length ratio of about one to four throughout his work.) He sharpened the outline contours by giving the profile an angular, as opposed to a rounded, edge, and he increased the interest of the rear and also the profile by accenting the buttocks with a subtle curving incision. The Bastis Master also displays in his superb name-piece a special sensitivity to the sensuousness and proportions of the female form: this is perhaps unique among folded-arm figures in having hips that are wider than the shoulders.

There is no denying that the Bastis Master's works resemble those of the Goulandris Master. A simple comparison of the illustrations should be sufficient to underscore this fact (fig. 47). Indeed, in my doctoral dissertation I erroneously went so far as to regard the small figure in Naxos as an early, if slightly atypical, work of the Goulandris Master and I even suggested that the Bastis Master's larger Naxian figure [2] and the name-piece [4] might represent a further refinement of the Goulandris Master's mature style as seen, for example, in the larger of his name-pieces. These errors were made before I recognized the Fort Worth piece [3] to be intermediate between the Bastis Master's smallest and largest figures. It is clear now that the Bastis Master was a major sculptor in his own right and that there are in all his works significant differences from those of the Goulandris Master—for example, in the shape of the head and feet, in the complete separation of the feet almost as far as the heels, and in the shoulder and pubic angles.

110

FIG. 47. A comparison of figures attributed to the
Goulandris and Bastis masters: *a*) [2] / [1]; *b*) [27] /
[4]; *c*) [2] / [1]; *d*) [27] / [4]; *e*) [22] / [3]. The
Goulandris Master's work appears first in each pair.

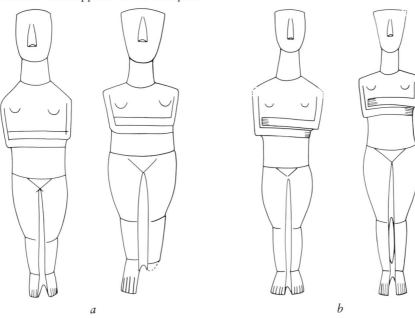

a

b

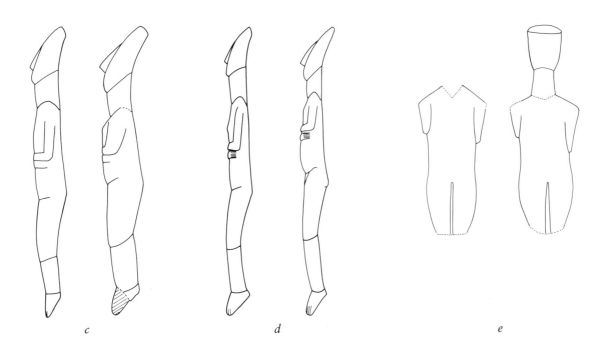

c

d

e

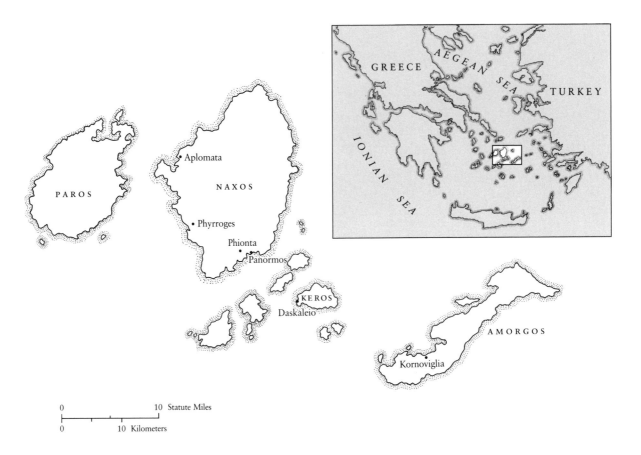

FIG. 48. Find-places of works attributed to the four late Spedos-variety masters discussed in chapter 5. Paros— (Goulandris). Naxos— (Goulandris), (Steiner); *Aplomata:* Goulandris, Naxos Museum; *Phyrroges:* Naxos Museum; *Phionta:* Naxos Museum, Bastis; *Panormos:* (Goulandris). Keros— (Goulandris), (Naxos Museum), (Bastis), (Steiner); *Daskaleio:* Goulandris. Amorgos— *Kornoviglia:* (Goulandris).

The similarities, on the other hand, cannot have been fortuitous, making it likely that the two sculptors were compatriots in touch with each other. So strong is the resemblance of the early and middle works carved by the Bastis Master to figures from comparable stages of the Goulandris Master's development – note, for example, the absence of the spine and the shape of the face on [3] – that it is tempting to imagine that the two men were brothers. One might suppose that they began their careers working side by side, eventually moving apart to work and grow independently, while still maintaining enough contact to mature along parallel lines.

The two Bastis Master figures in the Naxos Museum were found in 1948 in the cemetery of Phionta in southern Naxos where Kontoleon confiscated the contents of a number of graves just after they had been opened by looters. (Unfortunately, it is not known if the two figures were found in the same grave.) His name-piece is said to have been found on Naxos also,[84] while the Fort Worth piece belongs to the "Keros hoard."

The Late Spedos-Variety Masters: Interrelationships

It is of considerable interest to note that three of the four late Spedos sculptors discussed in this chapter are represented at documented sites on Naxos. The pattern of distribution of their works shows an interesting relationship. The Goulandris and Naxos Museum masters are represented at Aplomata, the Bastis and Naxos Museum masters at Phionta (fig. 48).[85] The stylistic relationship of the Goulandris and Bastis masters is evident even if their works have not been found in close association in a controlled excavation. The Bastis and Goulandris masters (as well as the Naxos Museum and Steiner masters) are represented in the "Keros hoard," however.

It is worth pointing out, furthermore, that the Goulandris and Naxos Museum masters are two of only three late Spedos sculptors whose works have been unearthed at Aplomata where most of the figures correspond to the early Spedos variety, a few to the slightly earlier Kapsala variety, and one or two to the still earlier precanonical type. The graves in which the three late Spedos sculptors' works were buried were presumably among the last of the cemetery to have been dug, and it seems unlikely that they or their contents would have been of significantly different date from each other. The Phionta cemetery, on the other hand, was, as far as one can determine (it is unpublished), a small burial ground that was in use over a relatively short period – perhaps only a generation or two. At least the figures found there all seem to belong to the late Spedos variety.

The factors mentioned here point to an essential interrelatedness and perhaps to the contemporaneity, or overlap, of at least three of the four sculptors. If we knew more about the find-places of the Steiner Master's figures, it is likely that he would fit into this picture quite nicely also. It is probably no coincidence, for example, that works of the Steiner [1], Naxos Museum [10], and Goulandris [10] masters were all present in the group of objects confiscated in 1965 from a Naxian smuggler.

It seems clear, then, that the Naxos Museum, Goulandris, and Bastis masters, and probably the Steiner Master, too, all came from the same island though each one probably resided in a different community. In the final chapter the question of their origins will be explored in greater detail.

Chapter Six

Five Late Classical Sculptors

THE SCHUSTER MASTER
[Pls. 40, 41; Checklist, p. 162]

A NUMBER of works can be attributed to an excellent sculptor named after the late owner of the only complete figure from his hand now available for study [2]. (A piece in the British Museum [5] missing the lower legs was preserved to its full length in 1850 when drawings of it were made.[86]) The representation of the female in a pregnant state was the image this sculptor preferred.

Typologically the Schuster Master's figures could be characterized as a combination of the late Spedos and the Dokathismata varieties, for he has fused into an easily recognized and extremely harmonious style bold curving aspects derived from the former with angular elements and upper body width more appropriate to the latter. The execution is controlled and precise throughout, with all forms and details clearly and carefully defined. (The figure in the British Museum [5] appears to have less sharply articulated lines than the others, but this impression may be caused by the manner in which the piece has chipped and weathered.)

The distinctive outlines of the figures with their rhythmic alteration of curving and angular contours – see the profile views especially – are closely similar to each other insofar as the figures are preserved, and allowing for slight variations in the shoulder angle. The profile axis is somewhat more broken than that of the average late Spedos- or Dokathismata-variety figure. The proportions are also very similar from piece to piece, with the exception of the shoulder and chest width. The latter is much more pronounced – about one-third the length – on the Sainsbury [7] and Kahane [4] figures and on the very fragmentary torso [3] than on either the name-piece or the figure in the British Museum [5] where it exceeds the normal one-quarter of the length only slightly.

Because of their essential similarity in proportions, it is possible to estimate the original sizes of the damaged works. The figures range in length from about 24–25 cm for a headless piece in Athens [1] to an estimated 60–62 cm or more than twice the size for the piece in the

Israel Museum [12]. The figure without head and neck in the Sainsbury Collection [7] and the figure to which belonged the head in the Goulandris Collection [11] originally measured about 45–47 cm.

The figures appear to have been designed roughly in four parts though no logical or consistent proportion of the length was used to determine the maximum width. With the exception of the Sainsbury figure [7], the angular aspects of the outline, specifically the shoulders, seem to have benefited from the application of the harmonic system. Internal details conform more accurately than the shoulders: angle A or $(A + B)/2$ was used for the pubic triangle, while angle B was used to describe the V-shaped incision at the back of the neck.

Most of the individual forms and details are executed in the same way from piece to piece. Especially noteworthy as hallmarks of the Schuster Master's style when considered together are the head with broad curving top and crescent-shaped ridge at the back – the angular head of the Kahane figure [4] differs appreciably from the others; the long aquiline nose; a curving neckline in front, a V-shaped one on the rear; narrow arms, the forearms arching subtly to accent the swelling of the belly and modeled in relief on the larger works; a rather large deep pubic triangle, bisected at its apex by a continuation of the leg-cleft; well-defined knees; and a deeply grooved leg-cleft that continues precisely as far as the buttock line, created by a change in planes. (A mannerism used with particular effect by the Schuster Master is the delicate arching of the feet seen in the name-piece. This is less pronounced on the figure in Athens [1] and in the profile view drawing of the British Museum figure [5] already mentioned.)

Very few differences of detail can be observed. Of the two most notable ones, one was apparently a function of size, the other of proportional disparity. Thus, the only figure with incised fingers, the Sainsbury piece [7], is the only one large enough to have an arm width of at least 1 cm that allowed for the incision of five delicate fingers of even width. Knowing that he could probably not achieve the same result in a more confined space, this meticulous sculptor did not even attempt to represent the fingers on his smaller works.

The exaggerated width of the upper torso on the Sainsbury [7] and Kahane [4] figures and the torso fragment [3] must have prompted the somewhat unusual rendering of the left forearm. Because the elbows on these figures stand out so far from the comparatively narrow midsection, the sculptor, in an effort to balance the length of the arms, made the left one shorter than usual – that is, he did not continue it all the way across the full width of the figure to meet the right upper arm as he did on the two works with somewhat less exaggerated upper body width [2, 5] (and, indeed, as nearly all other sculptors did in their work).

One other slight difference that has to do with torso breadth may be observed on the rear of the figures. On four of them [3, 4, 6, 7] the upper arms were made much wider than in front so that the back, which is carved in a slightly higher plane, could form a continuous line with the hips and legs. This method of treating the rear can be seen on many broad-chested Dokathismata-variety figures, but on his name-piece the Schuster Master used a different approach: instead of making the upper arms wider on the rear, he indicated their separation from the torso by wedge-shaped grooves.

116

Despite a considerable disparity in size, the works illustrated here display a uniformly strong sense of balance and proportion in all their dimensions, which indicates that they belonged to the mature phase of a master craftsman and were probably carved in close chronological proximity to one another. The name-piece, though relatively small, stands out not only as a beautifully preserved piece that, incidentally, is carved in an unusual white marble with gray mottling, but as one of the masterpieces of Cycladic sculpture. This sculpture and the Kahane figure [4] must have belonged to the very pinnacle of their sculptor's career.

To date only one of the Schuster Master's sculptures has turned up in controlled circumstances. This fragmentary work was recovered on Keros, opposite the islet of Daskaleio [6]. Of the other pieces safely attributable to his hand, several, including the Sainsbury figure [7] and probably the Kahane piece [4], as well as [8], [9], [10], belong to the "Keros hoard," but nothing at all is known about the origins of the rest.

THE ASHMOLEAN MASTER
[Pls. 42, 43; Checklist, p. 163]

Four well-preserved figures in Budapest, Houston, Athens, and Oxford can be ascribed to the hand of a sculptor named after the collection that houses the largest one. A talented sculptor of pregnant females of the Dokathismata variety, the Ashmolean Master worked the marble in three different scales. His smallest figure, in Budapest, has a length of only 23.7 cm while his name-piece [4], with a length of 75.9 cm, is more than three times as long and, incidentally, the largest Dokathismata-variety work known. The two other figures, in the de Menil [2] and Goulandris [3] collections, are very similar to each other in size, with lengths of 36.7 and 39.1 cm, respectively. Their scale is thus half that of the name-piece.

The outlines of the three smaller figures are remarkably similar to each other. Unlike the Schuster Master, when making the shoulders of his figures very broad, the Ashmolean Master tapered the upper torso so that the elbows do not stand out markedly from the body and the inner line of the upper arms bears a natural relationship to the outline of the lower part of the figure. The outline contours of the name-piece differ from those of his other works chiefly because he made the shoulders of this figure much narrower in proportion to the overall length (only 21 percent as compared to a range of 29 to 32 percent for the others). Perhaps the slab of marble he chose for this unusually long figure was slender from the start. In any case, with such a narrow shoulder width he had no need to taper the upper body, with the result that the upper arms are nearly parallel.

The profile axis of the four figures is straight, and the contours are very similarly treated. The individual forms and details show a marked resemblance throughout and, although not unusual individually, their combined presence and the particular way in which they are rendered help to make the Ashmolean Master's style easily recognizable. One should note especially the shield-shaped face with pointed chin and long aquiline nose; the V-shaped incision

117

at the neckline; the upper arm incisions that begin well below the shoulders, the right one consistently lower than the left; the carefully modeled forearms, without fingers, that curve gently and taper to accent the slight bulge of the abdomen; the ankle grooves (not visible on the name-piece because of a break at this point); the rather straight feet with only four toes per foot incised on three of the figures [1, 3, 4]; and on the back a single continuous groove of approximately even depth and width that extends from the apex of the neckline to the ends of the feet.

Uniformity of appearance from piece to piece is also the result of the sculptor's consistent application of the harmonic system; the right shoulder/upper arm angles and the pubic triangle all conform to angle B.

In overall appearance the de Menil and Goulandris figures [2, 3], which are carved in the same scale, resemble each other particularly closely. This is partly due to the fact that they were carefully planned in the same way according to the four-part canon. The Budapest piece [1] was also planned in four parts, but slightly differently: its midpoint occurs at the forearms rather than at the abdomen. The midpoint of the name-piece, on the other hand, occurs just above the apex of the pubic triangle (fig. 49). Curiously, this figure was designed quite differently from the others and not according to the usual application of the canon. It consequently lacks the balanced proportions that have come to be associated with Cycladic sculpture of the second phase – a harmony of conception admirably exemplified by the mid-size figures from the Ashmolean Master's hand.

FIG. 49. The planning of figures attributed to the Ashmolean Master: *a*) [1]; *b*) [2]; *c*) [3]; *d*) [4]

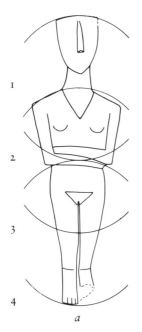

All four of these works are, regardless of the differences noted, stamped with the un-mistakable imprint of a well-developed personal style. However, they appear to represent different stages of the sculptor's artistic development.

To an earlier phase – though probably not the very beginning of his career – one might assign the Budapest figure. This piece is not only small and unassuming, but it is also rela-tively stocky and unrefined in appearance. The incised details are not all precisely executed, especially the leg-cleft in front and the spine and neckline in back, and the shoulders are awkwardly asymmetrical. In profile the figure is comparatively thick: for example, at the thickest point, from the abdomen to the buttocks, it is 10.7 percent of the length as com-pared to 6.3 percent for the Goulandris figure [3]. As noted in the discussion of the Goulan-dris and Bastis masters, the thickness of a figure appears to be jointly dependent upon its size and on the sculptor's level of experience. Although there is more than a 15 cm discrepancy in their length, the actual measurement at the profile's widest point is almost exactly 2.5 cm on both the Budapest and Goulandris figures carved by the Ashmolean Master, while at their narrowest points both have a thickness of about 1.8 cm. To have made the smaller figure much thinner would have meant risking fracture. The relative lack of refinement that re-sulted, both with respect to the thickness of the piece as a whole and in the frontal width of such parts as the neck and ankles, to some extent also reflects the sculptor's relative in-experience. For if one compares the Budapest figure with the Schuster Master's name-piece, one finds that although the two are carved in nearly the same scale – they differ in size by 5.5 cm – the latter displays none of the stockiness or awkwardness of the Ashmolean Master's small-scale work. On the contrary, his surviving works show that he was able to carve the marble in a variety of sizes with equal skill. It is for this reason that one should consider the Schuster Master's name-piece a mature work, while the Budapest figure one should view as belonging to a comparatively early stage of the Ashmolean Master's development.

Having achieved reasonable proficiency carving works of modest dimensions, the Ash-molean Master may have gone on to experiment on a larger, less constricting scale. Of the four surviving figures, the name-piece was perhaps the next one to have been carved, al-though a number of other figures may well have been produced by the sculptor between the Budapest figure and this one. While this very large image suffers from a certain inelegance of proportion, due to a lack of careful planning rather than from a coarseness related to small-ness of scale, it, too, shows that the sculptor had not yet perfected his approach. And al-though the name-piece is more carefully carved and detailed than the Budapest figure, the two works share characteristics indicative of a lack of finish, particularly on the rear, not seen on the two other figures. These include a quite superficially incised spine and leg-cleft and the unusual (though not unprecedented) absence of any definition of the upper arms on the back.

To an advanced stage if not the acme of the Ashmolean Master's artistic development belong the figures in the de Menil and Goulandris collections [2, 3]. These works, which were probably carved at a brief interval, display a harmony of proportion in all their dimensions and a refinement of individual forms not seen in the very small or the very large figures from his hand. Their medium size seems to have suited this sculptor especially well. The two works exhibit also a higher degree of meticulousness in the execution of details. In this regard the de Menil figure is particularly fine: alone of the four works, this piece has five toes on each foot; it also lacks the incision overruns that can be seen on the Goulandris figure at the right upper arm line and the pubic triangle.

It could perhaps be argued that the Budapest figure does not necessarily represent an earlier developmental phase, but was simply a small commission, produced around the same time as the de Menil and Goulandris figures, on which the master did not lavish a great deal of attention. From a slightly different point of view, on the other hand, it might be argued that the name-piece, because of its unusually large size, should be considered later than all the other figures since quite often the largest works of a sculptor appear to be his best ones. It seems likely, however, that the de Menil and Goulandris figures, which in terms of artistic quality represent a much greater degree of accomplishment than either the Budapest or the name-piece, were preceded by less masterfully conceived and executed figures through which the sculptor would have gained experience and refined his style. It was perhaps also necessary for him to try carving in a number of different scales until he found one that best suited his approach. The Budapest and Oxford figures fall naturally into place if one views them as just such preliminary pieces that served the important artistic purpose of preparing their obviously gifted sculptor for his best work.

The Ashmolean Master's name-piece was acquired toward the end of the last century on Amorgos.[87] The de Menil figure, which was acquired much more recently than the name-piece, is said to have come from Naxos, while the Goulandris piece was reputedly found on Keros. A further connection with this island may be seen in a damaged pair of feet and calves from the "Keros hoard" [5]. This fragment belonged to a figure with a length of about 37 cm — that is, the size of the de Menil and Goulandris figures. The piece resembles the lower legs and feet of the Goulandris figure particularly closely, especially in profile. Four toes appear to have been incised on the long delicate left foot; the right foot is too badly damaged for toes to be counted.

THE BERLIN MASTER
[Pls. 44, 45; Checklist, p. 163]

Two figures — masterworks both — can at present be attributed to a sculptor named after the location of the better preserved one. Carved with great skill and care, the images differ appreciably in size: the name-piece has a length of 43 cm, while the better-known work [2], in Athens, measures 68.6 cm. Both are unusually large for the Dokathismata variety; the latter is, after the Ashmolean Master's name-piece, the second largest known example of this variety.

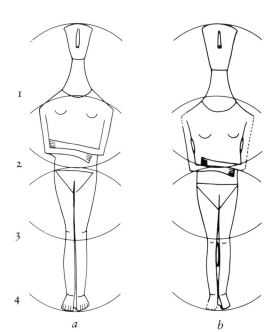

FIG. 50. The planning of figures attributed to the Berlin Master: *a*) [1] name-piece; *b*) [2]

Like the Schuster Master, this artist's highly individualistic approach to the pregnant female form combines elements of two different styles, but whereas the Schuster Master's work seems to have been influenced more by the Spedos variety, that of the Berlin Master is closer in concept to the Dokathismata. His figures have the broad angular upper body and narrow elongated lower torso and legs of the Dokathismata variety though their outline contours show curves that are reminiscent of the Spedos variety. The single sweeping curve that begins at the head and continues down the widening neck and long sloping shoulder, accented by the counter curve of the low neckline, and the series of undulating curves that begin at the waist and continue without interruption to the feet, though not without parallels, are unsurpassed in all of Cycladic sculpture for their controlled refinement of line and masterful execution.

The name-piece shows a much straighter profile axis than the large figure with its remarkably elongated, backward-tilting head and slightly flexed knees. The pregnant condition is defined on the name-piece not by any protrusion of the belly, but by the elegant curve of the forearm and hand above it. The other figure has a very slight abdominal bulge that is accented by the curving arm above. (A break just below the top of the pubic triangle alters the present appearance of this figure slightly.) Viewed in profile, the legs of both works are, curiously, thinner through the thighs than the calves.

The proportions and planning of the two figures differ somewhat: the midpoint of the length occurs slightly above the top of the pubic triangle on the name-piece, at the top of the right forearm on the figure in Athens (fig. 50). Thus, the former has somewhat longer legs proportionally than the latter. Although the shoulders of the Athens figure are damaged – they and the left upper arm have been restored in plaster – the width at this point appears to have been the same in relation to the length on both works. A four-part plan seems to have been followed in each case, but not with the precision one often finds among Spedos-variety figures. And while the unusually sloping shoulders do not conform to either of the primary harmonic angles or any of the familiar angle combinations – they are actually $B + (A/4)$ – the pubic triangle is drawn to the exact specifications of angle A.

The incised details are rendered with particular finesse, especially the neckline on the front and narrow arms that widen very slightly at the hands to make room for the delicate fingers. Apart from such minor differences as the fact that the left hand extends as far as the right upper arm on the name-piece but not on the Athens figure – a disparity seen in the work of the Schuster Master also – individual forms and details of the two figures are rendered in virtually identical fashion, with two very interesting, if obvious, exceptions. On the Athens figure the leg-cleft is perforated for a short distance between the calves, and the arms are separated from the sides by means of similar perforations, which effectively eliminate the excessive breadth of the upper torso. However, on the name-piece, which is 25.6 cm shorter than the Athens figure, the sculptor chose neither to remove a portion of the membrane connecting the legs nor to disconnect the arms. Like the Schuster Master on most of his works and like other Dokathismata-variety sculptors, the Berlin Master widened the upper arms on the rear of this figure, so that the lines of the back flow imperceptibly into those of the legs. Viewed from the front, however, the torso is unnaturally broad. One can only surmise that he did not attempt perforations on this figure because he did not consider the refinement worth the considerable risk of causing irreparable damage to what would have been a nearly finished work. The risk in this case, particularly in the area of the very narrow and consequently extremely fragile arms, would have been greater because of the figure's smaller size.[88] (Very few figures with arm perforations, including the larger work by the Berlin Master whose left upper arm is missing, have survived to the present with their arms intact.) In any case, this is perhaps the only example in which two figures of one sculptor show this discrepancy.

Regrettably, the find-places of these splendid works are not known. The only possible clue to their sculptor's origins may be locked in the secret of the "Keros hoard," for a tiny fragment from this assemblage, comprising the lower part of the face, with chin line, and the upper part of the neck of a figure comparable in size to the name-piece may also have been carved by the Berlin Master [3?].[89] Inasmuch as the two full figures are clearly works of their sculptor's maturity, there must have been a substantial number of pieces carved before them. It is hoped, therefore, that other works attributable to the Berlin Master will one day turn up in the course of systematic excavation, possibly answering the question of his origins.

THE STAFFORD MASTER

[Pls. 46, 47; Checklist, p. 164]

We turn now to an accomplished sculptor of Chalandriani-variety female figures, named after the collection that contains one of the best preserved pieces, and perhaps the finest example, attributable to his hand. A mere glance at the illustrations should be sufficient to show that the figures in the Stafford [1], Woodner [2], and Louvre collections [3], and the privately owned torso [6] were carved by one person – an artist with a very confident and boldly stylized approach to the human form.

The complete or nearly complete figures – the ends of the feet of [4] are slightly damaged – assignable to this sculptor are almost identical to each other in size (26.1–28.1 cm). The first four are virtually identical to each other in outline contours, proportions, planning, and details (although some of the details of the Woodner piece [2] have been obliterated as the result of cleaning with acid that has also had the effect of reducing the thickness and edges of the work). A fifth well-preserved work [5], on the other hand, resembles these figures quite closely in some respects, but not at all in others, and it is therefore not quite as clear that it was carved by the same sculptor. This figure will be discussed separately later on. The torso [6] that belonged originally to a somewhat smaller figure with an estimated length of about 23 cm differs from the members of the core group in the rendering of the incised details. Two heads – one in the Erlenmeyer Collection [7], the other in Naxos [8] – belonged to figures that were about the same length.

The outline contours of the core group members and the torso insofar as it is preserved consist of a pleasing contrast of curving and angular elements. The continuous arc formed by the outline of the head, neck, and long sloping shoulder, along with the very shallow chin, are coincidentally, quite reminiscent of the Berlin Master's work, and are characteristics found on the figures of one or two other sculptors as well.[90] Their combined presence in the works of sculptors that are otherwise very different in concept indicates that they are the products of a common stylistic trend, although it is possible that one of these sculptors actually influenced the other. One might even speculate that the Stafford Master served as an apprentice to the Berlin Master.

The profile views of the core figures and the torso fragment show considerable modeling along a straight axis. Here one can appreciate how skilled and daring the Stafford Master was: at its slenderest point the torso fragment has a thickness of only 0.55 cm, while the larger Louvre [3] and Smeets [4] pieces have a thickness at comparable points of slightly more than 1.2 cm. Not surprisingly, none of the figures, except the name-piece, has survived to the present without sustaining a fracture at this most vulnerable place.

The complex of individual forms and details that, along with the outline and shallow chin already mentioned, help to identify the Stafford Master's highly distinctive style include: an unusually long ridgelike nose that bisects nearly the entire face and, except on the Woodner figure [2] (and on one other privately owned, unpublished core member), merges at its lower end with the contour of the face rather than projecting from it; a neck V indicated by a change in planes rather than incision; prominent wide-spaced breasts; a broad, compressed pubic triangle; fan-shaped feet, held at an acute angle, that are very long when viewed in profile and from the rear; on the back a total absence of any markings save the superficially incised leg-cleft.

Unlike many if not most Chalandriani-variety figures, the works of the Stafford Master were planned with great care and precision (figs. 18a, 51a). They were evidently designed, with the aid of a straight edge, according to a division of the length into five equal parts, with the shoulder width equivalent to two of these units. The harmonic system appears also to have been used consistently to determine the angular aspects of the design and to control the outline at important points: angle B was used to describe one or both shoulders in each case and usually also the pubic triangle (fig. 51b). All five pieces, moreover, have a vague X-shaped design on the flat surface of the chest, formed by the rising planes of the neck and breasts. Here, too, the harmonic system may have been employed to determine the exact placement of the breasts and elbows. Indeed, the possible use of the hypothetical protractor on the chest of these figures suggests what might have been the original configuration of such a device, since the entire system seems to have been brought into play: from a single point of origin both complementary angles and their bisections appear to contribute to the organization of the composition (fig. 51c, d).

The differences observable among the members of the core group are negligible. The Louvre figure [3] is perhaps slightly less well executed than the others if one compares, for example, the rendering of the leg-cleft. This detail is very straight and precisely centered on the name-piece and the Smeets figure [4] but not on the Louvre piece. Moreover, the continuous head/neck/shoulder curve is more graceful and fluid on the other works, particularly on the name-piece and the Woodner figure [2]. It is not clear just how the forearms were treated on the Woodner piece or on the Louvre figure. (On the latter all but their lowest boundary is at present obscured by plaster used to mend a break across the figure.) Presumably they were originally similar to the gently curving, sharply tapered forearms effectively defined on the name-piece by an incised diagonal line, and meant by their slight curves to reinforce the impression of pregnancy suggested by the light swelling of the short midsection and pubic area.

Curiously, on the torso fragment the diagonal forearm line was never incised. And strangely enough, although the main mass of the figure is executed with great skill and delicacy, the incision work shows a number of false starts and overruns. One might speculate that this torso as well as the two small heads [7, 8], which have rather amorphous noses, belonged to pieces carved some time before the slightly larger works that seem to represent the Stafford Master's style at its apex.

It seems reasonable to suppose that [5] is also from the Stafford Master's hand. This

FIG. 51. The planning of a figure attributed to the
Stafford Master [3] (*a*) and the effect of the harmonic system hypothetical harmonic protractor
(*d*) on the design of the sculptor's name-piece [1]
(*b*, *c*)

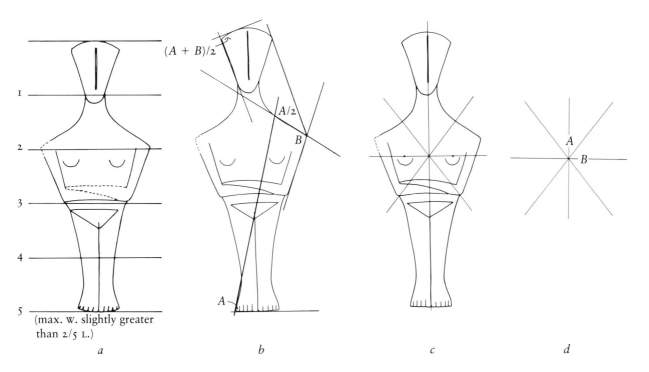

a   *b*   *c*   *d*

piece is only slightly shorter than the core group members although it is somewhat narrower across the shoulders and narrower as well as straighter across the top of the head than they are. It is also much flatter and, in profile, almost entirely without contour except at the top of the head, which resembles that of the core figures. Unlike them, this piece seems not to have been planned according to any logical division of the length into equal units, and while the harmonic system appears to have been used for certain aspects of the outline, such as the head angle and the neck/shoulder angle, the shoulder/upper arm angle does not conform to the system and the pubic triangle is best described by the angle combination $(A + B)/2$ (a right angle) rather than angle B as used on the core figures.

The most striking differences besides the contourless profile are, of course, the treatment of the upper torso and arms and the feet. Indeed, if these were the only portions of the figure preserved one would not think to attribute them to the same hand as the other works. The forearms, rendered in reverse (right *above* left instead of right *below* left), appear somewhat tentative and slack. Yet they show a slight taper that suggests that they might represent a step in the evolution of the stylized convention of the diagonal line used with such authority and grace on the Smeets and Stafford pieces. The head/neck/shoulder curve is present on this figure, too, but it lacks the bold sweeping quality of this contour as seen, for example,

125

on the name-piece. The top of the head also lacks the strong curve of the core figures, but, incidentally, shares its straightness with the small head in Naxos [8]. Like the core members, this figure lacks any incision work on the back except for the superficial leg-cleft. The feet are perhaps not carved according to the sculptor's original intention. They look as if they might have broken (during the carving process presumably) and been reshaped in a drastically shortened form.[91] If this was the case, the figure, as initially conceived, would have been even closer in size to the four core members and its feet might have borne a closer resemblance to theirs. One might view this figure as representing a formative stage in the development of the Stafford Master's ultimately taut, highly disciplined, and mannered approach to the human form as epitomized by his name-piece.

Only one of the eight images attributed to the Stafford Master was found in the course of systematic exploration. This is the small unpublished head [8] just mentioned, which was recovered by Doumas on Keros. Of the other works, the Louvre piece [3] is said to have come from Naxos, the name-piece from Paros – both were acquired early in the century – while the Erlenmeyer head [7], the torso fragment [6] (carved in an unusual fine-grained gray marble), and the "early" figure [5] belong to the "Keros hoard," an association that, incidentally, should lend support to the attribution of the "early" work to the hand of the Stafford Master.

THE DRESDEN MASTER
[Pls. 48, 49, 50; Checklist, p. 164]

Three works have been attributed to a Chalandriani-variety sculptor named after the location of the only completely preserved image [5] in this group that includes a headless figure in the Erlenmeyer Collection [6] and the lower part of another privately owned piece [8]. In addition, three female figures in Athens [1], Geneva [7], and a private collection [4], as well as two partially preserved females in Keos [2, 3] should probably also be viewed as the products of this sculptor's hand.

Like the Goulandris Hunter/Warrior Master, a sculptor of Chalandriani-variety figures discussed in chapter 3 (pls. 11, 12), the Dresden Master fashioned at least one armed male figure [5] as well as standard female representations. Five out of seven of these [2, 3, 4, 6, 8] show a pattern of grooved abdominal bands on the front. The iconographic range seen in this sculptor's work is reminiscent of that of two much earlier sculptors, the Doumas and Athens Museum masters, who not only carved figures of both sexes but who also made their females both with and without abdominal bands (pls. 14, 18).

In size the Dresden Master's work ranges from a diminutive 11.3 cm to as much as 26 or 27 cm. The name-piece and the headless female in Basel [6] were originally nearly identical in their dimensions, with a length of about 23 cm. (The name-piece measures 22.8 cm.)

In their severe outline contours and in their proportions the male and the Erlenmeyer figure [6], insofar as it is preserved, are also nearly identical. So similar are they, in fact, that if one were to superimpose the outline of one on that of the other the correspondence would be nearly exact. The lower figure fragment [8] is somewhat bulkier, but otherwise quite similar to the other two works, and the bold parallel grooving of the abdominal bands is especially similar to that of the hair on the name-piece.

One of the most striking elements of the Dresden Master's style is his way of depicting the head and neck. On the name-piece the head is massive and, in profile, mushroomlike; on the three completely preserved females [1, 4, 7] the head shape is triangular. The neck of all the well-preserved works is curiously thick and bulging. Its profile width is greatest on top and is equal to or greater than that of any part of the body. The downward taper of the neck is especially exaggerated on the name-piece. On all four complete works the neck has an angular midline down the front that forms the apex of the V incised on the essentially two-dimensional body. The beginning of a similarly treated neck can be seen also on three of the incomplete pieces [2, 3, 6].

The Dresden Master appears to have planned his figures according to a simple, if unusual, division of the length into three equal parts (figs. 18b, 52). The maximum width tends to vary somewhat from piece to piece with the result that certain figures [4, 7] have a much stockier build than that of the name-piece whose shoulder width is equivalent to only slightly more than one-third of its length. Within the first division, or third, of the design there is also considerable diversity in the amount of space allotted to the head in relation to the neck. Such proportional variations as well as the difference in male and female head shape and, of course, the iconographic distinctions are largely responsible for the dissimilarities observ-

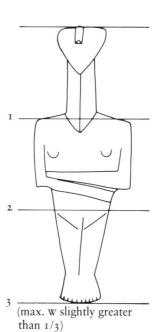

FIG. 52. The planning of a figure attributed to the Dresden Master [1]

(max. w slightly greater than 1/3)

127

able among the Dresden Master's works. He was, however, quite consistent in his use of the harmonic system, choosing angle B for the shoulder, angle A for the neck V, and the angle combination $(A + B)/2$ for the pubic V, almost without fail.

Since the name-piece [5] and the Erlenmeyer female [6] are nearly exact replicas of one another in outline, proportions, and the placement of details on the surface, one might well wonder if a somewhat more elaborate design was used in the initial stages of their manufacture. In an earlier discussion of the Dresden Master,[92] I suggested that the three-part schema may have been subdivided to form a grid of four by twelve squares, in which the head (minus the curious projecting knob ears) was made two squares wide by two squares long, and in which the width of the male at his belt and the width of the female at the top of the pubic area was also made two squares wide, while the same important aspects of the design of both figures were made to coincide with the horizontal divisions of this hypothetical grid.

Such a grid plan would have particular appeal in explaining the close similarity of the two figures had they been carved in significantly different sizes, as an error in the original publication of the female had led me to believe they were. But since they were nearly identical in size and most probably belong to the same phase of their sculptor's career, and were therefore likely to have been made close together in time – it is quite possible, despite their allegedly different find-places, that they were conceived originally as companion pieces – it should not be necessary to postulate that a formal grid plan was involved. It is possible that the sculptor actually had one of the figures in front of him while he worked on the other, or he may have worked on the two figures simultaneously. In such circumstances the simple three-part plan, the careful application of the harmonic system – particularly the angle B – along the outline, and the sculptor's practiced eye, should have been sufficient to produce two such similar images.

The Dresden Master appears to have been very much an individual among the sculptors of his time. The unparalleled top-heavy form of the head of his name-piece, the disproportionately thick and bulging neck on all his complete works, as well as his use of a three-part plan have all been noted. Most obvious, and apparently unprecedented, is the discrepancy in the treatment of the face on his male and female figures. On his name-piece this sculptor shares with the Goulandris Hunter/Warrior Master an unusual interest in facial detail that he depicts in similar fashion. The hair "combed" straight back from the forehead is paralleled on the male figure, now lost, also tentatively attributed to the Goulandris Hunter/Warrior Master.[93] But, unlike the females of this sculptor, the Dresden Master's have plain faces. His name-piece is, moreover, the most elaborately accoutred of all the late classical hunter/warriors that at present number seven.[94] His is the only complete surviving example of four that have a baldric running diagonally from the right shoulder, with the left forearm bent so as to lie parallel to it. (Compare the position of the arm and baldric on the Goulandris figure [pl. 11A.1; fig. 11f, g].) The Dresden Master's treatment of the typical Cycladic leaf-shaped dagger as a triangular termination of the right forearm appears, however, to be unique.

Despite the differences already noted and despite the fact that characteristics such as the triangular head or the bulging neck that comes to a point in front can be found in the work of other sculptors, too, certain features taken together make the Dresden Master's style easily recognizable. These include: small, wide-spaced breasts; tapered forearms; on the female figures a broad, low-placed pubic V bisected by the leg-cleft as far as, or nearly as far as, the lowest of the series of abdominal folds, or, in the case of the figures without folds [1, 7], nearly as far as the right forearm; a leg-cleft that terminates in front at the ankles; short stubby feet treated as a single fanlike unit; notched toes; upper arms separated from the back of the torso by means of wedge-shaped depressions; and a slight horizontal protrusion to indicate the buttocks. Another salient characteristic of the Dresden Master's style is his distinctive treatment of the profile. The curious bulging contours of the neck have already been mentioned. A similar convexity occurs along the front line of the legs, ending in a narrowing at the ankles.

Two of the female figures [6, 8] exhibit four abdominal bands, while the two Kean figures have three [2,3], and the fifth figure [4] two. In view of his fondness for parallel grooves seen on these figures and in the coiffure of the name-piece, one might well wonder if the Dresden Master also made marble vessels of the sort ornamented with a similar pattern of grooves (pl. VC, D).[95]

In basic structure and form as well as important details, such as the leg-cleft that begins at the lowest abdominal band and ends (as on all the other figures) at the ankles, the Kean figures [2, 3] are quite similar to the Erlenmeyer work [6]. They are, however, smaller, having belonged to figures that measured about 17 or 18 cm; their proportions differ somewhat as do also the low placement of their larger breasts; the incised detail is less precise and in general the outline is less sharply defined – impressions that may be due, in part at least, to the considerable weathering they have suffered (and possibly to handling as well), but certainly also to less careful workmanship. In short, the Kean pieces ought perhaps to be assigned to an earlier phase of the Dresden Master's career than his name-piece or the Erlenmeyer figure, which may be considered his best work. The three complete females [1, 4, 7], along with the lower figure fragment [8], should perhaps be placed between the Keos fragments and these, since they are more boldly executed than the former and less refined than the latter.

The fragmentary figures from Keos (along with a leg/foot fragment that may also have belonged to a piece carved by the Dresden Master),[96] though found in the course of excavation at Ayia Irini did not come from a clear Early Cycladic II context, and certainly not from a sepulchral one. The more damaged piece was found in conjunction with architectural remains dated to the Middle or Late Bronze Age settlement, suggesting that it at least may have been handled and used by inhabitants of Ayia Irini for purposes other than those for which it was originally intended. Although a quantity of fragmentary Cycladic figures of various types have been found at this site, nearly all of them out of context, as yet there is no evidence for a strong marble-working tradition on Keos during the first two phases of the Early Bronze Age. It is fair to assume, therefore, that either the Dresden Master's works found on

Keos were imported or that the Dresden Master was an itinerant artisan who found his way to Keos. The figure in Athens [1], which was reputedly found on Ios, should probably also be viewed as an import or the product of a wandering sculptor. Although a number of figures have been reported from this island, there are few documented examples, and evidence for a marble-working industry there is not conclusive.

The find-places of two of the figures attributed to the Dresden Master are not known [4, 7]. His name-piece, however, is said to have been found on Amorgos sometime early in this century or at the end of the last. The Erlenmeyer figure [6] and the privately owned lower figure fragment [8] belong to the "Keros hoard." As mentioned above, it is plausible that because of their close resemblance the hunter/warrior and the Erlenmeyer female may have been conceived originally as companion pieces. Whether or not they were actually acquired by the same person in the Early Bronze Age cannot, of course, be determined, but it is worth speculating that the male may actually have been found on Keros also and merely acquired by its modern purchaser on Amorgos, the more frequented of the two islands.[97] If this was the case, then it is possible that the two images were originally deposited together on Keros, though clearly they were not actually found together.[98] If, however, the provenances attached to the Dresden Master's works are all accurate, he would hold the distinction of having had his works disseminated to more islands in the archipelago than any other known sculptor.

Summary in Numerical Terms

Before going on to consider further the question of provenance, it might be useful to put into approximate and no doubt temporary perspective the numerical importance of the sculptors of folded-arm figures discussed in this book.

At present one can estimate a total of roughly twelve hundred extant Cycladic folded-arm figures (including those Chalandriani-variety images with uncanonical arm arrangements), or substantial fragments of such figures. Of these, the vast majority belong to the Spedos variety. The thirteen sculptors discussed in this chapter and the preceding one, with the three sculptors whose works are illustrated in pls. 6, 11, and 13, were, with their known works, together responsible for roughly 15 percent of this total. Bearing in mind that we do not know exactly how many different sculptures are represented among the many fragments preserved from the hand of the Goulandris Master, it is certainly noteworthy that this most prolific sculptor of all was alone responsible for between 5 and 8 percent of the total number of folded-arm figures now known.

With few exceptions, the sculptors chosen for discussion here are those to whom several works can be attributed. There are, in addition, perhaps twenty artists by whom at least two figures (mostly either unpublished or published in front view only) can be identified,[99] as well as a much smaller number to whom more than two can be assigned. This picture is certain to change as further excavation and research are undertaken.

Chapter Seven

Ending on a Geographical Note

As has already been mentioned, Cycladic sculpture has been found on many of the islands in the archipelago. In each phase of the Early Bronze Age, however, a seemingly limited number of these stand out as major centers for the production and use of marble objects. In the first phase Paros with her smaller neighbor, Antiparos, appears to have dominated though Naxos held a prominent place this early, too. Of the three sculptors of Plastiras-type figures discussed, one, the Doumas Master, seems firmly rooted on Paros, his work having also been found on the nearby coast of Naxos. The schematic groups discussed in chapter 3 are from Paros and Antiparos; the two documented groups with both schematic and Plastiras-type figures from Naxos, while from Naxos and Paros, reputedly, came the two groups of transitional Louros-type figures. Naxos, Keros, and Amorgos are the islands most frequently cited as sources of marble objects belonging to the second phase: of the ten grave groups of this date discussed or at least mentioned in chapter 3, for example, five are Naxian in origin, while one each was unearthed on Thera, Ano Kouphonisi, Keros, and Amorgos; the tenth is said to have been recovered on Amorgos as well.

The individuals whose works were identified and discussed in chapters 5 and 6 were selected for their typological range within the classical period and for their artistic interest and merit as exemplified by a number of different examples. They were not chosen because their works were found on any particular island or islands, nor was preference given to sculptors whose figures come from documented excavations. From the point of view of provenance, therefore, these sculptors represent as random a selection as is currently possible, given the Cyclades' very incomplete and uneven archaeological record. And yet, from a consideration of these masters' work there emerges a clear and consistently circumscribed pattern of distribution.

131

The Pattern of Distribution

Of the thirteen sculptors discussed in the two previous chapters, the work of five has been found in the course of systematic exploration on Naxos, that of three on Keros, and that of one each on Crete and Keos. These last should probably be viewed as imports. If we include the reputed provenances, as seems justified in the case of Naxos and Keros particularly, the position of Naxos, with works of nine of the thirteen sculptors, becomes still stronger, while Keros, if all the attributions are correct, appears just as prominent as Naxos (fig. 53).

FIG. 53. The distribution of works attributed to the sculptors discussed in chapters 5 and 6

	PAROS	NAXOS	KEROS	AMORGOS	KEOS	IOS	CRETE
Kontoleon	□	■	X				
Israel Museum		■	X				
Copenhagen		□	□	□			
Fitzwilliam				□			■
Steiner		□	□				
Naxos Museum		■	□				
Goulandris	□	■	■	□			
Bastis		■	□				
Schuster			■	○			
Ashmolean		□	□	□			
Berlin			○				
Stafford	□	□	■				
Dresden			□	□	■	□	

■ Figure(s) from documented source(s)

□ Figure(s) with reputed find-place(s)

X Sculptor perhaps too early to be represented

○ Attribution based on small fragment with reputed find-place

132

ENDING ON A GEOGRAPHICAL NOTE

Paros

Amorgos, Paros, and, in one case, Ios also enter the picture if reputed find-places are taken into account. However, the Parian provenances may be less secure since two of the three are attached to figures that have come to light fairly recently. Despite its size and central location, its relative abundance of arable land, and rich resources of marble, surprisingly few objects from the second Early Cycladic phase have been unearthed on Paros, at least in documented excavations, and not many are said to have been found there.

Amorgos

Although frequently mentioned as the source of marble objects – particularly male figures and unusually large sculptures – Amorgos, like Paros, has yielded relatively few figures and marble vessels from authorized excavations. Many objects – early acquisitions, principally in British museums – were obtained on Amorgos, but this fact is no guarantee that they were found there. It is quite possible that at least a number of these pieces had been brought to Amorgos from one of the smaller islands to the west. The most likely source, and the nearest, would have been Keros. Uninhabited now except for a few shepherds in summer, in 1928, for example, Keros had a population of only twelve. Any objects of note found there would have been taken to one of the larger, more frequented islands for sale to travelers. In the late nineteenth and early twentieth centuries, when Keros was under the authority of the monastery of Panagia Chozoviotissa on Amorgos, objects unearthed on Keros probably would have been brought to Amorgos. Now they would more likely find their way to Naxos or Athens. Objects brought to Amorgos and eventually sold there (or in Athens) could easily have "acquired" an Amorgian provenance. Keros was in fact considered so insignificant and little known that it is not uncommon for the most celebrated sculptures recovered there – the harper and the double pipes player in Athens – to be mentioned in the literature as having come from Amorgos. (Even today in Greek archaeological journals the small islands lying between Naxos and Amorgos are called "islands of Amorgos.")

Amorgos, on the other hand, enjoys a favorable position on the southeastern edge of the Cyclades where it probably served as a way station for maritime trade between Crete and Caria or the Troad. Amorgos itself seems to have possessed little in the way of mineral resources, apparently not even an abundance of white marble, nor perhaps was much of her terrain particularly suited to agriculture. It has been suggested that Amorgos was a shipping center for Melian obsidian being sent to the east in exchange for metal ores, perhaps chiefly tin, which was used to make Aegean bronze. Although the reasons for her relative wealth are not absolutely clear, evidence of it is abundant: vessels and jewelry of silver and tools and weapons of bronze are perhaps more plentiful in the graves of Amorgos than in those of any other island. Given this atmosphere of relative prosperity, one cannot ignore the reputation Amorgos has received for being rich in marble objects as well. But one must not rule out the

133

possibility that her marbles, like her metal objects perhaps, might not have been of local manufacture but rather the fruits of trade.

Naxos

It is significant in any case that five of the six sculptors in our group allegedly represented on Paros and/or Amorgos are represented also on Naxos, three of them – the Kontoleon, Goulandris, and Stafford masters – in excavations. The reasons for the preeminence of Naxos are evident. At 442 square kilometers, it is the largest as well as the most fertile and the most centrally located of the Cyclades. Moreover, it is endowed not only with limitless supplies of excellent marble but also with the best source in the Mediterranean basin of emery, which in its pure form, corrundum, is second only to diamond in hardness. (Small outcrops of this mineral are also found on southwest Paros as well as on Herakleia, Ios, and Sikinos.) It is not certain that emery, which was called "Naxian stone" in later antiquity, was in fact used by the Early Bronze Age sculptors. No workshops or tools of any kind made specifically for marble carving have been uncovered, but emery from Naxos was already being used for axes in the Neolithic settlement of Saliagos off Antiparos.[100] In addition, a Late Neolithic obsidian projectile point was found very near the present-day emery mines, and Doumas recovered a piece of the mineral in an Early Cycladic house at Avdeli nearby.[101] Clearly it was known, and we can probably assume that its qualities as a marble-working agent were investigated and appreciated early on. In any event, it should be safe to say that in the majority of cases marble objects found on Naxos were made by Naxian artists. Such a statement carries with it strong implications for the origins of the sculptors whose figures have been found on other islands in addition to Naxos.

Keros and the "Keros Hoard"

The work of seven of the thirteen sculptors appears to have been unearthed on both Naxos and Keros. With the exception of a half dozen fragments from works carved by the Goulandris Master, a fragmentary figure from the Schuster Master's hand, and a head fashioned by the Stafford Master, which have been found in the sanctioned investigations on Keros, all the other works said to have come from this island that are attributable to sculptors in our group (including additional works by the Goulandris, Schuster, and Stafford masters) belong to the so-called Keros hoard.

When it first came to light some twenty-five or thirty years ago, this assemblage consisted of 350 or more fragments of folded-arm figures, perhaps a dozen complete or very nearly complete figures (e.g., pls. 34 [4, 8], 46 [5]), several schematic ones of the Apeiranthos type, as well as a few complete and several fragmentary marble and clay vases, a substantial number of obsidian blades, at least one bone tube with incised decoration, and several stone and shell polishers. Except for a large group of figure fragments in the Erlenmeyer Collection, the hoard contents are now largely dispersed.

Among the three-hundred-odd broken figures I have been able to examine, the head and all body parts are well represented. The breaks have generally occurred at vulnerable points such as the neck/torso juncture, the pelvis, knees, and ankles. Some figures are more completely preserved than others and many consist of two or more adjoining pieces. It is probable, too, that in some cases nonadjacent fragments of the same sculpture survive. In nearly every example the break surfaces are weathered or encrusted, signifying that the damage to the sculptures did not occur recently. On the other hand, these weathered surfaces do not necessarily indicate that the fractures occurred in the Early Bronze Age, since the aging of the marble and the formation of encrustation can take place over a shorter period than forty-five hundred years.

The assemblage, which is a veritable treasure trove for the student of Cycladic sculpture, is reputed to have been the complete yield of finds from a single site. That the objects represent at least part of a unified group, which in terms of its size can conveniently be called a hoard, and not merely the remnants of various clandestine campaigns at different sites, need not be taken entirely on faith.

Several factors point to the contextual integrity of the material. First, virtually all the objects may be dated in the second Early Cycladic phase. The majority of the figure fragments belong to the Spedos variety produced in the first half of the phase but a substantial number belong also to the Dokathismata and Chalandriani varieties carved during the second half. When it first became known, the relative chronology and typological development of the various figure and vase forms had not yet been established, and it is therefore unlikely that a synthetic assemblage could have been made so pure at the time.

A large proportion of the fragments are similarly preserved: the surface of the marble is often free of encrustation and root marks; many pieces show dark specks as the result of aging; many are partially covered with a thin whitish deposit of calcium carbonate. Although actual paint is found on only a few of the heads in the group, there are numerous examples with paint "ghosts." A small but significant number, on the other hand, are badly weathered, the individual marble crystals exposed on their surfaces through long contact with wind and rain. It would seem, therefore, that a large number of the fragments at least had been deposited under similar conditions of soil and moisture, suggesting that they were found in close proximity to one another, while others would seem to have lain on the surface where they would have been easily noticed.

Finally, several sculptors are represented in the hoard by more than one work. Fully half of the nearly one hundred pieces now attributable to the hand of the Goulandris Master come from this assemblage. Six or seven pieces by the Naxos Museum Master, five or more each by the Steiner and Schuster masters, three by the Stafford master, and two each by the Copenhagen and Dresden masters also belong to the hoard. Although the works of one

135

sculptor may be found at different sites on the same island (e.g., the Naxos Museum Master) or even on different islands (e.g., the Doumas and Goulandris masters), the presence in the hoard of a large concentration of figures carved by a number of individual sculptors point to the essential integrity of the material. It is possible, but improbable, that a random accumulation of bits and pieces from various sources would contain so many works of the same artists.

The hoard is said to have been unearthed on Keros, one of several small islands lying southeast of Naxos that are known collectively as "the desolate isles" (Erimonisia). There is no knowing how reliable this information might be, and yet the archaeological evidence does strongly suggest that the find-place of the hoard was indeed Keros rather than any of the other small islands (some of which are rumored to have yielded quantities of Early Cycladic marble objects) or any of the major Cyclades.

In 1963, Doumas undertook an investigation of a site on the southwest coast of Keros, opposite the islet of Daskaleio (which it is thought was connected to it in the Early Bronze Age by a strip of land now submerged). There he found a great many fragmentary figures and vessels of marble as well as an abundance of potsherds.[102] These were strewn about the surface, in the fill, at no consistent depth, rather like potatoes in a field. In 1967, Zapheiropoulou continued the surface clearing begun by Doumas, and again found a wealth of very similar fragments scattered haphazardly over the site. A complete folded-arm figure was found at that time.[103]

Taken together, the Daskaleio finds included, besides this complete work, portions of figures of the Spedos, Dokathismata, and Chalandriani varieties, as well as a number of schematic statuettes of the Apeiranthos type, huge quantities of stone vase fragments, potsherds, obsidian blades, and at least one stone polisher. All of these finds can be dated to the second phase, with the possible exception of some pottery which may be slightly later. The sculptural material definitely recovered on Keros is in fact so similar to that of the hoard that the two groups of objects are virtually indistinguishable from each other. Moreover, the work of at least four sculptors, including the Goulandris, Schuster, and Stafford masters, is present in both sets of finds.[104] Of particular interest is the fact that both archaeologists attested to clear and abundant signs that clandestine activities had taken place at the site prior to the commencement of their investigations in 1963. Moreover, islanders from nearby Kouphonisi report that large quantities of figure fragments were indeed "exported" from Keros some two decades or more ago. Thus, although absolute proof in the form of joining pieces from the two groups is still lacking, it is nevertheless very tempting to identify the hoard as the fruits of the unauthorized activities opposite Daskaleio.

Although the types of finds and the state of their preservation are nearly identical in the two groups, there are nevertheless important differences. At Daskaleio, both clay and stone coarse wares were found mixed together with the usual fine wares normally associated with burials. Moreover, there was a significant discrepancy in the relative frequency of the basic classes of object: whereas the systematic clearing of the site yielded far more marble vase fragments than figures, as well as a plethora of potsherds, the objects in the hoard were over-whelmingly figurative; vases and vase fragments, both clay and marble, were few in number. This disparity can be explained as follows: the objects removed from the site illicitly were, for the most part, those considered to have some value on the antiquities market, and there-fore, although the looters collected some obsidian blades and fine vase fragments lying in their path or mixed in with figure fragments, they did not specifically seek them out and apparently shunned the coarser wares altogether. This, in turn, would explain the fact that *relatively* few figure fragments – I have counted roughly three hundred – were found in the subsequent sanctioned campaigns. We know that the finds from this site are incomplete because of the ample evidence of unauthorized digging; we may surmise that the finders of the hoard did not collect all the existing fragments of stone vessels, since at all controlled excavations of Early Cycladic sites that have yielded stone objects vases clearly outnumber figures. It is precisely this class of object, largely missing from the hoard, which was super-abundant at Daskaleio, many hundreds and probably thousands of marble vase fragments having been recovered in the course of the investigations there. It seems, therefore, that a single assemblage composed of the two sets of material makes better sense than either con-sidered separately and incompletely. Moreover, it is likely that many if not all the sculptors represented in the Kerian material carved both types of object.

Interpreting the material and identifying the nature of the site is no easy matter. The evidence at Daskaleio is unclear since Doumas and Zapheiropoulou did not find a typically preserved cemetery: there was no sign of individual graves and few traces of bones, and the finds were widely and illogically scattered. Moreover, an isolated building and much building rubble were also found there. At some unknown date (but possibly in connection with the eruption of the Thera volcano in the middle of the second millennium B.C.), the site may have suffered a geological disturbance with subsequent erosion and illicit digging adding to the disarray of the place. An earthquake or landslide might also account for the damaged state of most of the finds, although it alone does not explain the apparent absence of a great many joining pieces. However, the effect of such a landslide on the steep slope of the site, whatever its cause, apparently was to expose to view a great many of the finds, thus opening the way to destruction of a different sort. For example, a woman who lived on Keros more than sixty years ago related to me how she and her playmates used figure fragments in tossing games, while the men of the community would grind them into powder to clean and polish their knives. There is no telling what the extent of such human interference at the site might have been over the millennia nor is there any way of knowing what effect such acts of innocent vandalism and possibly of iconoclasm as well, and more recently of wholesale looting, may have had in distorting our perception of its original Early Bronze Age state.

Whatever its subsequent history, the fact remains that, with the exception of the coarse wares normally considered domestic items and one marble vessel type – the dove tray – to date documented only on Keros,[105] both the Daskaleio find and the hoard contain only types of objects virtually exclusively associated with burials. This is presumably the find-place of the harper and double-pipes player in Athens that were reported to have come from a grave along with two canonical folded-arm figures (pl. 10).[106] Besides the figures and common stone and clay vase forms, there are fragments of lamp models, or dummies (magical substitutes), as well as small pots filled with blue pigment from Daskaleio, and from the hoard there is an incised bone tube. The first have been interpreted as symbolic light sources for the dead, while the last were, like the little pots, used as canisters for pigments considered important for the symbolic renewal of life beyond the grave. Colin Renfrew has, however, recently suggested that the site opposite Daskaleio served not as a cemetery but as a large open-air sanctuary. An attractive hypothesis in a number of respects, it clearly needs to be tested through detailed excavation and geological and topographical exploration.[107]

Whatever the purpose of the site, it is indeed amazing to find so many marble objects on Keros. Only about fifteen kilometers square, for the most part inhospitable to farming, and, with the possible exception of sweet water, lacking in natural resources, Keros is a largely gray marble island that probably could never have supported a population of more than one or two hundred people at any given time. One can only surmise that the importance in the Early Bronze Age of this bit of terra firma lay in its easy accessibility to the other southern Cyclades and perhaps also in its position as a stepping-stone for mariners traveling between the southern islands (especially Melos and Thera), the Greek mainland, or Crete and the coast of Asia Minor, perhaps specifically Caria from which the name Keros (also known as Karos, and in antiquity as Keria or Kereia) is likely to have been derived. Its chief natural asset, at Daskaleio on the east coast (when this islet was connected to Keros) and at Glyphada on the south coast, were small safe harbors, something of a rarity in this region of the windswept Cyclades. The fortuitous combination of favorable location and sheltered anchorage or beaching place may have been the basic ingredients necessary to transform what would otherwise have been the impoverished and isolated home of a handful of farmers and fishermen eking out a meager existence into a common meeting ground and trading place, a kind of prehistoric Delos.

On a secular level, Keros may have been part of a close-knit "neighborhood" of small and varied islands lying between Naxos and Amorgos or it may have been an important link in a mercantile network that would have included the relatively affluent communities of southeast Naxos and probably Amorgos. (The latter, like Keros, seems to have prospered despite an apparent lack of abundant natural resources.) On a spiritual plane, there may have been an added and especially potent ingredient to explain the choice of this site for a special purpose; for the imposing skyline of southwestern Keros, when approached from Naxos and Kouphonisia, distinctly resembles a reclining giantess not unlike a Cycladic figure in form. On the summit, or "navel," of what looks like the pregnant belly of this giantess there is, apparently, a deep and treacherous cave. Such phenomena are not likely to have been overlooked or ignored at the time, and one might reasonably suppose, therefore, that the inhabitants of the region believed Keros to be a massive natural incarnation of the life force represented in their figures. As such, it would have been the ideal place for a Pan-Cycladic (or, in

138

effect, a southern Cycladic) sanctuary or, on the grounds that burial there would afford the best protection in the hereafter, a communal cemetery. (The small fortified settlement on the hill of Daskaleio islet might have served as a lookout and protection for this place rather than as an ordinary habitation site, although it is also possible that it is slightly later in date than the site opposite.)[108]

Speculation and fantasy aside, some such explanation is essential to account for the presence in so small a place of enormous quantities of nonessential "luxury" items, be they grave furnishings or shrine offerings. At present, these objects are the only sign that Keros flourished in the Early Cycladic period. The island as a whole has yet to be properly explored, but it can hardly have supported more than one or two marble specialists at any one time. And yet the incidence of marble objects on this small island rivals that of the major Cyclades and exceeds by far that of any individual site. (This holds true even if one considers only the objects found in the sanctioned investigations on Keros.) Even at the generous rate of two sculptors per generation of twenty years, over a period spanning as much as four hundred years or so, one can account for no more than a total of about forty resident sculptors producing figures and vessels. The material, however, suggests that several times this number of marble carvers were represented there. The presence on one small island of works by such a large number of sculptors strongly implies that the *majority* of them were produced in a number of different settlements and only subsequently brought there.

The other alternative, which Zapheiropoulou has proposed, is that Keros must have been an exception to the one- or two-artist-per-village rule, that it must have been an important marble-working center that supported a substantial number of sculptors in each generation.[109] Alone, the population figures estimated for Keros should preclude such a possibility. For, if this theory were correct, marble working would have had to have been the primary industry of the island, and we would have to assume that the many objects found on Keros represent only a small percentage of the total output of the artisans who worked there. Presumably most of their products would have been exported to other islands in exchange for commodities essential to the support system of their small, largely barren island, a high percentage of whose population would have consisted of craftsmen. Indeed, it should follow that with this hypothetical artists' colony Keros would not only have been of all the Cyclades a chief, if not *the* cardinal producer of marble goods, but that it would have been able to supply the major part of the entire Cycladic demand for such objects for several centuries.

The Center of the Circle

This argument brings us back to the sculptors discussed in chapters 5 and 6 and the conclusion anticipated earlier. Although the Goulandris Master is the only sculptor whose work has been recovered by archaeologists from both Keros and Naxos, the available information suggests that work of the Copenhagen, Naxos Museum, Steiner, Bastis, Ashmolean, and

Stafford masters has also been found on both these islands. The Naxian connections of the Naxos Museum and Bastis masters are assured. Indeed, as we saw, figures carved by the former have been found in three different cemeteries on Naxos.

It hardly seems necessary to ask if Naxians would, as a rule, have imported marble objects from another island such as Keros. Bringing marbles to Naxos would have been tantamount to carrying the proverbial coals to Newcastle. On the contrary, it is much more logical to suppose that the majority of the figures found on Keros – and perhaps also those found on marble-poor Amorgos – were made in communities on Naxos, probably in those along her eastern and southeastern coasts.[110] Indeed, if there had been nuclei of sculptors anywhere, one would expect them to have been on Naxos whose abundance of raw materials, relative affluence, and numbers could most easily have generated groups of craft specialists had the demand for their works been great enough. The most that one can show, however, and that only occasionally, is the apparent relationship to each other of two or three sculptors based on stylistic grounds and/or similarity of find-place. This was suggested in the case of the Kontoleon and Israel masters who worked near the beginning of the classical phase; in the case of the Goulandris, Bastis, and Naxos Museum masters who flourished around the middle of the phase; and for the Berlin and Stafford masters who worked near its end. It is probably no coincidence that five of these seven sculptors can be firmly tied to Naxos.[111] In fact, no other island except Keros has yielded more than two or three figures attributable to any one artist of the classical phase, at least not from documented sources.

Although there is no evidence that the demand for marble goods was anywhere sufficient to support groups of sculptors working together in ateliers, developing schools or styles peculiar to their groups or to their islands – not even if one could show that most marble products were made on Naxos and exported to other places – it seems clear at this point that in the second phase of the Early Bronze Age, Naxos was the epicenter of the marble-working craft and the home of many of the finest and most industrious sculptors of the Cyclades.

140

EPILOGUE

W I T H the exception of the Goulandris Master, the *relative* scarcity of works attributable to individual Cycladic artists implies that a great many sculptures from their hands remain to be found in the islands, while others may be "buried" in little-known collections. There is much still to be learned about both the development of individual masters' styles and about the distribution of their works. As the lists of these sculptors' oeuvres continue to grow, additional stages in their artistic careers should be revealed. For example, certain sculptors such as the Metropolitan Museum Master or the Berlin Master, known now only by two or three masterworks, may also, in time, be represented by images fashioned during their formative years. It is probable, too, that as new pieces come to light, others that have been known for some time but have not been attributed will be recognized as the works of particular sculptors. Gradually the 4,500-year-old jigsaw puzzle should begin to take shape.

Approximately 1,500 or 1,600 Cycladic figures of all types are known at present. If, as it is believed, they were produced over a period of roughly 600 or 700 years (2900 or 2800–2200 B.C.), then, in the present state of affairs, we can account for a hypothetical production rate of only less than three figures per year. Surely the Cyclades have many secrets still to be revealed. It is hoped that measures will be taken to ensure that a high proportion of future finds will be recovered in the course of systematic exploration, and that soon after they will be published and made available for further study. Only in this way will certain important questions pertaining to individual Cycladic sculptors in particular, as well as to the distribution, function, development, and chronology of Cycladic sculpture in general receive further elucidation.

ABBREVIATIONS

AAA: *Athens Annals of Archaeology*

ACC: Thimme, J., gen. ed. *Art and Culture of the Cyclades in the Third Millennium B.C.* Chicago, 1977.

Aegean Islands: *Greek Art of the Aegean Islands*. Metropolitan Museum of Art. New York, 1979.

AJA: *American Journal of Archaeology*

American Private Colls.: *Ancient Art in American Private Collections*. Fogg Art Museum. Cambridge, Massachusetts, 1954.

Brouscari: Brouscari, M. "Collection P. Canellopoulos: Antiquités Cycladiques." *Bulletin de Correspondence Hellénique* 105 (1981): 499–535.

Burial Habits: Doumas, C. *Early Bronze Age Burial Habits in the Cyclades*, Studies in Mediterranean Archaeology, vol. 48. Göteborg, 1977.

Caskey 1964: Caskey, J. L. "Excavations in Keos, 1963." *Hesperia* 33 (1964): 314–35.

Caskey 1971: Caskey, J. L. "Marble Figurines from Ayia Irini in Keos." *Hesperia* 40 (1971): 113–26.

Classical Art: *Classical Art from a New York Collection*. André Emmerich Gallery. New York, 1977.

Cycladica: Fitton, J. L., ed. *Cycladica: Studies in Memory of N. P. Goulandris*. Proceedings of the Seventh British Museum Classical Colloquium, June 1983. London, 1984.

D.: Diameter

Deltion: *Archaiologikon Deltion*

Deltion, Chronika: *Archaiologikon Deltion, Chronika*

Doumas-Goulandris Coll.: Doumas, C. *The N. P. Goulandris Collection of Early Cycladic Art*. Athens, 1968.

Early Art: *Early Art in Greece: The Cycladic, Minoan, Mycenaean and Geometric Periods*. André Emmerich Gallery. New York, 1965.

EC: Early Cycladic

Emergence: Renfrew, C. *The Emergence of Civilisation: The Cyclades and the Aegean in the Third Millennium B.C.* London, 1972.

Fellmann: Fellmann, B. "Frühe Idole in den Münchner Antikensammlungen." *Münchner Jahrbuch der Bildenen Kunst* 32 (1981): 7–24.

Fitton: Fitton, J. L. "Perditus and Perdita: Two Drawings of Cycladic Figurines in the Greek and Roman Department of the British Museum." In *Cycladica: Studies in Memory of N. P. Goulandris*, edited by J. L. Fitton, pp. 76–87. London, 1984.

H.: Height

Jahrbuch B-W: *Jahrbuch der Staatlichen Kunstsammlungen in Baden-Württemberg*

Kontoleon 1970: Kontoleon, N. M. "Anaskaphai Naxou." *Praktika tis en Athinais Archaiologikis Etaireias tou Etous 1970*, pp. 146–55.

Kontoleon 1971a: Kontoleon, N. M. "Anaskaphai Naxou." *Praktika tis en Athinais Archaiologikis Etaireias tou Etous 1971*, pp. 172–80.

Kontoleon 1971b: Kontoleon, N. M. "Naxos." *Ergon tis Archaiologikis Etaireias kata to 1971*, pp. 174–85.

Kontoleon 1972a: Kontoleon, N. M. "Anaskaphai Naxou." *Praktika tis en Athinais Archaiologikis Etaireias tou Etous 1972*, pp. 143–55.

Kontoleon 1972b: Kontoleon, N. M. "Naxos." *Ergon tis Archaiologikis Etaireias kata to 1972*, pp. 88–100.

L.: Length

Lambrinoudakis: Lambrinoudakis, V. "Anaskaphai Naxou." *Praktika tis en Athinais Archaiologikis Etaireias tou Etous 1976*, pp. 295–308.

Marangou: Marangou, L. "Evidence for the Early Cycladic Period on Amorgos." In *Cycladica: Studies in Memory of N. P. Goulandris*, edited by J. L. Fitton, pp. 99–115. London, 1984.

NG: Doumas, C. *Cycladic Art: Ancient Sculpture and Ceramics of the Aegean from the N. P. Goulandris Collection*. National Gallery of Art. Washington, D.C., 1979.

Papathanasopoulos: Papathanasopoulos, G. A. "Kykladika Naxou." *Archaiologikon Deltion, Meletai* 17 (1961–62): 104–51.

PCP: Davis, J. L., and Cherry, J. F., eds. *Papers in Cycladic Prehistory*. Monograph 14, Institute of Archaeology, University of California. Los Angeles, 1979.

PGP: P. Getz-Preziosi

PGP, ECS: Getz-Preziosi, P. *Early Cycladic Sculpture: An Introduction*. Malibu, 1985.

PGP, GM: Getz-Preziosi, P. *The Goulandris Master*. Athens, forthcoming.

PGP 1975: Getz-Preziosi, P. "An Early Cycladic Sculptor." *Antike Kunst* 18 (1975): 47–50.

PGP 1978: Getz-Preziosi, P. "Addenda to the Cycladic Exhibition in Karlsruhe." *Archäologische Anzeiger*, 1978, pp. 1–11.

PGP 1980: Getz-Preziosi, P. "The Male Figure in Early Cycladic Sculpture." *Metropolitan Museum Journal* 15 (1980): 5–33.

PGP 1981: Getz-Preziosi, P. "Risk and Repair in Early Cycladic Sculpture." *Metropolitan Museum Journal* 16 (1981): 5–32.

PGP 1982: Getz-Preziosi, P. "The 'Keros Hoard': Introduction to an Early Cycladic Enigma." In *Antidoron Jürgen Thimme*, edited by D. Metzler and B. Otto, pp. 37–44. Karlsruhe, 1982.

PGP 1984a: Getz-Preziosi, P. "Nine Fragments of Early Cycladic Sculpture in Southern California." *J. Paul Getty Museum Journal* 12 (1984): 5–20.

PGP 1984b: Getz-Preziosi, P. "Five Sculptors in the Goulandris Collection." In *Cycladica: Studies in Memory of N. P. Goulandris*, edited by J. L. Fitton, pp. 47–71. London, 1984.

Pres.: Preserved

Preziosi/Weinberg: Preziosi, P. G., and S. S. Weinberg. "Evidence for Painted Details in Early Cycladic Sculpture." *Antike Kunst* 13 (1970): 4–12.

Pryce: Pryce, F. N. *Prehellenic and Early Greek Sculpture: Catalogue of Sculpture in the Department of Greek and Roman Antiquities in the British Museum I*, pt. 1. London, 1928.

Renfrew 1967: Renfrew, C. "Cycladic Metallurgy and the Aegean Early Bronze Age." *American Journal of Archaeology* 71 (1967): 1–20.

Renfrew 1969: Renfrew, C. "The Development and Chronology of the Early Cycladic Figurines." *American Journal of Archaeology* 73 (1969): 1–32.

Safani: *The Art of the Cyclades: An Exhibition of Sculpture and Artifacts of the Early Cycladic Period, 3000–2000 B.C.* Safani Gallery. New York, 1983.

Tsountas 1898: Tsountas, C. "Kykladika I." *Archaiologike Ephemeris*, 1898, cols. 137–212.

Tsountas 1899: Tsountas, C. "Kykladika II." *Archaiologike Ephemeris*, 1899, cols. 73–134.

Xanthoudides: Xanthoudides, S. A. *The Vaulted Tombs of Mesara*. London, 1924.

Zapheiropoulou 1968a: Zapheiropoulou, P. "Kyklades, Anaskaphika: Erevnai—Periodeiai." *Archaiologikon Deltion, Chronika* 23 (1968): 381 (Keros).

Zapheiropoulou 1968b: Zafiropoulou, F. "Cycladic Finds from Keros." *Athens Annals of Archaeology* 1 (1968): 97–100.

Zapheiropoulou 1979: Zapheiropoulou, P. "Protokykladika Eidolia tis Naxou." In *Stili: Tomos eis Mnimin Nikolaou Kontoleontos*, pp. 532–40. Athens, 1979.

Zapheiropoulou 1983: Zaphiropoulou, P. "Un cimitière du Cycladique Ancien à Epano Kouphonissi." In *Les Cyclades: Matériaux pour une étude de géographie historique*, edited by C. and G. Rougement, pp. 81–87. Paris, 1983.

Zervos: Zervos, C. *L'art des Cyclades du début à la fin de l'age du bronze*. Paris, 1957.

NOTES

1. A. Malraux, *Picasso's Mask* (New York, 1976), p. 136.

2. I am grateful to Christos Doumas for allowing me to include photographs of two of the pieces in Naxos. See pls. 38–39 [1, 2].

3. With very few exceptions I have personally examined the many figures included in both the plates and the line drawings and have resisted all temptation to reproduce figures of unusual types or unusually large size – forgers' favorites – that I have not had an opportunity to study "in the flesh." Even so, one can expect a skeptical reaction to some of the more unusual pieces, at least, on the part of some readers, particularly those who find it difficult to accept as incontestably genuine sculptures that do not come from documented excavations or whose pedigrees do not extend back into the last century.

4. *ACC*, no. 453. E. M. Bossert, "Die gestempelten Verzierungen auf frühbronzezeitlichen Gefässen der Ägäis," *Jahrbuch des Deutschen Archäologischen Instituts* 75 (1960): 14–15, figs. 11*a*–*b*, 12.

5. A figure-of-eight figurine in Bonn acquired in Naxos in 1901 may have been an import from the Troad. See *ACC*, no. 50. (See also Doumas-Goulandris Coll., no. 303.)

6. An allegedly EC figurine of wood in an Irish private collection (E. Melas, ed., *Greek Islands*, trans. R. Stockman [New York, 1985], p. 162) is apparently not of Early Bronze Age or Cycladic origin. On the possible use of wooden figures, see R. L. N. Barber, "Early Cycladic Marble Figures: Some Thoughts on Function," in *Cycladica*, p. 11. See also p. 35 (discussion).

7. See *ACC*, no. 13 (illustrated here in fig. 3) and fig. 31 (a piece housed in the museum at Eleusis but acquired on Amorgos; see K. G. Kanta, *Eleusis: Myth, Mysteries, History, Museum* [Athens, 1979], p. 108).

8. The only examples to be unearthed in a systematically excavated cemetery (Aplomata on Naxos) are, however, from an Early Keros-Syros context – that is, slightly later. See Kontoleon 1972*a*, pl. 135. A complete precanonical figure from this cemetery is unpublished.

9. On the Plastiras-type figure illustrated in pl. 1*B*, similar perforations were begun but not completed, evidently because the sculptor did not wish to take the chance of causing irreparable damage to the piece. See *ACC*, no. 72 (text).

10. The reader will note that, when giving dimensions, the height (H.) is referred to in the case of standing and seated types, the length (L.) in the case of reclining ones.

11. *ACC*, no. 153; PGP 1980, no. 10.

12. See *ACC*, no. 257 (text).

13. See PGP 1980, p. 32, note following no. 25. Other examples not illustrated here in fig. 12 include: (1) a torso fragment of a left-hand figure with the left hand of the right-hand figure indicated at the base of its neck, as in figure 12*b* (Naxos, Archaeological Museum KE.63.58, unpublished); (2) a torso fragment of a right-hand figure with the right arm of the left-hand figure indicated across its back, as in fig. 12*c* (Naxos, Archaeological Museum AE.76/0155, Aplomata, Grave 27, Lambrinoudakis, pl. 195d, e); and (3) a complete right-hand figure with the right arm of the left-hand figure across its back (Goulandris Collection 330; NG, no. 135; PGP 1981, p. 23). In addition to the double figures

illustrated here, at least two of the four fragmentary bases recovered on Keros originally held two pairs of feet. See Zapheiropoulou 1968b: 98, 100, fig. 2.

14. See *ACC*, no. 281. Strange, but not without precedent, is the "double entendre" of the representation that seems at once torso and face. See R. J. Almansi, "The Face-Breast Equation," *Journal of the American Psychoanalytical Association* 8 (1960): 60–66. See also the discussion of the Metropolitan Museum Master in chap. 4.

15. See *ACC*, figs. 80, 82; nos. 343, 366, 368. J. Thimme, "Badisches Landesmuseum: Neuerwerbungen 1980," *Jahrbuch B-W* 20 (1982): 126.

16. In at least two other cases musician figures are said to have been found with marble vessels – goblets, plain bowls, and spouted bowls – although these are not carved in the same scale as the figures. *ACC*, app. 4, pp. 584–85.

17. Tsountas 1898, cols. 156–65.

18. *Burial Habits*, pp. 73–130.

19. Papathanasopoulos, pp. 104–14, 138–44, 148–49.

20. Ibid., pp. 114–29. The cemetery at Spedos was further explored in 1948 by Kontoleon.

21. Stephanos actually reported finding ten folded-arm figures at Spedos, but Papathanasopoulos in his examination of the finds could not account for five of them nor could he determine in which graves the missing figures were found. It is possible that three figures in Athens (6140.12 [pl. 21[1]], 6140.14 [fig. 5d], and 6140.15 [pl. 23[3]]) may be among the "missing" figures from Spedos.

22. Kontoleon 1970, 1971a, 1972a; Lambrinoudakis. Aplomata vies only with the site opposite the islet of Daskaleio on Keros (discussed in chap. 7) for the distinction of having the greatest concentration of marble objects. It is, however, far from certain that the latter was also a cemetery.

23. Tsountas 1898, cols. 152–53.

24. Tsountas 1899, cols. 77–115. See *Burial Habits*, p. 128. Doumas dug an additional eight graves (mostly plundered), finding two marble vases. Stephanos also excavated on Syros, where he recovered twenty-three stone vessels and one figure. Individual grave groups have not been identified among his finds. (I am indebted to Saul Weinberg for giving me his notes made many years ago in the National Archaeological Museum in Athens. It is from them that this information was gleaned.)

25. Tsountas 1898, cols. 154–55.

26. The localization of certain individuals on specific islands or the determination that certain ones were itinerant craftsmen who used local raw material could perhaps be effected through a comparison of isotopic signatures. Such a study would, however, require the cooperation of a great many museums and collectors, for small samples would have to be taken from several hundred sculptures and marble samples would have to be collected from many island sites. Moreover, a study of this kind could be complicated, if not made impossible, by the fact that the Early Bronze Age sculptor probably did not use specific quarries, since, as Renfrew has pointed out, pieces of raw material suitable for these relatively small figures could be found almost anywhere on the marble-rich islands. (I have observed such random selection of marble by present-day marble carvers on Naxos.) See N. Herz and D. B. Wenner, "Tracing the Origins of Marble," *Archaeology*, September–October 1981, pp. 15–21.

27. For the figure in Athens, see *Aegean Islands*, no. 11. For a profile view of the figure illustrated in pl. X, see PGP, *ECS*, fig. 4. A very large torso in the Bowdoin College Museum of Art (whose breaks apparently also occurred in antiquity) is, incidentally, very similar, insofar as it is preserved, to the figure shown in pl. X (see PGP, *ECS*, figs. 33–34), and it is very likely that they were the products of the same hand. It is conceivable that this sculptor also carved the work in Athens.

28. *Cycladica*, p. 35. This sword was found near two Cycladic figures placed facedown on top of each other and covered with a marble bowl. The objects came from a cemetery deposit but not from a grave (Zapheiropoulou 1983, pp. 86–87, figs. 17, 18). The figures are mentioned briefly in chap. 3. (Zapheiropoulou [1983, pp. 83–84] also mentions having found on Ano Kouphonisi a deliberately (?) bent bronze dagger covered by three marble bowls.)

29. M. J. Mellink, "Excavations in Karatas-Semayük," *AJA* 71 (1967): 254.

30. On the symbolic association of figure and vessel, which is most obvious in the case of the anthropomorphic stone beakers (pl. IVA) and the clay vessels of frying pan shape (e.g., *ACC*, fig. 89), see E. Neumann, *The Great Mother*, Bollingen Series (Princeton, 1955), p. 120.

31. See, e.g., *ACC*, nos. 475ff. E. Atzeni, "Vornuraghenzeit," in *Kunst und Kultur Sardiniens vom Neolithikum bis zum Ende der Nuraghenzeit*, ed. J. Thimme, pp. 15–44 with fig. 16 and nos. 1–12, 14 (Karlsruhe, 1980). O. Höckmann, "The Cyclades and Their Eastern Neighbours," *ACC*, pp. 155–63; O. Höckmann, "The Cyclades and the Western Mediterranean," *ACC*, pp. 163–72; O. Höckmann, "The Neolithic and Early Bronze Age Idols of Anatolia," *ACC*, pp. 173–84; O. Höckmann, "Zur Kykladischen Harfenspielerfigur

von Keros," *Boreas: Munstersche Beiträge zur Archäologie* 5 (1982): 33–48. C. Renfrew, "The Cycladic Culture," *ACC*, p. 26.

32. Contrary to popular opinion, which views it as an obdurate medium, marble, measuring only 3 on the Mohs scale, is relatively easy to carve, especially when freshly cut. It also tends to break along relatively straight planes, making raw blocks and slabs easy to find or to hew. These same qualities, however, also cause marble to fracture and splinter easily, wherefore, in the absence of modern tools, the block or slab had to be reduced gradually by a careful, time-consuming process.

33. The reconstructions offered here are based primarily on measurements taken from photographs. By reducing the surface to two dimensions, the photograph can be said to simulate the plane surface of the raw marble slab on which the sculptor plotted his design. However, one must be very careful in selecting photographs to use for this purpose, for distortions result when measurements are taken from photographs that are not shot in true perspective. (Slight distortions are inevitable in any case in photographs of all figures except perhaps very flat ones.) A project designed to test the proportionality of Cycladic sculpture by a more rigorous method is being developed by Jack De-Vries, a doctoral candidate at the University of Amsterdam.

34. See also *ACC*, fig. 60.

35. The virtually identical design of the chairbacks of two chronologically disparate works – the precanonical harper in New York (pl. III*A*) and an early Spedos-style seated female from Aplomata (Kontoleon 1971*a*, pls. 214–15) – suggests that an existing wooden chair pattern served as a model. (See PGP 1980, p. 15 with n. 23 and fig. 20*a, b*.)

36. The duck motif is seen also on much later representations: e.g., on the finials of the lyre in the celebrated fresco from the Mycenaean palace at Pylos (M. L. Lang, *The Frescoes*, vol. 2, *The Palace of Nestor at Pylos in Western Messenia* [Princeton, 1969], pl. 126, 43H6) – a very similar lyre is depicted on the Agia Triada sarcophagus in Herakleion – and on the ivory arm of a lyre dated to ca. 600 B.C. in Berlin (J. Boardman, *Greek Sculpture: The Archaic Period* [New York and Toronto, 1978], fig. 53). Moreover, the classical Greek words for musical instruments – *phorminx* (lyre), *syrinx* (panpipes), *salpinx* (trumpet) – were probably pre-Greek in origin and may have been the names used in the Early Bronze Age Cyclades.

37. See also *ACC*, figs. 62–65; PGP 1980, figs. 30–31.

38. The participants in these experiments were students of Karen Foster at Wesleyan University and of Jeremy Rutter at Dartmouth College. I am grateful to all of them for their help with the project.

39. See A. Badawy, *Ancient Egyptian Architectural Design: A Study of the Harmonic System*, University of California Publications. Near Eastern Studies 4 (1965). (Note: this publication contains a removable clear plastic sheet on which the harmonic system is printed. The use of such an aid greatly facilitates an inspection of angles in Cycladic sculpture as it can easily be laid over photographs, thus obviating the need for actual measurement.) D. A. Preziosi, "Harmonic Design in Minoan Architecture," *Fibonacci Quarterly* 6 (1968): 370–84. See also W. Hoffer, "A Magic Ratio Recurs Throughout Art and Nature," *Smithsonian* 6, no. 9 (December 1975): 110–24.

40. E.g., PGP 1975, pl. 20, 4–6; Brouscari, no. 2, fig. 17.

41. This is true for another, similar work (*ACC*, fig. 24).

42. Krassades 117: Tsountas 1898, col. 162. Pyrgos 103: Tsountas 1898, col. 159. Akrotiri 5: *Burial Habits*, p. 86. Akrotiri 20: *Burial Habits*, p. 93. Plastiras 9 (name-grave): *Burial Habits*, pp. 98–100.

43. Papathanasopoulos, pp. 132–37.

44. Aplomata 13: Kontoleon 1971*a*, pp. 178–79. Spedos 10: Papathanasopoulos, pp. 114–19. Ano Kouphonisi pair: Zapheiropoulou, "Early Cycladic Finds from Kouphonisi," *AAA* 3 (1970): 51 with fig. 1. Zapheiropoulou 1983, pp. 86–87, figs. 17, 18. Aplomata 23: Kontoleon 1972*a*, pp. 150–53. Lambrinoudakis, pp. 296–99.

45. Harper pairs: *ACC*, nos. 254–55; PGP in *ACC*, pp. 90–91; PGP 1980, nos. 11–14.

46. U. Köhler, "Praehistorisches von den griechischen Inseln," *Athenische Mitteilungen* 9 (1884): 156–59.

47. Chalandriani 307: Tsountas 1899, col. 111. Dokathismata 14 (name-grave): Tsountas 1898, cols. 154–55. Spedos 16: Papathanasopoulos, pp. 124–25.

48. A figure, acquired in Athens in 1907 and now in the Ashmolean Museum (Renfrew 1969, pl. 2f, III.8) was for a time thought to belong to the original group of seven (Renfrew 1969, p. 8), but Papathanasopoulos (p. 136n.93) mentions that the group was still intact in 1926.

49. The names chosen for individual sculptors are either, as in this case, those of the excavators who have unearthed important examples of their work or those of museums (or the cities in which the mu-

seums are located) or private collections that house particularly fine and/or well-preserved pieces attributable to their hands.

50. This is possible to do with confidence in at least two cases: a figure in the Goulandris Collection (no. 344; NG, no. 32) is closely similar to 6140.7 (pl. 3A.2), while another statuette (ACC, no. 80) is a near replica of 6140.11 (pl. 3A.5).

51. Two other very similar small Plastiras-type figures can be ascribed to the hand of the Missouri Master. See PGP in ACC, pp. 83–84, fig. 68, and no. 75. (The sculptor may also have carved a small unpublished marble beaker [University of Missouri Museum of Art and Archaeology 64.67.4] reputedly found with the name-pieces.)

52. Renfrew 1967, pp. 5, 18, nos. 12–14, pl. 3. ACC, no. 457.

53. Kontoleon 1970, pl. 194; 1971a, pls. 211b, 214–5 (the three from Grove 13; see also Archaeology 30 [1977], ill. on p. 278); 1972a, pl. 137.

54. See p. 158, Kontoleon Master: checklist [3, 4].

55. See note 28 above. Zapheiropoulou's excavations on Ano Kouphonisi also await final publication, wherefore it is not possible to illustrate or discuss the figures in detail here.

56. Thimme, on the other hand, regards these harpers as the work of two sculptors from the same workshop – one, responsible for pl. 9.2, working at the end of the transitional phase, the other at the beginning of EC II – the implication being that they represent two successive generations (ACC, pp. 496 [text of nos. 254–55], 584–85 [app. 4]). See also PGP 1980, pp. 15, 18.

57. In his account (see note 46 above), Köhler mentioned that the two female figures found with the musicians were "distinguished" by their size – that "the one whose entire length was preserved measured ca. 50 cm." The two female figures are perhaps identifiable. One of these appears to be a piece in the British Museum (1882.10-14.3 [Pryce A18]; ACC, no. 147). Recently Lesley Fitton brought to my attention the fact that faintly inscribed on the back of this figure are the notations: "found with 2 others: flute player and Apollo on chair" and "Amorgo." This early Spedos-variety figure, which is preserved to the knees, measures 25.3 cm, but would originally have had a length of at least 34 cm. While not large, it certainly exceeded the flutist, which stands a mere 20 cm high with its base.

The other figure that may well be from the group is in the National Archaeological Museum in Athens (no. 3913; Zervos, figs. 300–301). An early Spedos-variety figure also, it, too, is said to be from Amorgos and measures 55.3 cm, which accords well with Köhler's statement. Judging from its inventory number, it was acquired about the same time as the musician figures (nos. 3908 and 3910) – that is, in the early 1880s. (Note the similar date of acquisition of the British Museum piece.) The fact that Amorgos was given in both cases as the find-place rather than Keros is of little consequence, for at the time it was common to confuse Keros with Amorgos (see chap. 7).

Unfortunately, the identification of these figures was made too late to include illustrations and a detailed discussion here. Moreover, further study is needed before a reasonable conclusion can be reached as to whether the two works were carved by different sculptors or by one sculptor at different points in his career. Suffice it to say, though, that they do not bear a strong resemblance to either of the musician figures.

58. A second, slightly larger and in general more skillfully executed, though in many respects quite similar, male/female pair ought perhaps to be attributed to this sculptor as well – most probably to a more developed phase of his career. Known at present only from drawings made in the mid-nineteenth century and housed in the library of the Greek and Roman Department of the British Museum, it seems quite certain that these figures, too, were designed for use as companion pieces. See Fitton.

59. A figure in the Israel Museum (ACC, no. 219) could conceivably have been carved by the Tsountas Master as well. Its upper torso is similar to the torsos of the name-pieces, and in profile it is similar especially to the smaller name-piece.

60. Burial Habits, cf. pl. 28h (grave 5, Akrotiri) with pl. 34a (grave 6, Plastiras) and pl. 34d, e (grave 9, Plastiras).

61. Burial Habits, pls. 28d, e and pl. 34f.

62. Once considered a forgery (A. J. B. Wace, "Prehistoric Stone Figurines from the Mainland," Hesperia Supplement 8 [1949]: 423), this figure, after a long exile in storage, was recently put on display at the National Archaeological Museum.

63. See chap. 3, pp. 60, 63, with note 51 above.

64. See Kontoleon 1971b, fig. 218, first two figures on left.

65. To an even earlier stage perhaps may belong a small figure in Athens from (Spedos?) Naxos (fig. 5d) and at least two figures in Naxos (unpublished; possibly from grave 13 at Aplomata). It is conceivable, too, that the two figures in Oxford discussed in chap. 3 (pl. 5) are also from the Kontoleon Master's hand, in which case they would represent a similarly early stage of the sculptor's development.

66. See PGP 1981, no. 16. The figure in the Erlen-

meyer Collection (Kontoleon Master [7]) also has a somewhat unusually positioned repair hole in the left knee (PGP 1981, no. 15).

67. See note 21 above. The figures mentioned in note 65, which may be from this sculptor's hand, all have a Naxian provenance as well.

68. See note 21.

69. For a figure measuring 21.5 cm, apparently also from the Steiner Master's hand, see Steiner Master checklist, note.

70. A graphic example of weight reduction through narrowing may be seen in two very large works of nearly identical length attributed to a sculptor called the Karlsruhe/Woodner Master (PGP, *ECS*, pp. 70–72 with figs. 56–59). The narrower figure weighs 23 lbs, the broader one 35 lbs.

71. In the case of the Copenhagen Master, his smaller figures have a shoulder width that is about 21.5 percent of their length. That of his largest figure [4] is 20.8 percent, though if it had been completed according to the sculptor's original plan, the shoulder width would have been only about 17 percent of the overall length. It was doubtless the combination of narrowness and extreme thinness that caused this figure to break as it did.

72. Still larger originally were two fragmentary figures, most probably attributable to the Naxos Museum Master that, from the front at least, resemble [5] and [6] most closely. See Naxos Museum Master checklist, note.

73. Gilbert Ouy has suggested (personal communication) that the Naxos Museum Master may have used a foot of 31.07 cm divided into thirteen inches of 2.39 cm, further subdivided into eight smaller units. The lengths of the complete figures attributable to this sculptor, should the reader wish to experiment with them, are, as can best be determined at present: 18, 19.8, 21, 27.8, 39.5, 48, 50.8, 55, and 72 cm. One of the drawbacks to a serious and exact study of this kind is that Cycladic figures are rather frequently imprecisely measured. (Not all the measurements given in this book are my own, nor can I be certain that those that are are exact!) Generally, measurements are correct to within about 0.5 cm, but one can find greater discrepancies in the literature. An excellent device has recently been designed by DeVries specifically for taking precise measurements of Cycladic figures (see note 33 above). I am grateful to him for sending me the dimensions of the pieces he has measured.

74. Fellmann (pp. 19–20), recognizing the similarity of certain works [2, 4, 6, 11] here unhesitatingly attributed to different phases of one sculptor's career, merely raises the possibility that they might

belong to the same workshop. See also Zapheiropoulou 1979, p. 540 ("addendum").

75. The only experiments that shed any light at all on this question are valuable ones conducted by Elizabeth Oustinoff. Using tools made of materials available to the Early Bronze Age sculptor, she produced a small violin figurine by modifying a marble beach pebble. The task was accomplished in five hours. A Louros-type figurine took her thirty hours, while a small late Spedos-variety statuette required sixty hours. (See E. Oustinoff, "The Manufacture of Cycladic Figurines: A Practical Approach," *Cycladica*, pp. 38–47. PGP, *ECS*, figs. 43–44.) Presumably, as Oustinoff points out, an experienced sculptor would have taken less time.

76. See note 73 above. For the same reason it is also impossible to take precise measurements from front or rear view photographs of any but the flattest Cycladic sculptures.

77. The foot suggested by Ouy for the Goulandris Master is 31.7 cm divided into thirteen inches of 2.438 cm, perhaps subdivided into four smaller units. See note 73 above.

78. The occurrence of fingers on one hand only is, with one possible exception – also small – (*Antike Kunst* 8[1965]: pl. 20, 10) unparalleled and may have had to do with the difficulty of incising the correct number of fingers in a very small space.

79. It is unclear just where in the sculptor's development one should place the very small figure in Norwich [1], which is no more than half the size of the other relatively small and immature works attributable to his hand. Should one consider it an earlier effort than these others? The size alone should not necessarily lead to such a conclusion. However, if one considers the slightly smaller (15.7 cm) and quite asymmetrical figure represented in an advanced stage of pregnancy also in the Goulandris Collection (pls. 11A.3, 12A.3) to be a work of the master (see Goulandris Master checklist, note), a case could be made that it and the Norwich piece that it resembles in certain respects not associated with the sculptor's habitual style – a broad pubic triangle, broad leg-cleft, widely spaced feet, a broken profile, and a superficially incised spine – represent the earliest stage of the sculptor's development that can now be recognized. In these pieces we can see some of the characteristics that were to become hallmarks of his style (e.g., the rounded back), but his style as a whole – especially that of the pregnant figure – has not yet crystallized to the point of being easy to recognize. For example, the rendering of an advanced pregnant state was not an element of the sculptor's "formed" approach, and on this pregnant figure the

shoulders have only the beginning of the steep slope that was to become the norm in the Goulandris Master's work.

80. As mentioned in chap. 2, it is possible that all Spedos-variety figures once carried some painted detail. Certain figures attributable to other masters discussed in this chapter show clear paint ghosts on the head and/or face (e.g., the name-piece [6] and large head [7] of the Steiner Master or the figure in Athens carved by the Naxos Museum Master [2]).

81. See Goulandris Master checklist, note. Georgos Kastrisios, custodian of the Apeiranthos Museum, thinks these badly damaged pieces may have been found on Keros (see chap. 7).

82. Kontoleon, 1972a, pl. 134. It is tempting to think that the Goulandris Master also carved the marble vessels found in this grave. They include two footed bowls, a deep basin (of the sort found, incidentally, in abundance in the excavations on Keros) and a so-called frying pan (ibid., pls. 138B, C; 139a; 140).

83. On Paros and Amorgos as sources of figures, see discussion in chap. 7.

84. It is of interest to note that all the figures found at Phionta, including the two carved by the Bastis Master (and one carved by the Naxos Museum Master [1]) have a reddish surface, indicating probably that they were buried in iron-rich soil. A similar, albeit somewhat darker, patina is found on the Bastis Master's name-piece as well, which suggests that it, too, may have come from Phionta. Not coincidentally perhaps, a similar surface color is found on the figure carved by the Goulandris Master allegedly from Paros [26]. See note 83.

85. Note also that one of the works attributed to the Naxos Museum Master [6] came out of Greece through the same channels as two or three works of the Goulandris Master ([13, 32, and perhaps 15]). See note 84 also.

86. See Schuster Master checklist [4].

87. See Schuster Master checklist, note.

88. The frontal width of the upper arms is ca. 0.8 cm as compared to ca. 1.3 cm on the larger piece; the profile thickness of the arms is ca. 1.1 cm in comparison to ca. 1.6 cm on the larger work.

89. Not enough of the fragment is preserved to make a definite attribution – especially since other sculptors such as the Tsountas Master (pl. 13) treated the lower part of the face in similar fashion.

90. E.g., ACC, no. 221.

91. Cf. the feet of Copenhagen Master [4], chap. 5.

92. ACC, pp. 87ff.

93. See note 58 above. This hairstyle, also found on the male figure illustrated in fig. 8e, can be re-

garded as specifically appropriate to males. See Fitton, n. 17.

94. See PGP 1980, nos. 26–32. Add "Perditus": Fitton, fig. 2.

95. E.g., ACC, nos. 338–43.

96. See Stafford Master checklist, note.

97. See chap. 7. Cf. PGP in ACC, p. 87. Here I suggested, somewhat prematurely perhaps, that the Dresden Master might have been from Amorgos.

98. Possibly they were separated by a geological disturbance. See chap. 7.

99. See, e.g., notes 27, 70 above.

100. J. D. Evans and C. Renfrew, *Excavations at Saliagos Near Antiparos*, British School of Archaeology at Athens Supplementary vol. 5 (1968), pp. 65–66, 99–100. There is also evidence that Naxian emery was used in the manufacture of stone vases at Akrotiri (P. Warren, "The Stone Vessels from the Bronze Age Settlement at Akrotiri, Thera," *Archaiologike Ephemeris*, 1979, 104).

101. *Burial Habits*, p. 124. Doumas believes that Avdeli may actually have been settled for the purpose of mining the nearby emery. (C. Doumas, "Archaiotites kai Mnimeia Kykladon," *Deltion, Chronika* 18 [1963]: 279.)

102. C. Doumas, "Archaiotites kai Mnimeia Kykladon," *Deltion, Chronika* 19 (1964): 409–10.

103. Zapheiropoulou 1968a, p. 381. P. Zapheiropoulou, "Ostraka ek Kerou," *AAA* 8 (1975): 79–85. Zapheiropoulou 1979, no. 8, pl. 240. Additional investigations have been carried out by D. Hatzi-Vallianou ("Archaiotites kai Mnimeia Kykladon," *Deltion, Chronika* 30 [1975]: 327 [Keros]). See note 105 below.

104. The fourth is a sculptor of Dokathismata-variety figures known only from three fragments – one from the investigations on Keros (unpublished), two from the hoard (PGP 1984a, no. 8, figs. 30–33). I am indebted to C. Doumas and P. Zapheiropoulou for allowing me to examine their Kerian finds.

105. Zapheiropoulou 1968b, p. 100, figs. 5–6. Keros is the probable source of the examples in the Goulandris Collection (NG, nos. 131, 134).

106. See note 57 above. The cupbearer (pl. IIB) as well as several other complete figures in the Goulandris Collection may also come from the site.

107. See C. Renfrew, "Speculations on the Use of Early Cycladic Sculpture," *Cycladica*, pp. 27–28. See also pp. 33–34 (discussion). See also J. Thimme, "A Keros-Syros Deposit from Keros," *ACC*, p. 588.

108. See *Cycladica*, p. 33 (discussion).

109. Zapheiropoulou 1979, p. 540. Clearly some marble objects were made on Keros, as the finding

of a few unfinished pieces as well as pieces and numerous chips of white marble at the site strongly suggest. It would seem that most of these objects were made of imported marble (though the marble may have been brought from no further away than nearby Kato Kouphonisi – a possibility that, however, needs to be tested). Indeed, simple visual inspection as well as initial petrological testing suggest that the vast majority of the objects found on Keros were not made of Kerian stone – a more accurate determination could be made through further isotopic analysis – but, although some marble was evidently imported, for reasons given below it seems unlikely that a high percentage of the objects would actually have been made on Keros. See also note 111 below.

110. See *Burial Habits*, fig. 2. On this map of Naxos, Doumas includes sixty Early Cycladic sites,

of which more than half are situated along the eastern and southeastern coasts.

111. Taking the analogy of Delos one step further, one might suppose that, just as in the seventh century B.C., the majority of the monuments and dedications there were Naxian in origin, so on Keros the principal connection appears to have been with Naxos. And, if one speculates that the marble objects recovered on Keros were votives, one can readily imagine that, like the silver and tin votives (*tamata*) dedicated at the Feast of the Assumption on Tenos nowadays, some would have been acquired, presumably at an annual festival (*panegyri*), from local craftsmen working near the sanctuary; others would have been bought from artisans who had traveled to Keros for the occasion; while still others would have been brought by their owners from home.

APPENDIXES

Checklists of Figures Attributed to Sixteen Sculptors

T H E following inventories include previously published works, works illustrated here, and important works from unpublished excavations that can reasonably be attributed to each of the sculptors discussed in chapters 4 through 6. Other unpublished material (and pieces illustrated only in front view in auction or exhibition catalogs), as well as less secure attributions, are summarized in a note following the numbered entries.

The figures are listed more or less sequentially from the smallest to the largest, with the position of substantial fragments determined by estimates of their original dimensions. For the most part, less substantial fragments (e.g., heads) are listed after the better preserved works. (In a few cases where fragments were added late in the preparation of the book, they have been put near the end of the lists so as not to disturb the numbering drastically.)

The checklist numbers are bracketed throughout, so as not to confuse them with the plate and figure numbers.

THE DOUMAS MASTER

[Pls. 4*B*, 14, 15; figs. 15*a*, 27*b*]

[1] Naxos, Archaeological Museum 1990. Pres. H. 8.7 cm (most of legs missing). Grave 5, Akrotiri, Naxos. *Burial Habits*, p. 87. (Pls. 14, 15)

[2] Oxford, Ashmolean Museum AE.417. Pres. H. 8.6 cm (most of legs missing). "Lefkes, Paros." Renfrew 1969, p. 6, II.2. (Pls. 14, 15)

[3] Private collection. Pres. H. 10.1 cm (legs missing from below knees). Provenance unknown. *Classical Art*, no. 5. (Pls. 14, 15; fig. 27*b*)

[4] Geneva, Barbier-Müller Museum BMG 202-13. H. 13.4 cm. Provenance unknown. *ACC*, no. 77; PGP 1980, no. 2; PGP 1981, no. 8. (Pls. 14, 15)

[5] Dresden, Staatliche Antikensammlungen, Skulpturensammlung ZV.1991. Pres. H. 12.4 cm (legs missing from above knees). Provenance unknown. *ACC*, no. 74; PGP 1980, no. 3. (No illus.)

[6] Paros, Archaeological Museum 657. Pres. H. 11.2 cm (legs missing from below knees). Grave 9, Plastiras, Paros. *Burial Habits*, p. 99. Name-piece. (Pl. 4*B*.1)

[7] Paros, Archaeological Museum 659. H. 14 cm. Grave 9, Plastiras, Paros. *Burial Habits*, pp. 99–100. Name-piece. (Pl. 4*B*.2)

[8] Paros, Archaeological Museum 658. H. 15.3 cm

(after neck restoration). Grave 9, Plastiras, Paros. *Burial Habits*, p. 99. Name-piece. (Pl. 4*B*.3)

[9] Athens, National Archaeological Museum 4762. H. 31.5 cm. Grave 23, Glypha, Paros. Tsountas 1898, col. 155. (Pls. 14, 15; fig. 15*a*)

THE METROPOLITAN MUSEUM MASTER
[Pls. I*A*, 16, 17; figs. 4*b*, 7*a*, 33]

[1] Geneva, Barbier-Müller Museum BMG 202-75 (ex. J. Müller Collection). H. 18.3 cm. Provenance unknown. *ACC*, no. 66; PGP 1981, no. 5. (Pls. I*A*, 16, 17; fig. 33*b*)

[2] New York, Metropolitan Museum of Art 45.11.18. H. 21.8 cm (much of right foot missing). Provenance unknown. *ACC*, no. 65; PGP

1981, no. 4. Name-piece. (Pls. 16, 17; figs. 4*b*, 7*a*, 33*a*)

[3] E. Berlin, Staatliche Museen, Antikensammlung 8429. H. 23.5 cm (large holes aligned with spine modern). "Delos." *ACC*, no. 67. (Pls. 16, 17; fig. 33*c*)

THE ATHENS MUSEUM MASTER
[Pls. 18, 19, 20; figs. 8*a*, 34]

[1] Private collection. Pres. H. 18.2 cm (legs missing from above knees). Provenance unknown. PGP 1975, p. 48, *b*. (Pls. 18, 20)

[2] Athens, National Archaeological Museum 3919. H. 30.8 cm. "Amorgos." PGP 1975, p. 48, *a*; PGP 1980, no. 5. Name-piece. (Pls. 18, 19, 20; figs. 8*a*, 34)

[3] Oxford, Ashmolean Museum AE.151. Pres. H. 9.2 cm (lower torso and upper thighs only). "Amorgos." PGP 1975, p. 48, *c*; PGP 1981, no. 7. (Pls. 18, 20)

[4] Geneva, Barbier-Müller Museum BMG 202-59. Pres. H. 13.6 cm (head with part of neck only). Provenance unknown. PGP 1975, p. 48, *d*; PGP, *ECS*, pl. V*a*. (Pls. 19, 20)

THE KONTOLEON MASTER
[Pls. 21, 22; figs. 5*e*, 7*c*, 35]

[1] Athens, National Archaeological Museum 6140.12. L. ca. 17.5 cm. Spedos?, Naxos. (Pls. 21, 22; figs. 5*e*, 7*c*)

[2] Dominique de Menil Collection X 084. L. 18.9 cm. "Paros." *ACC*, no. 124. (Pls. 21, 22; fig. 35*a*)

[3] Naxos, Archaeological Museum 5461. L. 21.4 cm (most of left foot missing). Grave 13, Aplomata, Naxos. Kontoleon 1971*b*, fig. 218a (photo taken at a very poor angle). Name-piece. (No illus.)

[4] Naxos, Archaeological Museum 5463. L. 21.7 cm (left foot missing). Grave 13, Aplomata, Naxos. Kontoleon 1971*b*, fig. 218b (photo taken at a very poor angle). Name-piece. (No illus.)

[5] New York, Metropolitan Museum of Art 1977.187.10ab (bequest of Alice K. Bache). L. 30 cm (right foot missing). Provenance unknown. PGP 1981, no. 16. (Pls. 21, 22)

[6] Private collection. L. 31 cm. Provenance unknown. (Pls. 21, 22; fig. 35*b*)

[7] Basel, Erlenmeyer Collection. Pres. L. 17.2 cm (head/neck missing as well as legs from knees). Provenance unknown. PGP 1981, no. 15. (No illus.)

[8] Heidelberg, Archäologisches Institut der Universität St. 39. Pres. L. 17.8 cm (lower part missing from top of pubic area). Provenance unknown. R. Hampe and H. Gropengiesser, *Aus der Sammlung der Archäologischen Institutes der Universität Heidelberg* (1967) no. 1. (No illus.)

Note: Another work probably attributable to the Kontoleon Master is: Sotheby's (London) 10 July 1972, lot 172 (19.7 cm). I have not personally examined the figure, illustrated in the auction catalog in front view only. Other figures possibly from the hand of the Kontoleon Master include a small piece from Naxos – possibly Spedos – in Athens (fig. 5*d*), two unpublished figures possibly from grave 13 at Aplomata, and also, conceivably, the two figures "from Naxos" in Oxford illustrated in pl. 5. See note 65.

A large figure (47 cm to above the ankles) in the Paul and Marianne Steiner Collection (*ACC*, no. 157) was perhaps also carved by the Kontoleon Master. Its head form, which is rather similar to that of Naxos 163 (see Israel Museum Master checklist, note), differs markedly from the works listed here. Otherwise, it resembles [5] and [6], especially in profile.

A fragmentary work (Sotheby's [New York] March 1–2, 1984, lot 32) is perhaps also attributable to the Kontoleon Master. Finally, it is conceivable that the very large figure (69.4 cm to knees) illustrated in pl. VI*A* represents the acme of this sculptor's development. The head form is, again, quite different from that of the works listed above.

THE ISRAEL MUSEUM MASTER

[Pl. 23; fig. 36]

[1] Naxos, Archaeological Museum 164. Pres. L. 13.5 cm (legs missing from knees). Spedos, Naxos. (No illus.)

[2] Washington, D.C., Hirshhorn Museum and Sculpture Garden 1966.5186. L. 22.9 cm. Provenance unknown. (Pl. 23; fig. 36*a*)

[3] Athens, National Archaeological Museum 6140.15. Pres. L. 19 cm (legs missing from knees). Spedos?, Naxos. Zervos, fig. 109. (Pl. 23)

[4] Jerusalem, Israel Museum 74.61.206. L. 29 cm. Provenance unknown. *ACC*, no. 128. Name-piece. (Pl. 23; fig. 36*b*)

[5] Naxos, Archaeological Museum 165. L. 45.5 cm. Spedos, Naxos. (No illus.)

Note: Also to be attributed to the Israel Museum Master probably: Christie's (London), 24–25 April 1978, lot 484 (23.4 cm). I have not personally examined the figure, illustrated in the auction catalog in front view only. Another unpublished figure from Spedos may also be from the hand of the Israel Museum Master (Naxos, Archaeological Museum 163. L. 27 cm).

THE COPENHAGEN MASTER

[Pls. 24, 25; fig. 5*f*]

[1] Private collection. L. 56.2 cm (right foot restored). Provenance unknown. PGP 1981, pp. 19, 23; figs. 54–55. PGP 1984*b*, figs. 5–7, a. (Pls. 24, 25)

[2] London, private collection. L. 57.2 cm. Provenance unknown. Sotheby's (London), 15 July 1980, lot 135. PGP 1984*b*, figs. 5–7, b. (Pls. 24, 25; fig. 5*f*)

[3] Copenhagen, Danish National Museum 1624. Pres. L. 49.7 cm (legs missing from knees). "Amorgos." PGP 1984*b*, figs. 5–7, c. Name-piece. (Pls. 24, 25)

[4] Athens, Goulandris Collection 257. L. 70.7 cm. "Naxos." NG, no. 143 (L. 70 cm); Doumas, Goulandris Coll., no. 257 (L. 70.7 cm). PGP 1981, pp. 19, 23, figs. 52–53. PGP 1984*b*, figs. 5–7, d. (Pls. 24, 25)

[5] Private collection? Pres. L. 15.6 cm (head/neck only). "Keros." (Pl. 24)

[6] Private collection. Pres. L. 13.6 cm (head with trace of neck only). "Keros." Safani, no. 10 (photo taken after restoration). (Pl. 24)

Note: A large, privately owned, unpublished head, measuring 20.2 cm to the chin, can also be attributed to the Copenhagen Master.

THE FITZWILLIAM MASTER

[Pls. 26, 27; figs. 5g, 7d, 16a, 23d, 37]

[1] Stockholm, Medelhavsmuseet 62.10. L. 19.6 cm (left foot missing). Provenance unknown. A. Andrén, *Antik Skulpturi svenska samlinger* (Stockholm, 1964), pl. 1. (Pls. 26, 27; fig. 37a)

[2] New York, Christos G. Bastis Collection. L. 20.6 cm. Provenance unknown. (Pls. 26, 27; figs. 5g, 7d, 37b)

[3] Herakleion, Archaeological Museum 122. L. 23.8 cm. Communal tomb, Koumasa, Crete. Renfrew 1969, pl. 4c. (Pls. 26, 27; fig. 37c)

[4] Cambridge, Fitzwilliam Museum GR.33.1901 (gift of R. C. Bosanquet). L. 25.6 cm (nose missing). "Amorgos." *ACC*, no. 161. Name-piece. (Pls. 26, 27; figs. 16a, 23d)

THE STEINER MASTER

[Pls. 28, 29, 30; fig. 38]

[1] Tokyo, National Museum of Western Art S.1974-1. L. 34.5 cm. Provenance unknown. *Bulletin Annuel du Musée National d'Art Occidental* 9 (1975): 18–19. PGP 1984b, figs. 8–10, a. (Pls. 28, 29, 30)

[2] Naxos, Archaeological Museum 4674. L. 42 cm. "Naxos." Zapheiropoulou 1979, no. 9. This figure was stolen in 1977 and has not been recovered. (Pl. 28; fig. 38a)

[3] Basel, Erlenmeyer Collection. Pres. L. 22.7 cm (head/neck missing as well as legs from knees). "Keros." (Pls. 28, 29, 30)

[4] Athens, Goulandris Collection 654. L. 48 cm. Provenance unknown. NG, no. 49. PGP 1984b, figs. 8–10, b. (Pls. 28, 29, 30; fig. 38b)

[5] Private collection. L. 51 cm. Provenance unknown. PGP 1984b, figs. 8–10, c. (Pls. 28, 29, 30; fig. 38c)

[6] New York, Paul and Marianne Steiner Collection. L. 60.2 cm. Provenance unknown. PGP 1984b, figs. 8–10, d. Name-piece. (Pls. 28, 29, 30; fig. 38d)

[7] Private collection. Pres. L. 13.4 cm. (head with part of neck only). "Keros." Preziosi/Weinberg, pl. 5.2–3. (No illus.)

Note: Another complete work attributable in all likelihood to the Steiner Master is, at 21.5 cm, also the smallest: *Ancient Art* (Robin Symes Gallery, London, June 1971), no. 19. I have not personally examined the figure, illustrated in a small front view only. For this reason it is neither discussed nor listed above, but it is included in Appendix 2. At least three small unpublished heads from the "Keros hoard" are also probably from works carved by the Steiner Master.

THE NAXOS MUSEUM MASTER

[Pls. 31, 32, 33; fig. 39]

[1] Naxos, Archaeological Museum 169. L. 18 cm. Phionta, Naxos. PGP 1984b, figs. 11–13, a. Name-piece. (No illus.)

[2] Athens, National Archaeological Museum 6140.19. L. 19.8 cm. Grave 28, Phyrroges, Naxos. Papathanasopoulos, pp. 138–39 and pl. 72a; Preziosi/Weinberg, pl. 5.4–5. (Pls. 31, 32, 33)

[3] Naxos, Archaeological Museum 205. L. 21 cm. Aplomata, Naxos. PGP 1984b, fig. 2.2. Name-piece. (No illus.)

[4] Munich, Staatliche Antikensammlungen und Glyptothek, von Schoen Collection 262. L. 27.8 cm. Provenance unknown. Fellmann, no. 7 (Pls. 31, 32, 33)

[5] Private collection? Pres. L. 25 cm (head/neck missing). "Keros." (Pls. 31, 32, 33)

[6] Private collection. L. 39.5 cm. Provenance unknown. Fellmann, p. 20 and fig. 11. PGP 1984*b*, figs. 11–13, b. (Pls. 31, 32, 33)

[7] Naxos, Archaeological Museum 194. Pres. L. 42 cm (ends of feet damaged). Naxos. PGP 1984*b*, figs. 11–13, c. Name-piece. (No illus.)

[8] Naxos, Archaeological Museum 195. L. 48 cm. Naxos. PGP 1984*b*, fig. 2.3. Name-piece. (No illus.)

[9] New York, Woodner Family Collection. L. 50.8 cm. Provenance unknown. PGP, *ECS*, fig. 36. (Pls. 31, 32, 33)

[10] Naxos, Archaeological Museum 4676. L. 55 cm. "Naxos." Zapheiropoulou 1979, no. 13. Name-piece. (Pls. 31, 32, 33; fig. 39*a*)

[11] Athens, Goulandris Collection 598. L. 72 cm. "Naxos." NG, no. 145. PGP 1984*b*, figs. 11–13, d. (Pls. 31, 32, 33; fig. 39*b*)

Note: In addition, a pair of legs attributable to the Naxos Museum Master was found in the excavations at Aplomata (Naxos, Archaeological Museum 5943); another pair of legs in the Erlenmeyer Collection in Basel, at least three torso fragments, and one or two heads, all from the "Keros hoard" (and all unpublished) can also be ascribed to this sculptor. An upper torso fragment in Athens (Canellopoulos Museum 1401; Brouscari, no. 8) is perhaps also from his hand, and, like all his complete works, most probably belonged to a female figure (cf. Brouscari, p. 510).

Two partially preserved figures (61 cm to above the knees and 21 cm from the shoulders to the beginning of the right forearm) that originally measured more than 85 cm should probably also be attributed to the Naxos Museum Master (see Hotel Drouot [Paris] 14 November 1973, lot 35 [L. Salavin Collection]; Münzen und Medaillen Auktion 56 [Basel] 19 February 1980, lot 3). I have not personally examined these pieces, the first illustrated in the auction catalog in front view only. See note 72.

THE GOULANDRIS MASTER

[Pls. VII*D*, IX, 34, 35, 36, 37; figs. 5*h*, 7*e*, 40, 41, 42, 43, 44, 45, 47]

[1] Norwich, University of East Anglia, Sainsbury Centre for Visual Arts, 1955 UEA 343. L. 16.5 cm. Provenance unknown. PGP, *GM*, no. 1. (Pls. 34, 36, 37)

[2] Athens, Goulandris Collection 251. L. 33 cm. "Naxos." NG, no. 42. PGP, *GM*, no. 2. PGP 1984*b*, figs. 14–16, a. Name-piece. (Pls. 34, 36, 37; fig. 47*a, c*)

[3] New York, Arthur and Medeleine Lejwa Collection. Pres. L. 19.1 cm. (lower part missing from mid-abdomen). "Naxos." ACC, no. 174. (No illus.)

[4] San Francisco, Fine Arts Museums of San Francisco (William H. Nobel Bequest Fund) 1981.42. L. 33.4 cm. (repairs of breaks obscure neck and knee grooves and restoration at knees has perhaps altered original length so that figure is possibly slightly shorter now than originally). "Keros." PGP 1982, fig. 1 (pre-restoration photograph). PGP, *ECS*, figs. 60–61. PGP, *GM*, no. 3. (Fig. 41*a*)

[5] Norwich, University of East Anglia, Sainsbury Centre for Visual Arts 1961 UEA 342. Pres. L. 27.6 cm (legs missing from knees). Provenance unknown. ACC, no. 169. (No illus.)

[6] New York, Mrs. Allan D. Emil Collection. Pres. L. 32.4 cm (feet missing). Provenance unknown. PGP, *GM*, no. 13. ACC, no. 180. (Pls. 34, 36, 37)

[7] Naxos, Archaeological Museum 5800. L. 35.2 cm. Grave 23, Aplomata, Naxos. Kontoleon 1972*a*, pl. 136*a*; 1972*b*, fig. 85. PGP, *GM*, no. 4. (No illus.)

[8] Private collection. L. 38.2 cm (left foot missing). "Keros." ACC, no. 178 (head/neck missing). PGP, *GM*, no. 5. (Pls. 34, 36, 37)

[9] Dominique de Menil Collection CA 6018. Pres. L. 22.3 cm (head/neck missing as well as legs from knees). Provenance unknown. ACC, no. 179. (No illus.)

[10] Naxos, Archaeological Museum 4675. L. 39 cm (most of left foot missing). "Naxos." Zapheiropoulou 1979, no. 11. PGP, *GM*, no. 6. (No illus.)

[11] Thessaloniki, Archaeological Museum B.E. 10660. Pres. L. 21.3 cm (head/neck missing as well as legs from knees). Provenance unknown. *Deltion, Chronika* 24 (1969) pl. 299b. PGP, *GM*, no. 22. (No illus.)

[12] Athens, Canellopoulos Museum 2075. Pres. L. 13 cm (head/neck missing as well as much of upper torso and legs from upper thighs). Provenance unknown. Brouscari, no. 7, fig. 9. PGP, *GM*, no. 36. (No illus.)

[13] Private collection. L. 42 cm. Provenance unknown. PGP 1984*b*, figs. 14–16, b. PGP, *GM*, no. 7. (Pls. 34, 36, 37; fig. 40*a*)

[14] Naxos, Archaeological Museum KE.63.4 (2374). Pres. L. 14.8 cm (head with most of neck missing as well as lower part from mid-abdomen). Keros. PGP, *GM*, no. 29. (No illus.)

[15] Des Moines, Des Moines Art Center 64.3 (Coffin Fine Arts Trust Fund). Pres. L. 44.1 cm (ends of feet damaged). (Repair of break obscures neck groove.) Provenance unknown. *ACC*, no. 168. PGP, *GM*, no. 8. (No illus.)

[16] London, British Museum 84.12-13.6. Pres. L. 16.3 cm (head with most of neck missing as well as lower part from mid-abdomen). "Amorgos." Pryce, A22. PGP, *GM*, no. 33. (No illus.)

[17] Basel, Erlenmeyer Collection. Pres. L. 18.6 cm (abdomen/thighs only). "Keros." *ACC*, no. 176. (No illus.)

[18] Basel, Erlenmeyer Collection. Pres. L. 13.1 cm (torso only). "Keros." PGP 1984*a*, fig. 20. (No illus.)

[19] Basel, Erlenmeyer Collection. Pres. L. 15.6 cm (torso only). "Keros." PGP 1984*a*, fig. 21. (No illus.)

[20] Private collection. Pres. L. 18.5 cm (head/neck missing as well as legs from upper thighs). "Keros." *ACC*, no. 173. PGP 1984*a*, no. 5. (No illus.)

[21] Canberra, Australian National Gallery 1982.2232 (ex Maurice Bonnefoy Collection). L. 55 cm (probably ca. 54 cm originally; ends of feet incorrectly restored). Provenance unknown. Sotheby's (London) 12 July 1971, lot 132 (length given as 54.6 cm). PGP 1978, pp. 3–5 with figs. 5–6 (incorrect restoration of feet not taken into account). PGP, *GM*, no. 9. (Pls. IX*B*, 35, 36)

[22] Private collection. Pres. L. 29 cm (head/neck missing as well as legs from knees). (Repair of break obscures abdominal and pubic incisions.) "Keros." (Pls. 34, 37; fig. 47*e*)

[23] Zumikon-Zürich, Binia Bill Collection. Pres. L. 45 cm (legs, missing from knees, restored in plaster). (Repair of break obscures neck

groove.) Provenance unknown. *ACC*, no. 170. (No illus.)

[24] Private collection. Pres. L. 22 cm (head with part of neck missing as well as lower part from abdominal groove). "Keros." Preziosi/Weinberg, pl. 6, 5.6. PGP, *GM*, no. 34. (No illus.)

[25] Bloomington, Indiana University Art Museum 76.25 (gift of Thomas T. Solley). L. 60 cm. Provenance unknown. *ACC*, no. 167. PGP 1984*b*, figs. 14–16, c. PGP, *GM*, no. 10. (Pls. IX*A*, 36; figs. 5*h*, 40*b*, 41*b*, 45)

[26] New York, Christos G. Bastis Collection. L. 62.15 cm (restoration at neck and knees may have altered original length slightly). "Paros." PGP, *GM*, no. 11. (Pl. 35; figs. 42*b*, 43*a*)

[27] Athens, Goulandris Collection 281. L. 63.4 cm. "Naxos." NG, no. 46; color ill. on p. 6. PGP 1984*b*, figs. 14–16, d. PGP, *GM*, no. 12. Name-piece. (Pls. 34, 36, 37; figs. 7*e*, 40*c*, 42*c*, 44, 47*b*, *d*)

[28] Private collection. Pres. L. 34.3 cm (head/neck missing as well as legs from knees). "Keros." PGP, *GM*, no. 24. (Pls. 34, 35, 37)

[29] Karlsruhe, Badisches Landesmuseum 70/550. Pres. L. 10.2 cm (head/neck only). "Keros." *ACC*, no. 171. PGP, *GM*, no. 41. (Figs. 42*g*, 43*b*)

[30] Athens, Goulandris Collection 256. Pres. L. 11.2 cm (head/neck only). "Naxos." NG, no. 44. PGP, *GM*, no. 42. Name-piece. (No illus.)

[31] Columbia, University of Missouri Museum of Art and Archaeology 76.214. Pres. L. 11.7 cm (head/neck only). "Keros." *ACC*, no. 177. PGP, *GM*, no. 44. (Fig. 42*e*)

[32] Private collection. Pres. L. 13.4 cm (head/neck only). Provenance unknown. *Early Art*, no. 23. PGP, *GM*, no. 45. (Fig. 42*f*)

[33] New York, Paul and Marianne Steiner Collection. Pres. L. 14.5 cm (head/neck only). Provenance unknown. Safani, no. 11. (No illus.)

[34] Karlsruhe, Kurt Flimm Collection. Pres. L. 11 cm (head only). "Keros." *ACC*, no. 172; PGP 1978, fig. 1. (No illus.)

[35] Malibu, J. Paul Getty Museum 83.AA.316.2. Pres. L. 10.4 cm (part of head with small section of neck only). "Keros." PGP 1984*a*, no. 2. (No illus.)

[36] Copenhagen, Danish National Museum 4697. Pres. L. 24.6 cm (head/neck only). "Amorgos." *ACC*, pl. Va and p. 468. PGP, *GM*, no. 48. (Pl. VII*D*; fig. 42*h*)

[37] Basel, Erlenmeyer Collection. Pres. L. 5.1 cm (lower torso fragment). "Keros." *ACC*, no. 175. (No illus.)

Note: Numbers [38] through [51] constitute an addendum made late in the preparation of this volume. That is to say, they do not occur in their proper places within the main body of the checklist.

[38] New York, Paul and Marianne Steiner Collection. Pres. L. 26.8 cm (head/neck and feet missing). Provenance unknown. PGP, *GM*, no. 20. (No illus.)

[39] Private collection. Pres. L. 10.5 cm (head/neck missing as well as legs from upper thighs). Sotheby's (London), 9 July 1984, lot 190. PGP, *GM*, no. 25. (No illus.)

[40] Apeiranthos, Archaeological Museum 749. Pres. L. 10.5 cm (head/neck missing as well as lower part from mid-abdomen). "Panormos, Naxos." PGP, *GM*, no. 27. (No illus.)

[41] Private collection. Pres. L. 20.2 cm (lower part missing from mid-abdomen). "Keros." PGP, *GM*, no. 19. (No illus.)

[42] Athens, National Archaeological Museum 5390. Pres. L. 15 cm (head missing as well as lower part from mid-abdomen). "Naxos." PGP, *GM*, no. 28. (No illus.)

[43] Apeiranthos, Archaeological Museum 753. Pres. L. 12.2 cm (head/neck missing as well as lower part from mid-abdomen). "Panormos, Naxos." PGP, *GM*, no. 30. (No illus.)

[44] Apeiranthos, Archaeological Museum 754. Pres. L. 20.2 cm (upper part missing to left forearm; legs missing from knees). "Panormos, Naxos." PGP, *GM*, no. 35. (No illus.)

[45] Private collection. Pres. L. 44 cm (legs missing from knees). Provenance unknown. PGP, *GM*, no. 16. (Fig. 43*c*)

[46] Private collection. Pres. L. 52.5 cm (legs missing from knees). "Keros." PGP, *GM*, no. 17. (No illus.)

[47] Private collection. Pres. L. 9.9 cm (head/neck only). "Keros." PGP, *GM*, no. 40. (No illus.)

[48] Paris, Musée du Louvre 3094. Pres. L. 11.5 cm (head/neck only). "Kornoviglia, Amorgos." PGP, *GM*, no. 43. (No illus.)

[49] Private collection. Pres. L. 13.8 cm (head/neck only). "Keros." PGP, *GM*, no. 46. (No illus.)

[50] Norwich, University of East Anglia, Sainsbury Centre for Visual Arts (?)1970 UEA 410. Pres. L. 11.4 cm (lower calves and feet only). Provenance unknown. PGP, *GM*, no. 39. (No illus.)

[51] New York, François de Menil Collection. Pres. L. 13.5 cm (head/neck only). Provenance unknown. *The John and Dominique de Menil Collection* (The Museum of Primitive Art, New York, 1962), no. 32. (No illus.)

Note: See also Safani, no. 6 (head of Goulandris Master figure joined to partial figure from another hand; both fragments from "Keros hoard"); PGP 1984*a*, fig. 4 (at least two heads from "Keros hoard": top row, second and third from left). Besides many small and/or worn fragments of torsi and legs from the "Keros hoard" and a weathered head from Grave 23 at Aplomata (see n. 82) that may be from works of the Goulandris Master, there are a great many fragments, largely from the "Keros hoard," in the Apeiranthos Museum, and from the sanctioned investigations on Keros in the Naxos Museum that are attributable to his hand. It should be noted that among all the many fragments that can be ascribed to the Goulandris Master there are probably at least several cases in which two or more fragments from the same figure survive. Since the pieces are for the most part now widely dispersed, the prospect of finding joins is unlikely. It would probably be impossible in any case to identify as parts of one figure two nonadjoining fragments except by isotopic analysis.

Finally, it is conceivable that a very small complete figure in the Goulandris Collection (Pls. 11*A*.3, 12*A*.3; for profile view see NG, no. 72 or PGP, *ECS*, fig. 5) is also from the master's hand. Compare especially the rear view of this work with that shown in pl. 37[6]. (See note 79 and PGP, *GM*, nn. 5, 8.)

THE BASTIS MASTER

[Pls. 38, 39; figs. 25*b*, 46, 47]

[1] Naxos, Archaeological Museum 168. L. 22.5 cm (left foot missing). Phionta, Naxos. PGP 1981, pp. 25, 27–28; figs. 58–59. (Pls. 38, 39; figs. 46*a*, 47*a, c*)

[2] Naxos, Archaeological Museum 166. L. 50 cm. Phionta, Naxos. (Pls. 38, 39; fig. 46*b*)

[3] Fort Worth, Kimbell Art Museum AG70.2 (gift of Ben Heller). Pres. L. 41.8 cm (legs missing from knees). (Repair of break obscures groove at neck; this has been incorrectly restored in

back.) "Keros." C. C. Vermeule, *Greek and Roman Sculpture in America: Masterpieces in Public Collections in the United States and Canada* (Berkeley and Los Angeles, 1982), no. 2 (Pls. 38, 39; figs. 25*b*, 47*e*)

[4] New York, Metropolitan Museum of Art 68.148 (gift of Christos G. Bastis). L. 63.5 cm. "Naxos." ACC, no. 166. PGP 1981, pp. 25, 27–28; figs. 60–61. Name-piece. (Pls. 38, 39; figs. 46*c*, 47*b, d*)

THE SCHUSTER MASTER

[Pls. 40, 41]

[1] Athens, National Archaeological Museum 3917. Pres. L. 19.5 cm (head and perhaps part of neck missing; left foot incorrectly restored in plaster, being joined to the right foot by a membrane that extends too far toward toes). Provenance unknown. Zervos, fig. 252. (No illus.)

[2] New York, private collection (ex. M. Schuster Coll.). L. 29.2 cm. Provenance unknown. PGP 1978, pp. 5–7 (n.b., L. incorrectly given as 23 cm). Name-piece. (Pls. 40, 41)

[3] Private collection. Pres. L. 13.9 cm (head with part of neck missing as well as legs from upper thighs and part of right shoulder and arm). Provenance unknown. PGP 1978, p. 7, fig. 9. (No illus.)

[4] Zürich, Mr. and Mrs. Isidor Kahane Collection. Pres. L. 28.5 cm (lower legs and feet missing). "Keros?" (Pls. 40, 41)

[5] London, British Museum 1854.12–18.23. Pres. L. 26.9 cm (legs missing from above knees). Originally 37.6–38 cm. (Repair of break obscures neck groove.) Detailed, accurate 1:1 pencil and watercolor drawings made in 1850 (B.M. GR. 1955.8–20.3) show figure in unrestored state, with lower legs (damaged) and feet preserved to their full length. See Fit-

ton, p. 76 with fig. 1. Provenance unknown. PGP 1978, p. 5, *c.* (Pls. 40, 41)

[6] Naxos, Archaeological Museum KE.67/4186. Pres. L. 18 cm (head/neck missing as well as legs from ca. knees; both shoulders chipped). Keros. *Deltion, Chronika* 23 (1968): pl. 334*b* (photograph taken at poor angle). (No illus.)

[7] Norwich, University of East Anglia, Sainsbury Centre for Visual Arts 1977 UEA 668. Pres. L. 33 cm (head/neck and ends of feet missing). "Keros." R. Sainsbury, ed., *Robert and Lisa Sainsbury Collection* (Sainsbury Centre for Visual Arts, University of East Anglia, 1978), no. 495. (Pls. 40, 41)

[8] Malibu, J. Paul Getty Museum 83.AA.318.2. Pres. L. 7.3 cm (lower right upper arm to mid-thighs). "Keros." PGP 1984*a*, no. 6. (No illus.)

[9] Basel, Erlenmeyer Collection. Pres. L. 12.5 cm (head/neck and shoulders missing as well as legs from knees). "Keros." PGP 1984*a*, figs. 25–26. (No illus.)

[10] Basel, Erlenmeyer Collection. Pres. L. 7 cm (abdomen/thigh fragment). "Keros." PGP 1984*a*, fig. 27. (No illus.)

[11] Athens, Goulandris Collection 110. Pres. L. 9.5 cm (head with part of neck only). Prove-

nance unknown. Doumas-Goulandris Coll., no. 110; NG, no. 37. (No illus.)

[12] Jerusalem, Israel Museum 74.61.217. Pres. L. 12 cm (head with part of neck only). Provenance unknown. Unpublished. (Pl. 40)

Note: A number of other fragments from the "Keros hoard" can be attributed to the Schuster Master. At least one of two fragments apparently found on Amorgos (Chora Museum, nos. 204, 205) that I have elsewhere ascribed to the hand of the Ashmolean Master (PGP 1984*b*, p. 52 with n. 6; see also Marangou, p. 101, nos. 2, 3; figs. 21–22) ought probably to be attributed, rather, to the Schuster Master. The partially preserved head (Marangou, fig. 21) bears a strong resemblance to that of the Kahane figure [4] and, like it and other works of the Schuster Master, but unlike those of the Ashmolean Master that in certain other respects it however closely resembles (pls. 42, 43), this fragment shows clear incisions marking the juncture with the neck on the rear. (Incidentally, recent examination of the Kahane figure has shown that the head/neck, reattached at the base of the neck, definitely belongs to the same figure as the body despite its unusual angular form reminiscent of the Ashmolean Master's style.) The neck/shoulder fragment (Marangou, fig. 22) shows a shoulder slope more consistent with that seen in the work of the Schuster Master than with the much steeper slope used by the Ashmolean Master. On the other hand, the fragment has a V-shaped incision on the front of the neck similar to that found in the Ashmolean Master's work. (The Schuster Master consistently made this incision a curving one.) It is, therefore, not clear to which of these sculptors the small fragment should be attributed. See Ashmolean Master checklist, note.

THE ASHMOLEAN MASTER
[Pls. 42, 43; figs. 5*i*, 7*f*, 17*a*, 49]

[1] Budapest, Musée des Beaux-Arts 4709 (ex Paul Arndt Collection). L. 23.7 cm (end of left foot missing). Provenance unknown. ACC, no. 215. PGP 1984*b*, figs. 17–19, a. (Pls. 42, 43; fig. 49*a*)

[2] Dominique de Menil Collection CA 6326. L. 36.7 cm. "Naxos." ACC, no. 216. PGP 1984*b*, figs. 17–19, b. (Pls. 42, 43; figs. 17*a*, 49*b*)

[3] Athens, Goulandris Collection 206. L. 39.1 cm. "Keros?" NG, no. 146. PGP 1984*b*, figs. 17–19, c. (Pls. 42, 43; figs. 7*f*, 49*c*)

[4] Oxford, Ashmolean Museum AE.176. L. 75.9 cm (accurate measurement taken by J. DeVries; see note 73). (Repair of break obscures ankle grooves.) "Amorgos." ACC, no. 182. PGP 1984*b*, figs. 17–19, d. Name-piece. (Pls. 42, 43; figs. 5*i*, 49*d*)

[5] Private collection. Pres. L. 9.7 cm (calves with left foot only). "Keros." (Pl. 43)

Note: A neck-shoulder fragment in Amorgos (Chora Museum, no. 205; Marangou, p. 101, no. 3, fig. 22) is possibly from a relatively small, mature work of the Ashmolean Master (but see Schuster Master checklist, note).

THE BERLIN MASTER
[Pls. 44, 45; fig. 50]

[1] Berlin, Staatliche Museen Preussischer Kulturbesitz, Antikenmuseum 1978.4. L. 43 cm. Provenance unknown. U. Gehrig, "Ein Idol der Kykladen-Kultur," *Jahrbuch Preussischer Kulturbesitz* 15 (1980): 179–81. Name-piece. (Pls. 44, 45; fig. 50*a*)

[2] Athens, National Archaeological Museum 9606. L. 68.6 cm (end of right foot missing; shoulders damaged; left upper arm restored in plaster). Provenance unknown. Zervos, figs. 296, 298. (Pl. 44; fig. 50*b*)

Note: A fragment from the "Keros hoard" [3?] (Pres. L. 4.1 cm) consisting of the lower part of the head with the upper part of the neck may also have belonged to a figure carved by the Berlin Master (pl. 45).

THE STAFFORD MASTER
[Pls. 46, 47; figs. 18a, 51a–c]

[1] Cambridge, Mass., Fogg Art Museum L. 63. 1984 (on loan from Frederick Stafford Collection). L. 27 cm. "Paros." *American Private Colls.*, no. 127. Name-piece. (Pls. 46, 47; figs. 18a, 51b, c)

[2] New York, Woodner Family Collection. L. 27 cm (treated severely with acid). Provenance unknown. Unpublished. (Pls. 46, 47)

[3] Paris, Musée du Louvre MA 3093. L. 27.5 cm (repair of break across middle of figure obscures forearms). "Naxos." *ACC*, no. 225 (L. given as 27.5 cm, but 26.8 cm on photo furnished by the Louvre.) (Pls. 46, 47; fig. 51a)

[4] Private collection? (ex Henri Smeets Collection). Pres. L. 28.1 cm (ends of feet damaged slightly). Provenance unknown. *ACC*, no. 226. (No illus.)

[5] Private collection. L. 26.1 cm (possible reworking at chin). "Keros." PGP 1982, fig. 2. (Pls. 46, 47)

[6] Private collection. Pres. L. 10.3 cm (head and legs missing). "Keros." *ACC*, no. 224. (Pls. 46, 47)

[7] Basel, Erlenmeyer Collection. Pres. L. 4.9 cm (head with trace of neck only). "Keros." *ACC*, no. 223. (No illus.)

[8] Naxos, Archaeological Museum 4136. Pres. L. 5.2 cm (head with trace of neck only). Keros. (No illus.)

Note: A privately owned, unpublished figure measuring 26.8 cm is a near replica of the core figures [1 through 4].

THE DRESDEN MASTER
[Pls. 48, 49, 50; figs. 5j, 11f, 18b, 27g, 52]

[1] Athens, National Archaeological Museum 3916. L. 11.3 cm. "Ios." Zervos, fig. 115 [*sic*] (error for 111). (Pls. 48, 49, 50; fig. 52)

[2] Keos, Archaeological Museum K9.55. Pres. L. 12.1 cm (head/neck missing). Ayia Irini, Keos. Caskey 1971, no. 7. (Pl. 48)

[3] Keos, Archaeological Museum K3.1. Pres. L. 9.4 cm (head/neck missing as well as lower legs with feet). Ayia Irini, Keos. Caskey 1964, pl. 48h, i; Caskey 1971, no. 8. (Pl. 48)

[4] Private collection. L. 19 cm. Provenance unknown. (Pls. 48, 49, 50; fig. 5j)

[5] Dresden, Staatliche Kunstsammlungen, Skulpturensammlung ZV 2595. L. 22.8 cm. "Amorgos." *ACC*, no. 240; PGP 1980, no. 26. Name-piece. (Pls. 48, 49, 50; figs. 11f, 18b)

[6] Basel, Erlenmeyer Collection. Pres. L. 16.1 cm (head/neck missing). "Keros." *ACC*, no. 230. (Pls. 48, 50; fig. 27g)

[7] Geneva, Barbier-Müller Museum BMG 202-62 (ex P. Geneux Collection). L. 26.7 cm. Provenance unknown. *ACC*, no. 229. (Pls. 48, 49, 50)

[8] Private collection. Pres. L. 11 cm (upper part missing to top of abdomen; ends of feet damaged). "Keros." *ACC*, no. 231. (Pls. 48, 49, 50)

Note: A pair of lower legs with right foot from Ayia Irini on Keos may possibly be the work of the Dresden Master (K9.56; Caskey 1971, no. 9), and a head/neck fragment in the Keros hoard as well as a pair of legs and perhaps a head in Apeiranthos (Archaeological Museum 927, 939) said to be from Panormos, but possibly from Keros (see note 81) should also be attributed to his hand.

Size Range of Works Attributed to Sixteen Sculptors

THE following chart includes the dimensions (height or length), actual or estimated, of nearly all the works enumerated in Appendix 1. For the Goulandris Master, see p. 101. A few fragments have been excluded because it is not possible to estimate their original dimensions. With one exception (Steiner Master checklist), dimensions of figures cited in the checklist notes have not been included unless I have personally examined them and am reasonably certain of the accuracy of the attributions, and, in the case of fragmentary ones, can estimate their original sizes to within a few centimeters.

There are only two sculptures omitted from this chart that could affect it to any significant extent. These are the figure illustrated in pl. VI*A* (see Kontoleon Master checklist, note) and the fragments of large works mentioned in the Naxos Museum Master checklist, note). If these are in fact works of the Kontoleon and Naxos Museum masters, respectively, they would, with estimated lengths of ca. 85 cm, represent the largest known figures fashioned by these sculptors.

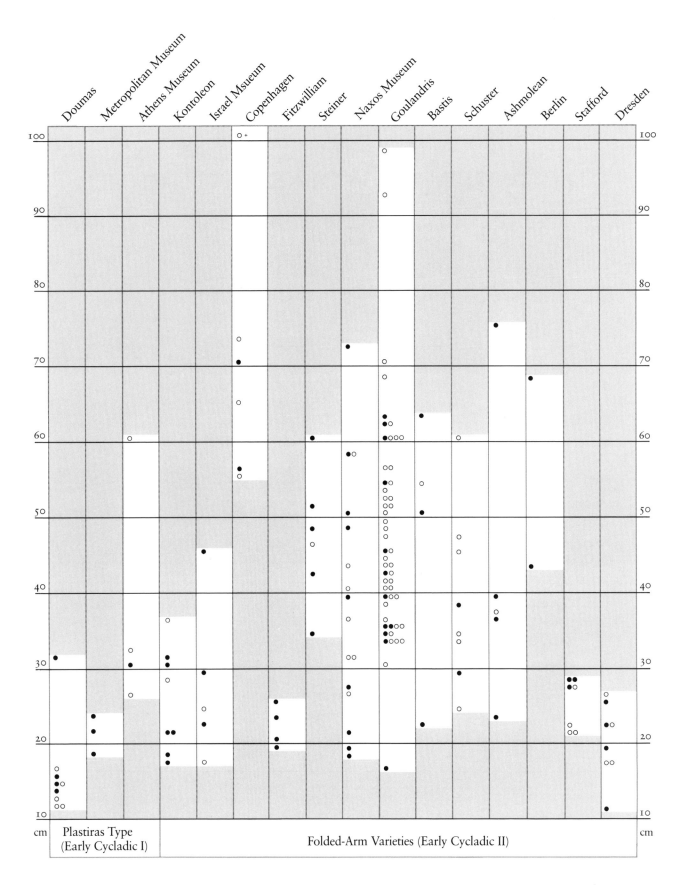

NOTE: Some of the termini are based on estimates of the original dimensions of incomplete figures.

- Complete figure
- ○ Estimated dimension based on comparison(s) with complete figures attributed to the same sculptor. In cases where two or more comparisons produce different dimensions (in most cases within 2–3 cm of each other) an average of these is recorded here.

BIBLIOGRAPHY

Extensive bibliographies of Early Cycladic studies can be found in C. Renfrew, *The Emergence of Civilisation* (London, 1972) and in J. Thimme, gen. ed., *Art and Culture of the Cyclades* (Chicago, 1977).

Barber, R. L. N. "Early Cycladic Marble Figures: Some Thoughts on Function." In *Cycladica: Studies in Memory of N. P. Goulandris*, edited by J. L. Fitton, pp. 10–14. London, 1984.

Barber, R. L. N., and MacGillivray, J. A. "The Early Cycladic Period: Matters of Definition and Terminology." *American Journal of Archaeology* 84 (1980): 141–57.

Bent, J. T. "Researches Among the Cyclades." *Journal of Hellenic Studies* 5 (1884): 42–58.

———. *Aegean Islands: The Cyclades, or Life Among the Insular Greeks*. London, 1885. New enlarged ed., edited by A. N. Oikonomides. Chicago, 1966.

———. "Discoveries in Asia Minor." *Journal of Hellenic Studies* 9 (1888): 82–87.

Betancourt, P., and Lawn, B. "The Cyclades and Radiocarbon Chronology." In *The Prehistoric Cyclades: Contributions to a Workshop on Cycladic Chronology Held in London, June 1983*, edited by J. A. MacGillivray and R. L. N. Barber, pp. 277–95. Edinburgh, 1984.

Bossert, E. M. "Die gestempelten Verzierungen auf frühbronzezeitlichen Gefässen der Ägäis." *Jahrbuch des Deutschen Archäologischen Instituts* 75 (1960): 1–16.

Branigan, K. *The Foundations of Palatial Crete: A Survey of Crete in the Early Bronze Age*. New York and Washington, 1970.

———. "Cycladic Figurines and Their Derivatives in Crete." *Annual of the British School of Archaeology at Athens* 66 (1971): 57–78.

———. "Metal Objects and Metal Technology of the Cycladic Culture." In *Art and Culture of the Cyclades in the Third Millennium B.C.*, edited by J. Thimme and P. Getz-Preziosi, pp. 117–22. Chicago, 1977.

Brouscari, M. "Collection Paul Canellopoulos: Antiquités Cycladiques." *Bulletin de Correspondence Hellénique* 105 (1981): 499–535.

Buchholz, H.-G., and Karageorghis, V. *Prehistoric Greece and Cyprus*. London and New York, 1973.

Caskey, J. L. "Greece, Crete and the Aegean Islands in the Early Bronze Age." In *Cambridge Ancient History*. Vol. 1, Part 2, edited by I. E. S. Edwards, C. J. Gadd, and N. G. L. Hammond, pp. 771–807. Cambridge, 1971.

———. "Marble Figurines from Ayia Irini in Keos." *Hesperia* 40 (1971): 113–26.

———. "Addenda to the Marble Figurines from Ayia Irini." *Hesperia* 43 (1974): 77–79.

Coleman, J. E. "The Chronology and Interconnections of the Cycladic Islands in the Neolithic Early Bronze." *American Journal of Archaeology* 78 (1974): 333–43.

———. "Early Cycladic Clay Vessels." In *Art and Culture of the Cyclades in the Third Millennium B.C.*, edited by J. Thimme and P. Getz-Preziosi, pp. 109–17. Chicago, 1977.

———. "Chronological and Cultural Divisions of the Early Cycladic Period: A Critical Appraisal." In *Papers in Cycladic Prehistory*, edited by J. L. Davis and J. F. Cherry, pp. 48–50. Los Angeles, 1979.

———. "Remarks on 'Terminology and Beyond.'" In *Papers in Cycladic Prehistory*, edited by J. L. Davis and J. F. Cherry, pp. 64–65. Los Angeles, 1979.

———. "'Frying Pans' of the Early Bronze Age Aegean." *American Journal of Archaeology* 89 (1985): 191–219.

Craig, H., and Craig, V. "Greek Marbles: Determination of Provenance by Isotopic Analysis." *Science* 176 (April 28, 1972): 401–3.

Davis, J. L. "A Cycladic Figure in Chicago from the 'Keros Hoard' and the Non-funereal Use of Cycladic Marble Figures." In *Cycladica: Studies in Memory of N. P. Goulandris*, edited by J. L. Fitton, pp. 15–23. London, 1984.

Davis, J. L., and Cherry, J. F., eds. *Papers in Cycladic Prehistory*. Monograph 14, Institute of Archaeology, University of California. Los Angeles, 1979.

Doumas, C. "Archaiotites kai Mnimeia Kykladon." *Archaiologikon Deltion, Chronika* 19 (1964): 409–12 (Keros/Naxos).

———. *The N. P. Goulandris Collection of Early Cycladic Art*. Athens, 1968.

———. "Notes on Early Cycladic Architecture." *Archäologischer Anzeiger*, 1972, pp. 151–70.

———. "Grave Types and Related Burial Practices During the Cycladic Early Bronze Age." In *The Explanation of Culture Change*, edited by C. Renfrew, pp. 559–63. Proceedings of a meeting of the Research Seminar in Archaeology and Related Subjects Held at the University of Sheffield. London, 1973.

———. "The Early Cycladic Period." In *History of the Hellenic World: Prehistory and Protohistory*, edited by G. A. Christopoulos and J. C. Bastias, pp. 106–15. University Park, Pennsylvania, 1974.

———. "Early Cycladic Architecture." In *Art and Culture of the Cyclades in the Third Millennium B. C.*, edited by J. Thimme and P. Getz-Preziosi, pp. 31–33. Chicago, 1977.

———. "Early Cycladic Burials." In *Art and Culture of the Cyclades in the Third Millennium B.C.*, edited by J. Thimme and P. Getz-Preziosi, pp. 33–36. Chicago, 1977.

———. "An Historical Survey of Early Cycladic Research." In *Art and Culture of the Cyclades in the Third Millennium B.C.*, edited by J. Thimme and P. Getz-Preziosi, pp. 185–91. Chicago, 1977.

———. *Early Bronze Age Burial Habits in the Cyclades*. Studies in Mediterranean Archaeology, vol. 48. Göteborg, 1977.

———. "Prehistoric Cycladic People in Crete." *Athens Annals of Archaeology* 9 (1977): 69–80.

———. *Cycladic Art: Ancient Sculpture and Ceramics of the Aegean from the N. P. Goulandris Collection*. National Gallery of Art. Washington, D.C., 1979.

———. *Cycladic Art: Ancient Sculpture and Pottery from the N. P. Goulandris Collection*. British Museum. London, 1983.

Dümmler, F. "Mittheilungen von den griechischen Inseln. I. Reste vorgriechischer Bevölkerung auf den Kykladen." *Athenische Mitteilungen* 11 (1886): 15–46.

Erlenmeyer, M.-L., and Erlenmeyer, H. "Von der frühen Bildkunst der Kykladen." *Antike Kunst* 8 (1965): 59–71.

Evans, J. D., and Renfrew, C. *Excavations at Saliagos Near Antiparos*. Annual of the British School of Archaeology at Athens, Supplementary Vol. 5. London, 1968.

Fellmann, B. "Frühe Idole in den Münchner Antikensammlungen." *Münchner Jahrbuch der Bildenen Kunst* 32 (1981): 7–24.

Fitton, J. L. "Perditus and Perdita: Two Drawings of Cycladic Figurines in the Greek and Roman Department of the British Museum." In *Cycladica: Studies in Memory of N. P. Goulandris*, edited by J. L. Fitton, pp. 76–87. London, 1984.

———, ed. *Cycladica: Studies in Memory of N. P. Goulandris*. Proceedings of the Seventh British Museum Classical Colloquium, June 1983. London, 1984.

Fotou, V. "Les sites de l'époque néolithique et de l'age du bronze à Naxos (recherches archéologiques jusqu'en 1980)." In *Les Cyclades: Matériaux pour une étude de géographie historique*, edited by C. and G. Rougement. Paris, 1983.

Gale, N. H., and Stos Gale, Z. "Cycladic Lead and Silver Metallurgy." *Annual of the British School of Archaeology at Athens* 76 (1981): 169–224.

———. "Lead and Silver in the Ancient Aegean." *Scientific American*, July 1981, pp. 176–92.

Getz-Preziosi, P. "An Early Cycladic Sculptor." *Antike Kunst* 18 (1975): 47–50.

———. "Early Cycladic Stone Vases." In *Art and Culture of the Cyclades in the Third Millennium B.C.*, edited by J. Thimme and P. Getz-Preziosi, pp. 95–108. Chicago, 1977.

——. "Cycladic Sculptors and Their Methods." In *Art and Culture of the Cyclades in the Third Millennium B.C.*, edited by J. Thimme and P. Getz-Preziosi, pp. 71–82. Chicago, 1977.

——. "Addenda to the Cycladic Exhibition in Karlsruhe." *Archäologische Anzeiger*, 1978, pp. 1–11.

——. "The Hunter/Warrior Figure in Early Cycladic Marble Sculpture." In *Papers in Cycladic Prehistory*, edited by J. L. Davis and J. F. Cherry, pp. 87–96. Los Angeles, 1979.

——. "The Male Figure in Early Cycladic Sculpture." *Metropolitan Museum Journal* 15 (1980): 5–33.

——. "Risk and Repair in Early Cycladic Sculpture." *Metropolitan Museum Journal* 16 (1981): 5–32.

——. "The 'Keros Hoard': Introduction to an Early Cycladic Enigma." In *Antidoron Jürgen Thimme*, edited by D. Metzler and B. Otto, pp. 37–44. Karlsruhe, 1982.

——. "The Goulandris Master." In *Cycladic Art: Ancient Sculpture and Pottery from the N. P. Goulandris Collection*, by C. Doumas, pp. 45–48. London, 1983.

——. "Five Sculptors in the Goulandris Collection." In *Cycladica: Studies in Memory of N. P. Goulandris*, edited by J. L. Fitton, pp. 48–71. London, 1984.

——. "Nine Fragments of Early Cycladic Sculpture in Southern California." *J. Paul Getty Museum Journal* 12 (1984): 5–20.

——. *Early Cycladic Sculpture: An Introduction.* Malibu, 1985.

——. *The Goulandris Master.* Athens, forthcoming.

Greek Art of the Aegean Islands. Metropolitan Museum of Art, New York, 1979.

Gwinnett, A. J., and Gorelik, L. "An Ancient Repair on a Cycladic Statuette Analyzed Using Scanning Electron Microscopy." *Journal of Field Archaeology* 10 (1983): 378–84.

Hatzi-Vallianou, D. "Archaiotites kai Mnimeia Kykladon." *Archaiologikon Deltion, Chronika* 30 (1975): 321 (Keros).

Havelock, C. M. "Cycladic Sculpture: A Prelude to Greek Art?" *Archaeology*, July/August 1981, pp. 29–36.

Higgins, R. A. "A Cycladic Idol." *The British Museum Quarterly* 36 (1972): 118.

Höckmann, O. "Zu Formenschatz und Ursprung der Schematischen Kykladenplastik." *Berliner Jahrbuch für Vor- und Frühgeschichte* 8 (1968): 45–74.

——. "The Cyclades and Their Eastern Neighbours." In *Art and Culture of the Cyclades in the Third Millennium B.C.*, edited by J. Thimme and P. Getz-Preziosi, pp. 155–63. Chicago, 1977.

——. "The Cyclades and the Western Mediterranean." In *Art and Culture of the Cyclades in the Third Millennium B.C.*, edited by J. Thimme and P. Getz-Preziosi, pp. 163–72. Chicago, 1977.

——. "Cycladic Religion." In *Art and Culture of the Cyclades in the Third Millennium B.C.*, edited by J. Thimme and P. Getz-Preziosi, pp. 37–52. Chicago, 1977.

——. "The Neolithic and Early Bronze Age Idols of Anatolia." In *Art and Culture of the Cyclades in the Third Millenniun B.C.*, edited by J. Thimme and P. Getz-Preziosi, pp. 173–84. Chicago, 1977.

——. "Zur Kykladischen Harfenspielerfigur von Keros." *Boreas: Münstersche Beiträge zur Archäologie* 5 (1982): 33–48.

Hope-Simpson, R., and Dickinson, O. *A Gazeteer of Aegean Civilisation in the Bronze Age, Vol. I: The Mainland and Islands.* Studies in Mediterranean Archaeology, vol. 52. Göteborg, 1979.

Köhler, U. "Praehistorisches von den griechischen Inseln." *Athenische Mittheilungen* 9 (1884): 156–59.

Kontoleon, N. M. "Anaskaphai Naxou." *Praktika tis en Athinais Archaiologikis Etaireias tou Etous 1970*, pp. 146–55.

——. "Anaskaphai Naxou." *Praktika tis en Athinais Archaiologikis Etaireias tou Etous 1971*, pp. 172–80.

——. "Naxos." *Ergon tis Archaiologikis Etaireias kata to 1971*, pp. 174–85.

——. "Anaskaphai Naxou." *Praktika tis en Athinais Archaiologikis Etaireias tou Etous 1972*, pp. 143–55.

——. "Naxos." *Ergon tis Archaiologikis Etaireias kata to 1972*, pp. 88–100.

Lambrinoudakis, V. "Anaskaphai Naxou." *Praktika tis en Athinais Archaiologikis Etaireias tou Etous 1976*, pp. 295–308.

Leekley, D., and Noyes, R. *Archaeological Excavations in the Greek Islands.* Park Ridge, New Jersey, 1975.

MacGillivray, J. A., and Barber, R. L. N., eds. *The Prehistoric Cyclades: Contributions to a Workshop on Cycladic Chronology.* Edinburgh, 1984.

Majewski, K. *Figuralna plastyka Cycladska. Geneza i rozwoj form.* (German summary: "Die Kykladische figurale Plastik, ihre Genesis und Entwicklung," pp. 102–17.) Archivum Towarzystawa we Lwow 6, 1935.

———. "Idole cycladzkie w nowszych badaniach (1935–1970)." *Archaeologia* 22 (1971): 1–37. (English summary: "Cycladic Idols in More Recent Research," pp. 39–41.)

Matthäus, H. "Ein Kykladenidol in Marburg: Bemerkungen zur Chronologie der kykladischen Frühbronzezeit." *Archäologische Anzeiger*, 1980, pp. 149–65.

Melas, E., ed. *Greek Islands*. Translated by R. Stockman. New York, 1985.

Mylonas, G. E. *Aghios Kosmas: An Early Bronze Age Settlement and Cemetery in Attica*. Princeton, 1959.

Oustinoff, E. "The Manufacture of Cycladic Figurines: A Practical Approach." In *Cycladica: Studies in Memory of N. P. Goulandris*, edited by J. L. Fitton, pp. 38–47. London, 1984.

Ouy-Parczewska, K., and Ouy, G. "Enquête iconométrique sur la statuaire égéene du 3ᵉ millenaire. . . ." *Jahrbuch der Staatlichen Kunstsammlungen in Baden-Württemberg* 19 (1982): 7–26.

Papathanasopoulos, G. A. "Kykladika Naxou." *Archaiologikon Deltion, Meletai* 17 (1961–62): 104–51.

Papathanas[s]opoulos, G. *Neolithic and Cycladic Civilization*. Athens, 1981.

Philippson, A. *Das ägäische Meer und seine Inselwelt. Die griechischer Landschaften*, vol. 4. Frankfurt am Main, 1959.

Preziosi, P. G., and Weinberg, S. S. "Evidence for Painted Details in Early Cycladic Sculpture." *Antike Kunst* 13 (1970): 4–12.

Renfrew, C. "Cycladic Metallurgy and the Aegean Early Bronze Age." *American Journal of Archaeology* 71 (1967): 1–20.

———. "The Development and Chronology of the Early Cycladic Figurines." *American Journal of Archaeology* 73 (1969): 1–32.

———. *The Emergence of Civilisation: The Cyclades and the Aegean in the Third Millennium B.C.* London, 1972.

———. "The Cycladic Culture." In *Art and Culture of the Cyclades in the Third Millennium B.C.*, edited by J. Thimme and P. Getz-Preziosi, pp. 17–30. Chicago, 1977.

———. "The Typology and Chronology of Cycladic Sculpture." In *Art and Culture of the Cyclades in the Third Millennium B.C.*, edited by J. Thimme and P. Getz-Preziosi, pp. 59–71. Chicago, 1977.

———. "Terminology and Beyond." In *Papers in Cycladic Prehistory*, edited by J. L. Davis and J. F. Cherry, pp. 51–63. Los Angeles, 1979.

———. "Introduction." In *Cycladic Art: Ancient Sculpture and Pottery from the N. P. Goulandris Collection*, by C. Doumas, pp. 9–26. London, 1983.

———. "From Pelos to Syros: Kapros Grave D and the Kampos Group." In *The Prehistoric Cyclades: Contributions to a Workshop on Cycladic Chronology*, edited by J. A. MacGillivray and R. L. N. Barber, pp. 41–53. Edinburgh, 1984.

———. "Speculations on the Use of Early Cycladic Sculpture." In *Cycladica: Studies in Memory of N. P. Goulandris*, edited by J. L. Fitton, pp. 24–30. London, 1984.

Renfrew, C.; Cann, J. R.; and Dixon, J. L. "Obsidian in the Aegean." *Annual of the British School of Archaeology at Athens* 60 (1965): 225–47.

Renfrew, C., and Peacey, J. S. "Aegean Marble: A Petrological Study." *Annual of the British School of Archaeology at Athens* 63 (1968): 45–66.

Rougement, C., and Rougement, G., eds. *Les Cyclades: Matériaux pour une étude de géographie historique*. Table ronde réunie à l'Université de Dijon les 11, 12, et 13 mars, 1982. Editions du Centre National de la Recherche Scientifique. Paris, 1983.

Sapouna-Sakellarakis, E. "Cycladic Jewelry." In *Art and Culture of the Cyclades in the Third Millennium B.C.*, edited by J. Thimme and P. Getz-Preziosi, pp. 123–29. Chicago, 1977.

Sakellarakis, I. A. "Anaskaphi Archanon." *Praktika tis en Athinais Archaiologikis Etaireias tou Etous 1972*, pp. 310–53.

———. "The Cyclades and Crete." In *Art and Culture of the Cyclades in the Third Millennium B.C.*, edited by J. Thimme and P. Getz-Preziosi, pp. 145–54. Chicago, 1977.

———. "Anaskaphi Archanon." *Praktika tis en Athinais Archaiologikis Etaireias tou Etous 1980*, pp. 400–401.

Samson, A. *Manika: Mia Protoelladiki Poli sti Chalkida, I*. Chalkis, 1985. (English summary: "Manika I: An Early Helladic Settlement and Cemetery Near Chalkis," pp. 377–92.)

Schefold, K. "Heroen und Nymphen in Kykladen-gräbern." *Antike Kunst* 8 (1965): 87–90.

Thimme, J. "Die religiöse Bedeutung der Kykladeni-dole." *Antike Kunst* 8 (1965): 72–86.

——. "Ein monumentales Kykladenidol in Karls-ruhe: Zur Typologie und Deutung der Idole." *Jahr-buch der Staatlicher Kunstsammlungen in Baden-Württemberg* 12 (1975): 7–20.

——. Catalogue introductions, entries, and appen-dices. In *Art and Culture of the Cyclades in the Third Millennium B.C.*, edited by J. Thimme and P. Getz-Preziosi, pp. 415–588. Chicago, 1977.

——. "Badisches Landesmuseum: Neuerwerbungen 1982. Antike." *Jahrbuch der Staatlichen Kunst-sammlungen in Baden-Württemberg* 20 (1983): 196–202.

Thimme, J., gen. ed., and Getz-Preziosi, P., trans. and ed. of English ed. *Art and Culture of the Cyclades in the Third Millennium B.C.* Chicago, 1977.

Treuil, R. *La Néolithique et le Bronze Ancien Egéens. Les problèmes stratigraphiques et chronologiques, les techniques, les hommes.* Bibliothèque des Écoles Françaises d'Athènes et de Rome 248. Paris, 1983.

Tsountas, C. "Kykladika I." *Archaiologike Ephe-meris*, 1898, cols. 137–212.

——. "Kykladika II." *Archaiologike Ephemeris*, 1899, cols. 73–134.

Vermeule, E. T. *Greece in the Bronze Age.* Chicago and London, 1964.

Weinberg, S. S. "Neolithic Figurines and Aegean In-terrelations." *American Journal of Archaeology* 85 (1951): 121–33.

——. "The Relative Chronology of the Aegean in the Stone and Early Bronze Ages." In *Chronologies in Old World Archaeology*, edited by R. W. Ehrich, pp. 285–320. Chicago, 1965.

——. "Anthropomorphic Stone Figurines from Neo-lithic Greece." In *Art and Culture of the Cyclades in the Third Millennium B.C.*, edited by J. Thimme and P. Getz-Preziosi, pp. 52–58. Chicago, 1977.

Wolters, P., "Marmorkopf aus Amorgos." *Athe-nische Mitteilungen* 16 (1891): 47–58.

Zafiropoulou, F. "Cycladic Finds from Keros." *Athens Annals of Archaeology* 1 (1968): 97–100.

Zapheiropoulou, P. "Kyklades. Anaskaphikai Erev-nai—Periodeiai." *Archaiologikon Deltion, Chronika* 23 (1968): 381 (Keros).

——. "Protokykladika Evrimata ex Ano Koupho-nisi." *Athens Annals of Archaeology* 3 (1970): 48–51. (English summary: "Early Cycladic Finds from Kouphonisi," p. 51.)

——. "Ostraka ek Kerou." *Athens Annals of Ar-chaeology* 8 (1975): 79–85. (English summary: "Some Fragments from Keros," p. 85.)

——. "Protokykladika Eidolia tis Naxou." In *Stili: Tomos eis Mnimin Nikolaou Kontoleontos*, pp. 532–40. Athens, 1979.

——. "Un cimitière du Cycladique Ancien à Epano Kouphonissi." In *Les Cyclades: Matériaux pour une étude de géographie historique*, edited by C. and G. Rougement. Paris, 1983.

——. "The Chronology of the Kampos Group." In *The Prehistoric Cyclades: Contributions to a Work-shop on Cycladic Chronology*, edited by J. A. Mac-Gillivray and R. L. N. Barber, pp. 31–40. Edinburgh, 1984.

Zervos, C. *L'art des Cyclades du début à la fin de l'age du bronze, 2500–1100 avant notre ère.* Paris, 1957.

INDEX

Abdominal grooves, 49, 51, 71, 78, 126–27, 129; fig. 27

Abstract figures. *See* Apeiranthos type; Schematic figures

Amorgos. *See* Figures, find-places of

Ano Kouphonisi. *See* Figures, find-places of

Antiparos. *See* Figures, find-places of

Apeiranthos type, 29, 60–61, 64, 134, 136; fig. 3

Arm perforations, 13, 17, 81, 122; figs. 8, 9*e*, 17*b*

Arms, folded arrangement of, 13–14, 17, 47, 49; fig. 25

Ashmolean Master, 117–20, 139

Athens Museum Master, 78–82, 126

Attenuation. *See* Figures, narrowing of large

Awl, 11, 35–36, 77, 81

Bastis Master, 108–13, 119, 139, 140

Berlin Master, 120–23, 140

Boring tool. *See* Awl

Chalandriani variety, 17–18, 39, 67–68, 135–36; figs. 3, 5*j*, 7*g*, 9, 11*e–h*, 18, 25*d*, 27*g*, 28*d*. *See also* Dresden Master; Stafford Master

Chronology, Early Cycladic, 7–8

Compass, hypothetical use of, 37–39, 41; figs. 15–16, 17*a*, 19–20, 24, 33–34. *See also* Design canons

Copenhagen Master, 88–90, 139

Craft specialization, 30, 36, 54–56, 65, 99–100, 139

Crete. *See* Figures, find-places of

Cupbearer type, 20, 23, 29

Damage, purposeful, 33

Death, attitudes toward, 5, 31

Delos. *See* Figures, find-places of

Design canons, 36; three-part (EC I), 37, chap. 4; four-part (EC I), fig. 15*b*; three-part (EC II), 39, 127, fig. 18*b*; four-part (EC II), 38, chaps. 5–6, fig. 16; five-part (EC II), 39, 124, fig. 18*a*, fig. 51

Despotiko. *See* Figures, find-places of

Dokathismata variety, 17, 21, 39, 61, 68, chap. 6, 135–36; figs. 3, 5*i*, 7*f*, 8*c–f*, 11*d*, 17, 26*b*, 27*f*

Doumas Master, 63–64, 71–74, 108, 126

Dresden Master, 126–30

Drios type, 11; fig. 27*e*

Emery, 5, 35, 134

Figures: late find-contexts of, ix, 32, 34, 129; meaning and function of, 31–33; narrowing of large, 52, 89, 94, 98; objects found with, 5, 7, 26–27, 29–30, 32–33; relationship to sculpture of other places, 33–34. *See also* Marble vessels

Figures, find-places of (actual or reputed)

—Amorgos, 30, 33, 81–82, 92, 108, 120, 130, chap. 7 esp. 133; Dokathismata, 29, 108; Grave 14, Dokathismata, 59, 60, 62; Kapsala, 29; Kornoviglia, 108

—Ano Kouphonisi, 33; deposit, 60, 66

—Antiparos, 81; Grave 117, Krassades, 27, 59, 60, 62

—Crete, 19, 92

—Delos (Rheneia), 78

—Despotiko: Grave 129, Leivadia, 27

—Ios, 130

—Keos, 30, 129; Ayia Irini, 32, 129
—Keros, 30, 32, 61, 67, 108, 120, chap. 7 esp. 133–40; Daskaleio Islet, 32; "Keros hoard," 90, 95, 98, 108, 112–13, 117, 120, 122, 126, 130, chap. 7 esp. 134–38; site opposite Daskaleio, 108, 117, 126, 136–39
—Melos, 30
—Naxos, 30, 60–61, 67, 81, 86–87, 95, 98, 108, 112, 120, 126, chap. 7 esp. 134, 140; Grave 5, Akrotiri, 60, 63, 73–74; Grave 20, Akrotiri, 60, 63; Aplomata, 29, 54, 97–98, 113; Grave 13, Aplomata, 29, 60–61, 64–65, 83; Grave 15, Aplomata, 61, 66; Grave 23, Aplomata, 61, 108; Grave 27, Aplomata, 61; Karvounolakkoi, 27; Grave 26, Louros Athalassou, 60; Panormos, 107; Phionta, 67, 98, 112–13; Phyrroges, 27; Grave 28, Phyrroges, 98; Spedos, 67, 87; Grave 10, Spedos, 60, 65; Grave 16, Spedos, 61
—Paros, 30, 72, 81, 86, 108, 126, chap. 7 esp. 133; Grave 23, Glypha, 60, 71–72; Lefkes, 72; Grave 6, Plastiras, 74; Grave 9, Plastiras, 27, 60, 63, 72, 74; Grave 103, Pyrgos, 27, 59–60, 62
—Syros, 30; Chalandriani, 29; Grave 307, Chalandriani, 61
—Thera, 30
Fingers: presence and/or neatness of, dependent on size, 51–52, 65, 72, 77, 81, 104, 116
Fitzwilliam Louros Master, 63
Fitzwilliam Master, 90–92
Folded-arm arrangement. See Arms, folded arrangement of
Frequency of marble objects, 27, 29–30, 130, 141

"Golden triangle." See Harmonic system
Goulandris Hunter/Warrior Master, 67–68, 126, 128; figs. 9f, 11g
Goulandris Master, 66, 99–113, 119, 134–36, 140

Harmonic system, 42–47, 62, chaps. 4–6
Harp player type, 20, 27, 30–31, 40–41, 61, 66–67; fig. 21
Headgear, 20, 74
Hunter/Warrior figures, 20, 23, 61, 67–68. See also Goulandris Hunter/Warrior Master

Incisions: false starts, 49, 124; overruns, 47, 49, 92, 124
Ios. See Figures, find-places of
Israel Museum Master, 86–87, 89, 140

Kapsala variety, 16, 29, 54, 60, 64–66; figs. 5d–e, 7c, 29. See also Israel Museum Master; Kontoleon Master
Keos. See Figures, find-places of
Keros. See Figures, find-places of

"Keros hoard." See Figures, find-places of, Keros
Kontoleon Master, 65, 83–87, 89, 140
Koumasa variety, 18–19, 92; fig. 10

Lead as material for figures, 9
Louros type, 11, 60, 62–63; figs. 5b, 11c, 13a, 23c, 27d

Male figures, 20, 23, 71, 78; figs. 8e, 11, 34. See also Cupbearer type; Harp player type; Hunter/Warrior figures; Three-figure group; Woodwind player type
Marble, 5, 7, 134; alabasterlike, 88, 90; gray, on Keros, 138; intractable medium, 36; islands lacking, 30, 133; mottled, 117; variety peculiar to some Kapsala figures from Naxos, 16, 64, 86
Marble vessels, 24–27, 29, 33, 74, 78, 81, 99, 134, 136–38
Master, definition of, 62
Melos. See Figures, find-places of
Mending. See Repairs, ancient
Metropolitan Museum Master, 74–80
Missouri Master, 63, 82; fig. 23a–b

Narrowing of large figures. See Figures, narrowing of large
Naxos. See Figures, find-places of
Naxos Museum Master, 95–99, 113, 135, 139–40
Neolithic figures, 9–10; figs. 3, 4a

Obsidian, 4–5, 26, 30, 35, 74, 134, 136–37

Painted details or paint ghosts, 53–54, 85, 87, 104–7, 135; figs. 29, 42–45
Paros. See Figures, find-places of
Planning of figures. See Design canons
Plastiras type, 9–11, 13, 51–53, 60, 63–64, chap. 4; figs. 4b, 5a, 7a, 8a–b, 11a–b, 15a–b, 23b, 27b–c, 28a
"Postcanonical" figures, 18
"Postpartum wrinkles." See Abdominal grooves
Precanonical type, 13, 52, 57; figs. 5c, 6, 7b, 28b
Pregnant state, depiction of, 49, 57, 67, 90, 109, 115, 117, 121; fig. 26. See also Abdominal grooves
Pumice: material for figures, 9; possible use as smoothing agent, 36

Repairs, ancient, 10–11, 13, 19, 31–32, 77, 79, 85; figs. 4b, 6d, 28a, 32, 33a–b

Schematic figures (EC I), 10, 60, 62–63; fig. 27a
Schuster Master, 115–17, 119, 121–22, 134–36
Sculptors' names, 147n.49

Seated female figures, 23, 29, 41, 60, 64, 66–67; fig. 30

Shell as material for figures, 9, 63–64

Shrines, possible, 26, 138–39

Size: possible controlling factors of, 33, 52; possible use of system of measurement to determine, 52–53, 95–96, 100–101

Spedos variety, 16; on Crete, 19

—Early, 16, 57, 60–61, 64–66; figs. 5f–g, 7d, 16, 25a, 25c, 26a, 28c. See also Copenhagen Master; Fitzwilliam Master; Israel Museum Master

—Late, 17, 67; figs. 5h, 7e, 25b. See also Bastis Master; Goulandris Master; Naxos Museum Master; Schuster Master; Steiner Master

Stafford Master, 123–25, 134–35, 140

Standardized system of measurement, possible use of, 52–53, 95–96, 100–101

Steiner Master, 92–95, 98, 113, 135, 139

Stephanos Master, 62

Syros. See Figures, find-places of

Thera. See Figures, find-places of

Three-figure group, 20, 23, 46–47, 57–58; fig. 24

Tools, figure-making, 20, 35–36. See also Awl; Emery; Pumice

Traditional formula. See Design canons

Tsountas Master, 68–69; fig. 23g

Two-figure types: "tandem," 23, 39–40, 57, 91; figs. 12a, 19; "side-by-side," 23, 61; fig. 12b–c

Violin figures. See Schematic figures

Wood as possible material for figures, 9–10, 31, 40–41

Woodwind player type, 20, 40, 61, 67; fig. 20

PLATES

A   B

PLATE I. Plastiras-type figures of the Early Cycladic I phase

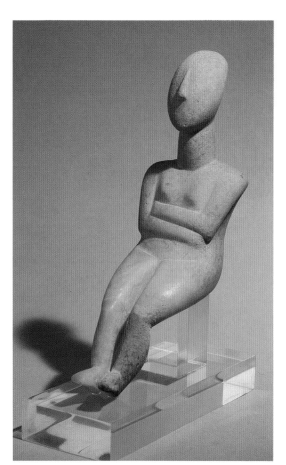

PLATE II.
Special figures of the Early Cycladic II phase

A

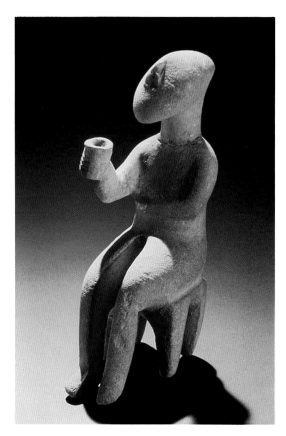

B

C

A

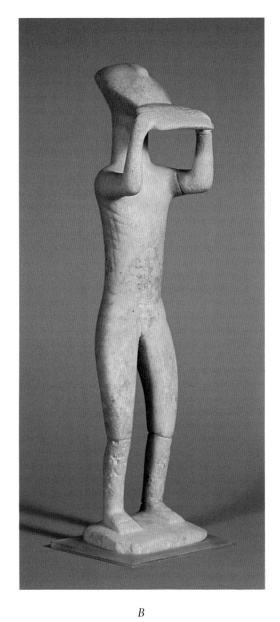

B

PLATE III. Musician figures

A

B

PLATE IV. Marble vases of the Early Cycladic I phase

C

D

A

B

PLATE V. Figure with "cradle" and three marble vases of the Early Cycladic II phase

C

D

A

B

PLATE VI. Figures with painted details

PLATE VII. Figures with painted (A, C, D) or unusual carved detail (B)

A

PLATE VIII. Musician groups of the Early Cycladic II phase

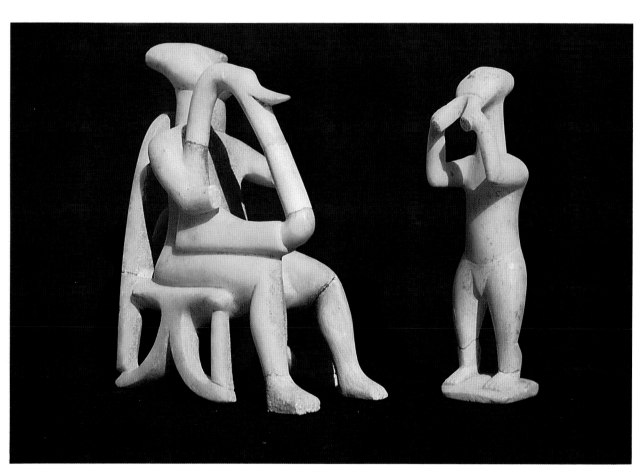

B

A

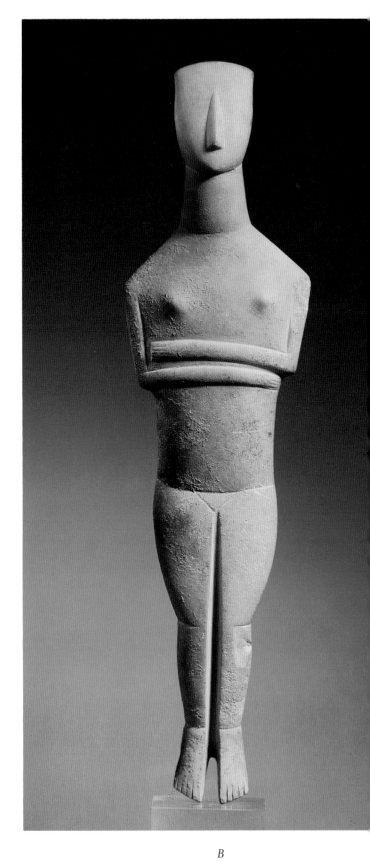

B

PLATE IX. Works attributed to the Goulandris Master

PLATE X. A nearly life-size figure

PLATE XI. Head of an unusually large, elongated figure

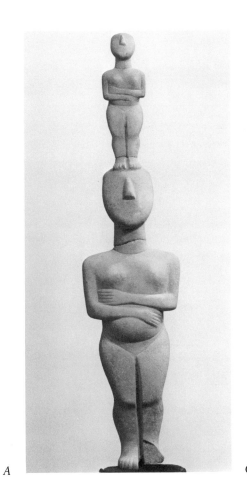

A

B

C

C

PLATE 1. One-piece compositions with two and three figures

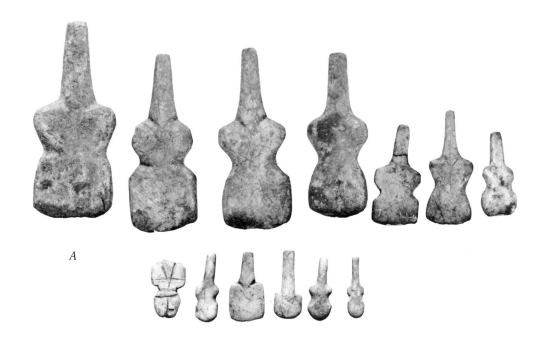

A

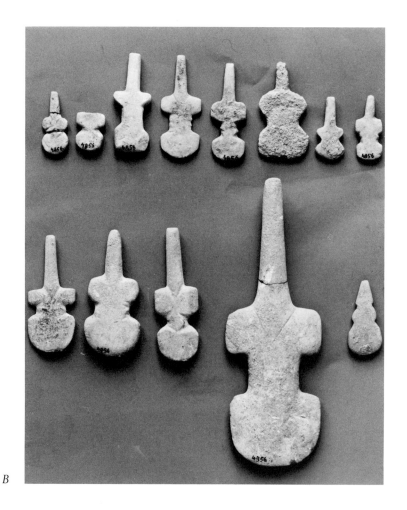

B

PLATE 2. Groups of figures from graves of the Early Cycladic I phase

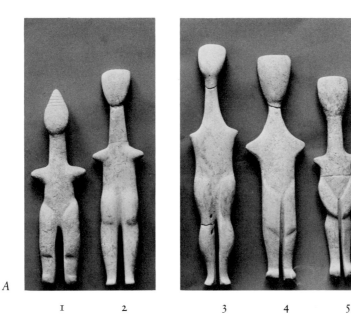

A

1   2   3   4   5

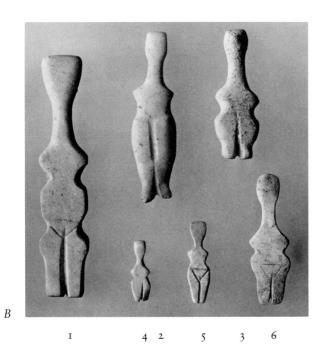

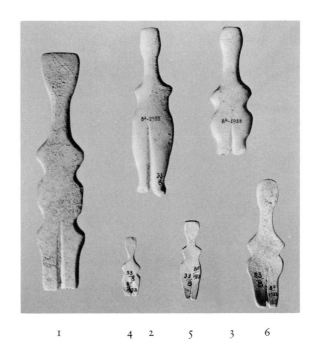

B

1   4   2   5   3   6   1   4   2   5   3   6

PLATE 3. Groups of figures from graves of the transitional phase

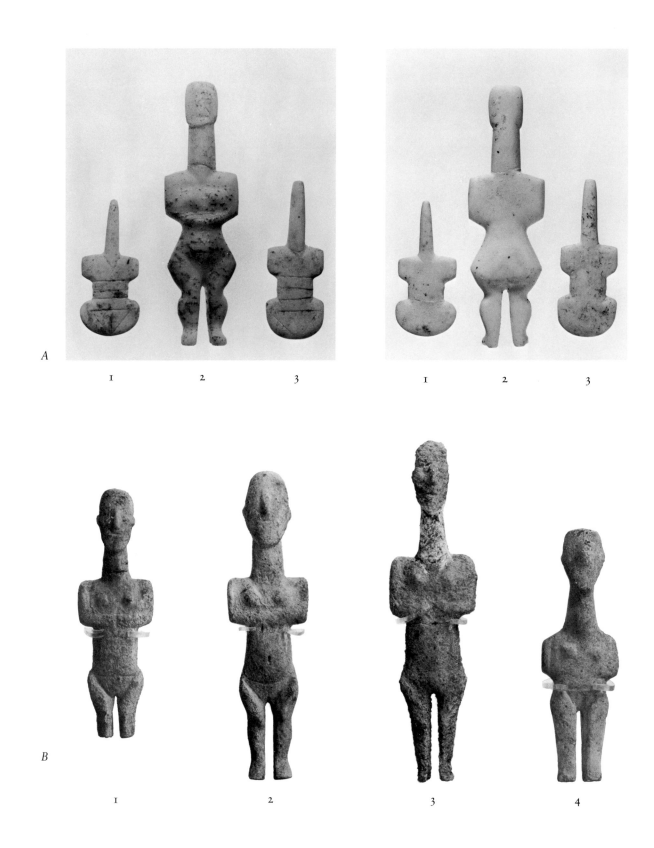

PLATE 4. Groups of figures from graves of the Early Cycladic I phase

I   I   I

2   2   2

PLATE 5. Two of three figures said to be from a grave on Naxos

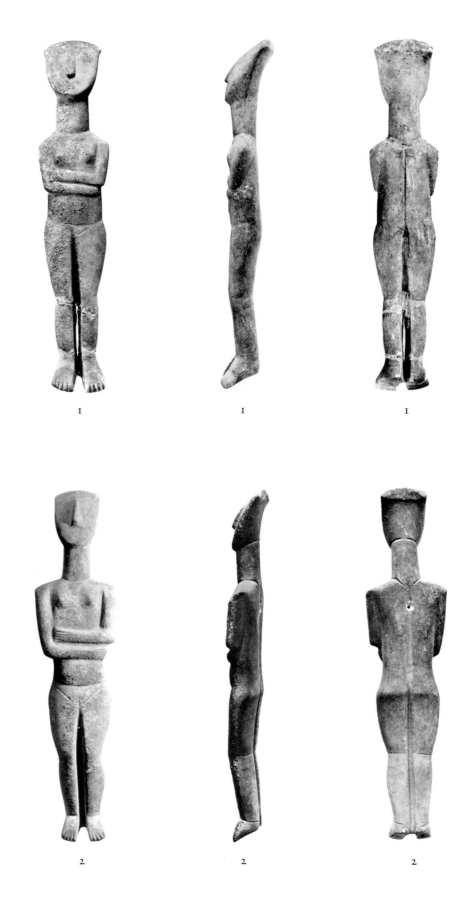

I   I   I

2   2   2

PLATE 6. The pair of figures from grave 10 at Spedos on Naxos

1   2

1   2

PLATE 7. A pair of harp players said to have been found together

1

2

1

2

PLATE 8. A pair of harp players said to have been found together

1

2

1

2

PLATE 9. A pair of harpers said to have been found in a grave on Thera

I

2

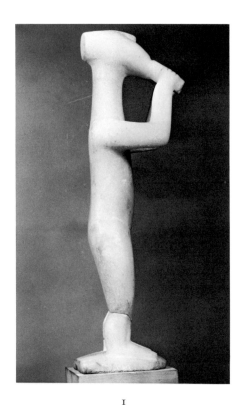

I

2

PLATE 10. The double pipes player and harper from a grave on Keros

A

1

2

B

A

3

4

C

PLATE II. A group of four figures said to have been found together on Naxos (*A*) and two related figures (*B*, *C*)

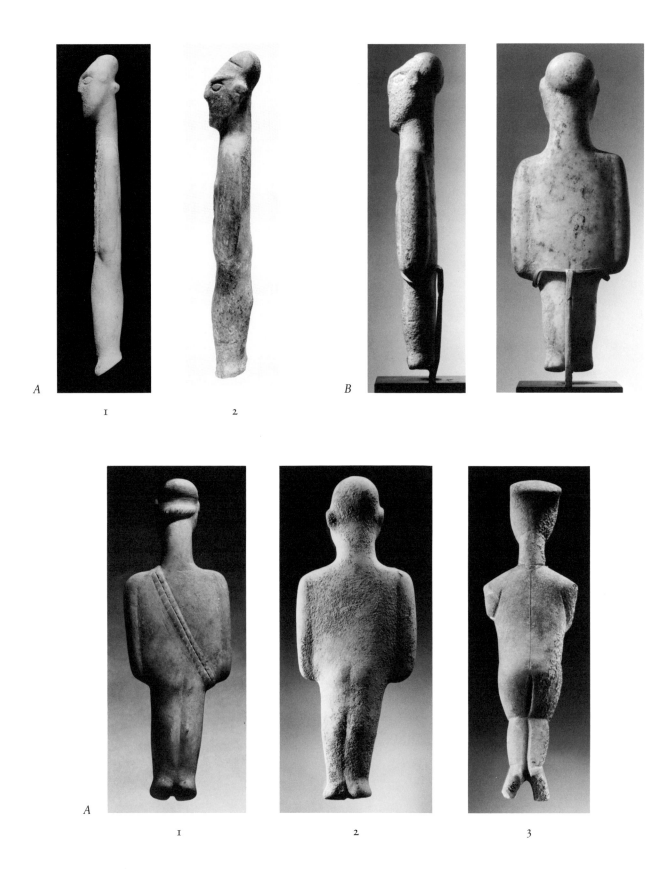

PLATE 12. Three of four figures said to have been found together on Naxos (*A*) and a related figure (*B*)

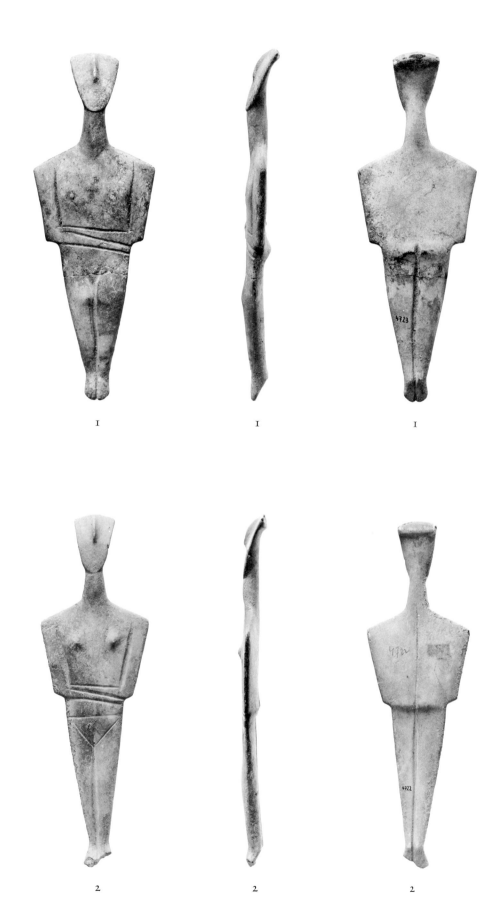

1   1   1

2   2   2

PLATE 13. The pair of figures from grave 14 at Dokathismata on Amorgos

[1] [2] [3]

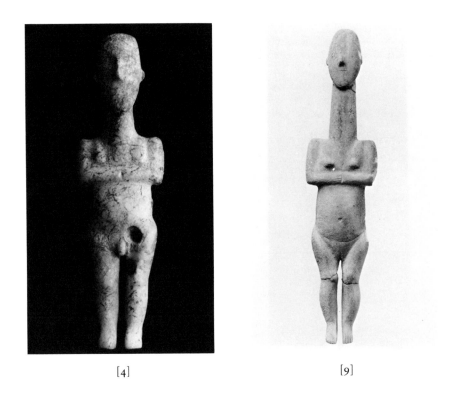

[4] [9]

PLATE 14. Works attributed to the Doumas Master

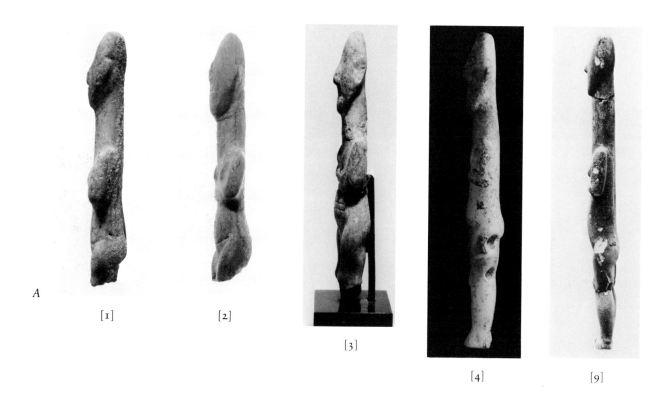

A

[1]   [2]   [3]   [4]   [9]

B

[2]   [3]   [4]   [9]

PLATE 15. Works attributed to the Doumas Master

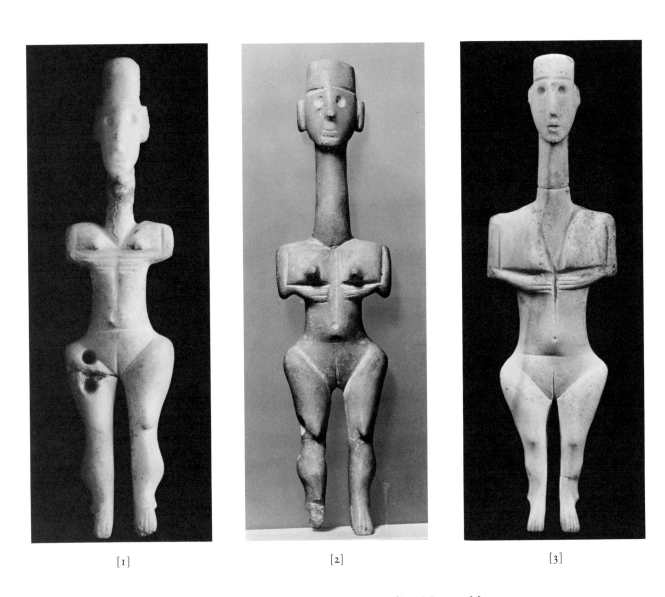

[1]   [2]   [3]

PLATE 16. Works attributed to the Metropolitan Museum Master

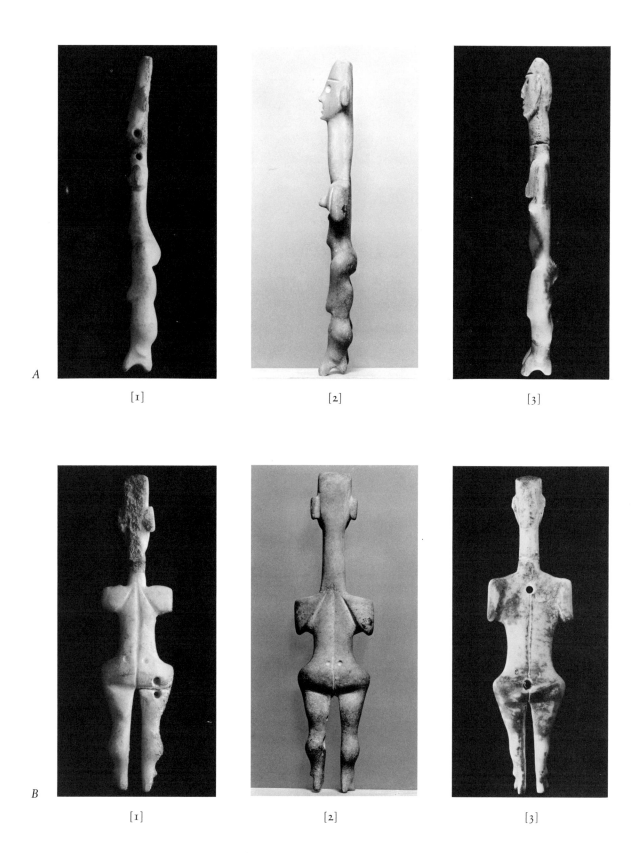

A

[1] [2] [3]

B

[1] [2] [3]

PLATE 17. Works attributed to the Metropolitan Museum Master

[1]

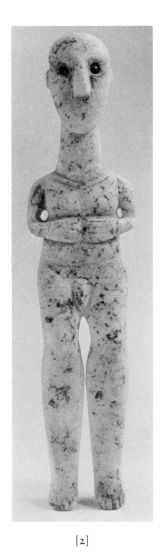

[2]

[3]

PLATE 18. Works attributed to the Athens Museum Master

[2]   [4]

PLATE 19. Works attributed to the Athens Museum Master

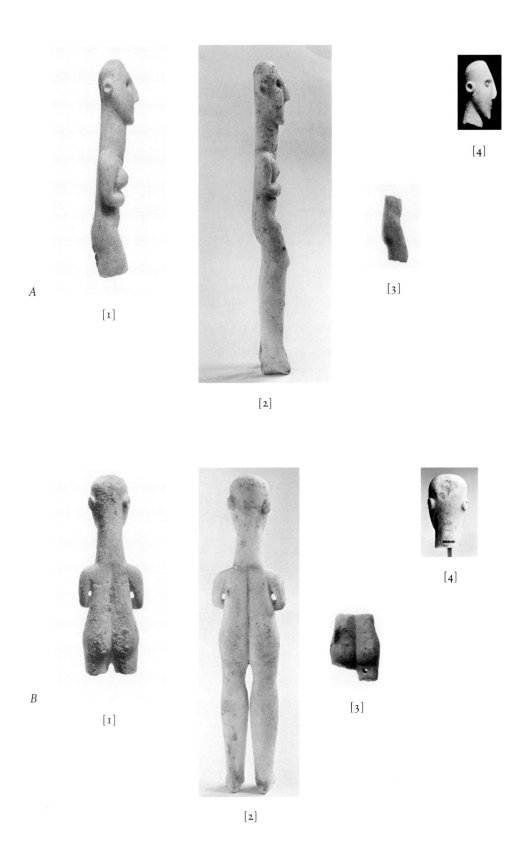

A

[1]

[2]

[3]

[4]

B

[1]

[2]

[3]

[4]

PLATE 20. Works attributed to the Athens Museum Master

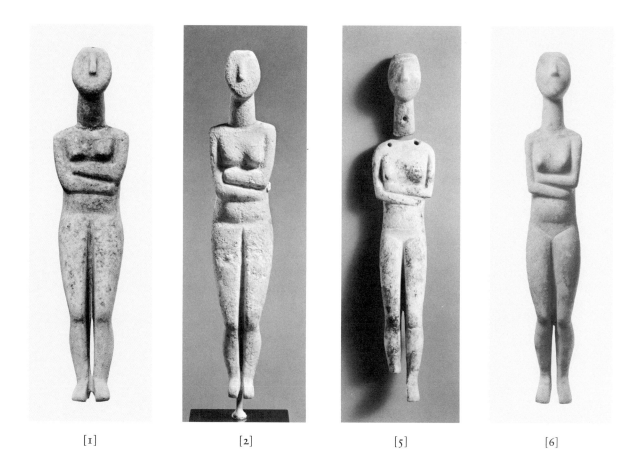

[1]   [2]   [5]   [6]

PLATE 21. Works attributed to the Kontoleon Master

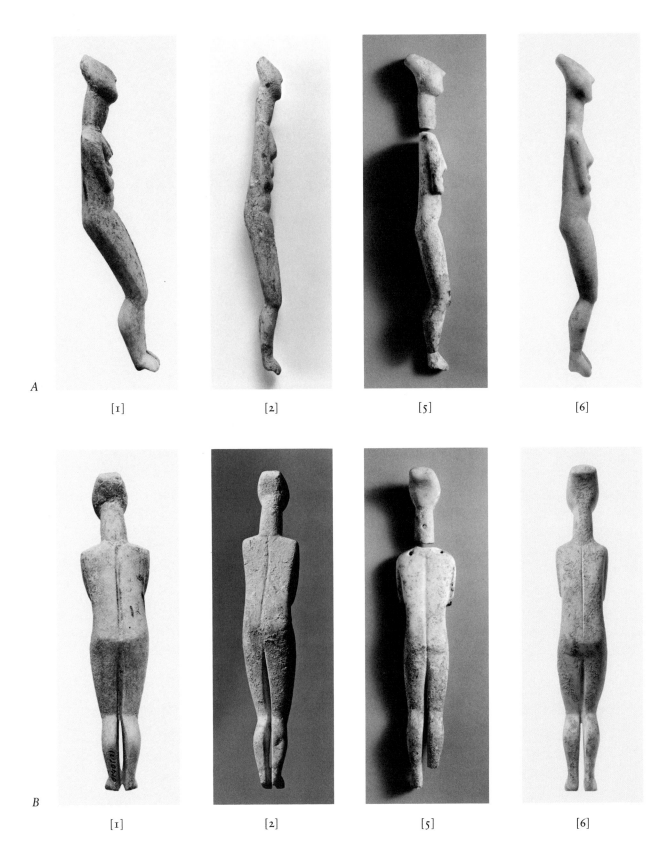

A

[1]   [2]   [5]   [6]

B

[1]   [2]   [5]   [6]

PLATE 22. Works attributed to the Kontoleon Master

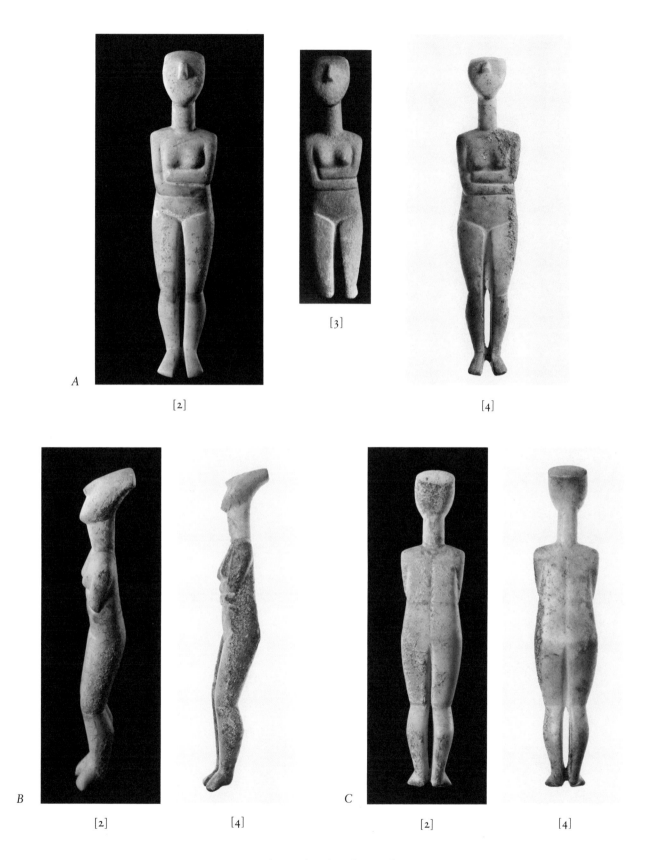

A [2] [3] [4]

B [2] [4]

C [2] [4]

PLATE 23. Works attributed to the Israel Museum Master

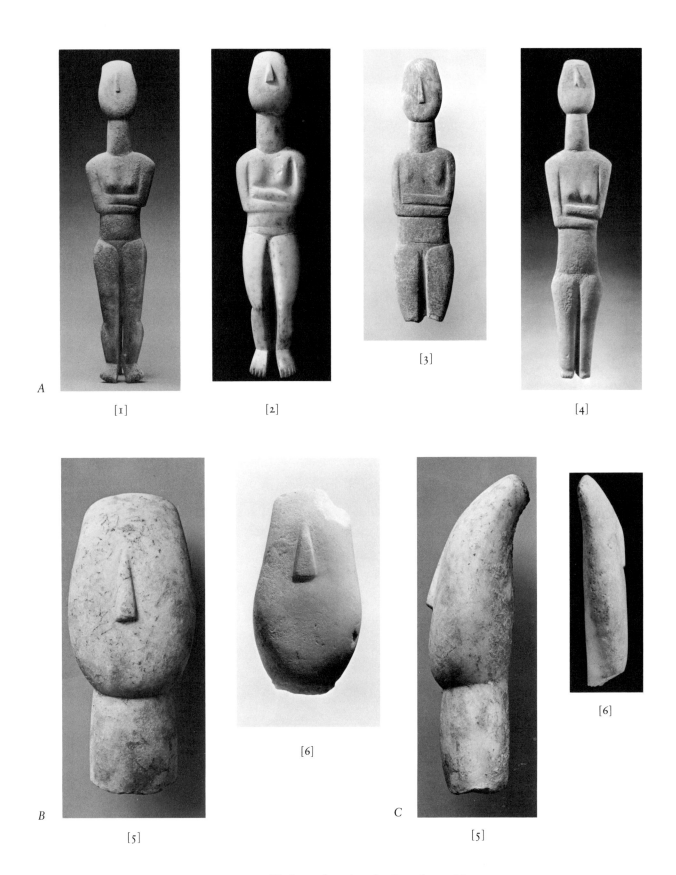

A

[1]　　　　　　[2]　　　　　　　[3]　　　　　　　　[4]

B
[5]

[6]

C
[5]

[6]

PLATE 24. Works attributed to the Copenhagen Master

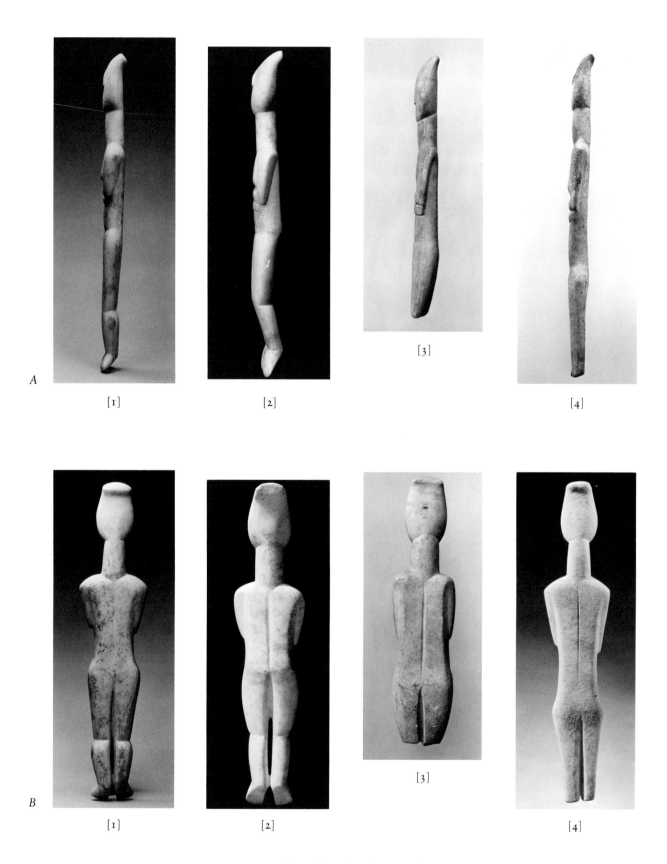

A

[1]   [2]   [3]   [4]

B

[1]   [2]   [3]   [4]

PLATE 25. Works attributed to the Copenhagen Master

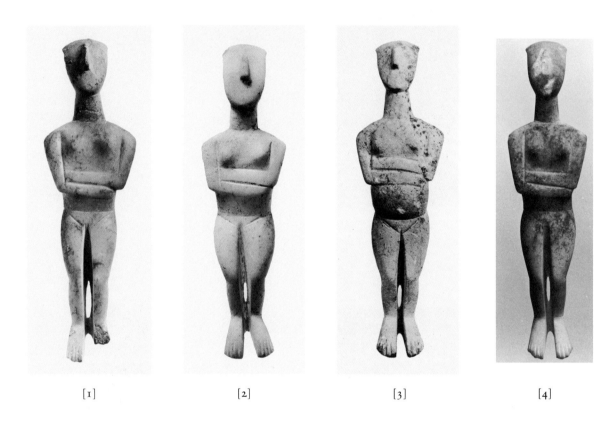

[1] [2] [3] [4]

PLATE 26. Works attributed to the Fitzwilliam Master

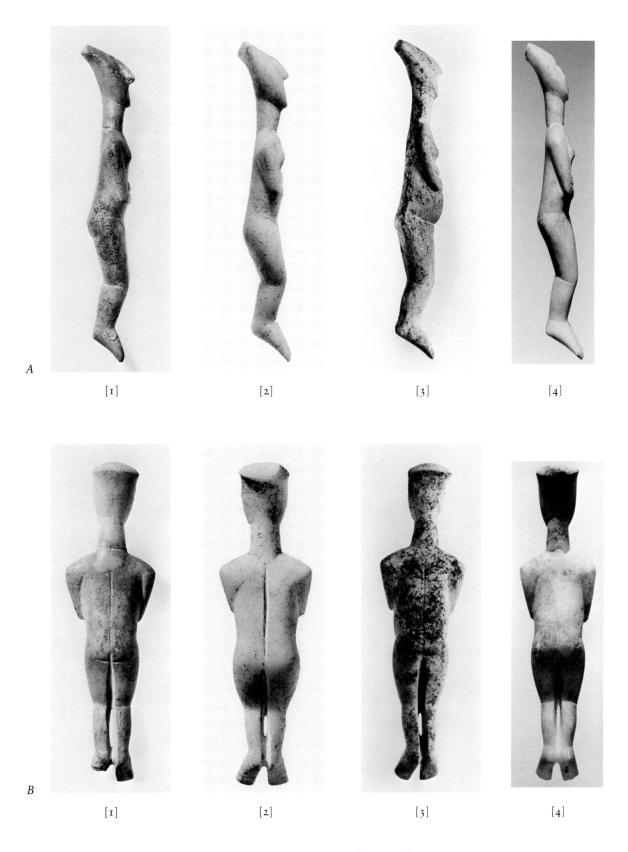

A

[1] [2] [3] [4]

B

[1] [2] [3] [4]

PLATE 27. Works attributed to the Fitzwilliam Master

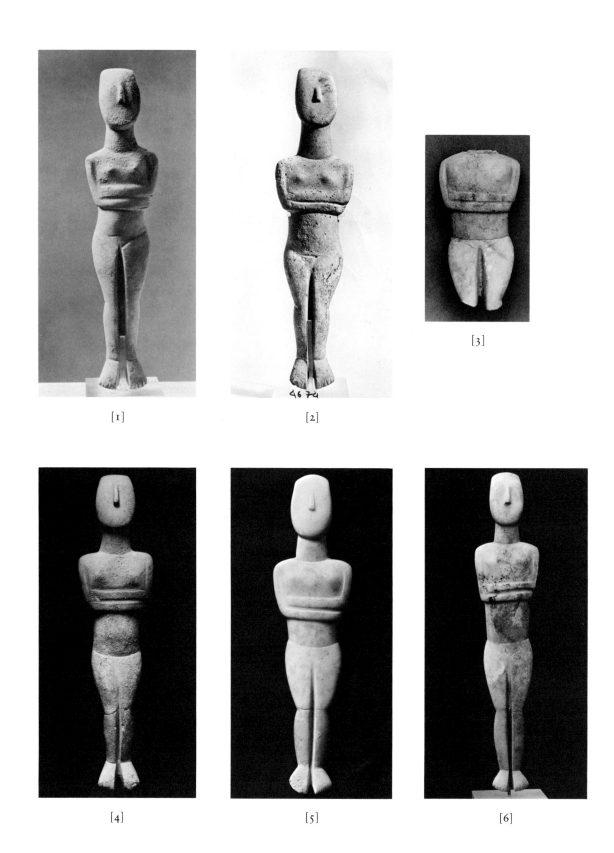

[1] [2] [3]

[4] [5] [6]

PLATE 28. Works attributed to the Steiner Master

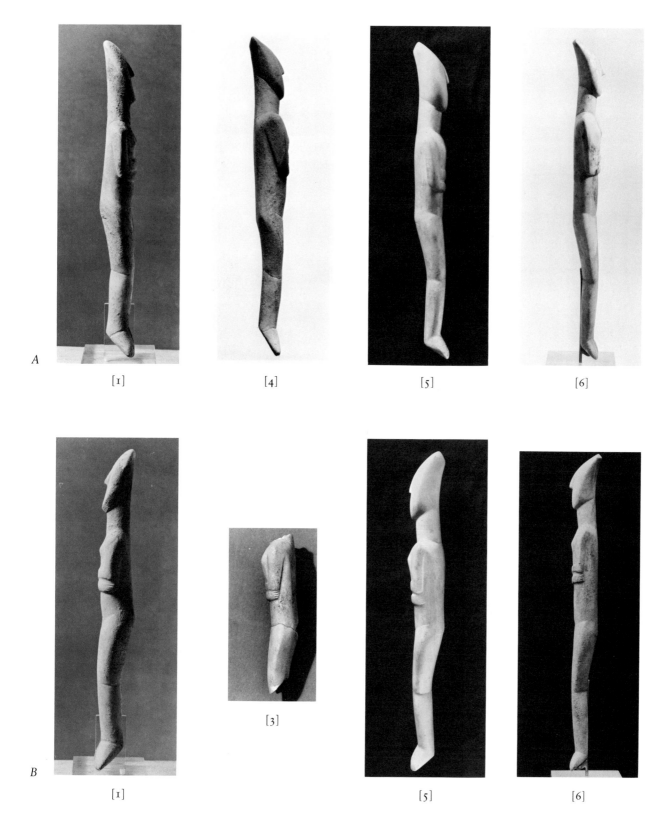

A [1] [4] [5] [6]

B [1] [3] [5] [6]

PLATE 29. Works attributed to the Steiner Master

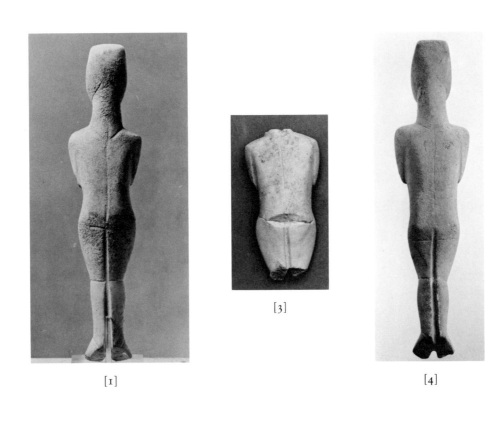

[1]

[3]

[4]

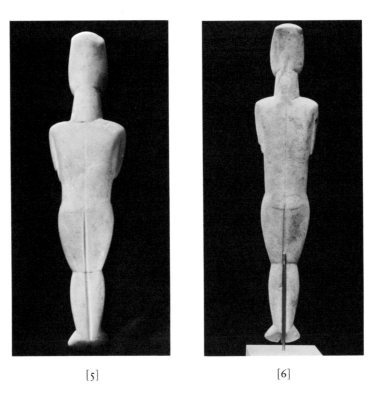

[5]

[6]

PLATE 30. Works attributed to the Steiner Master

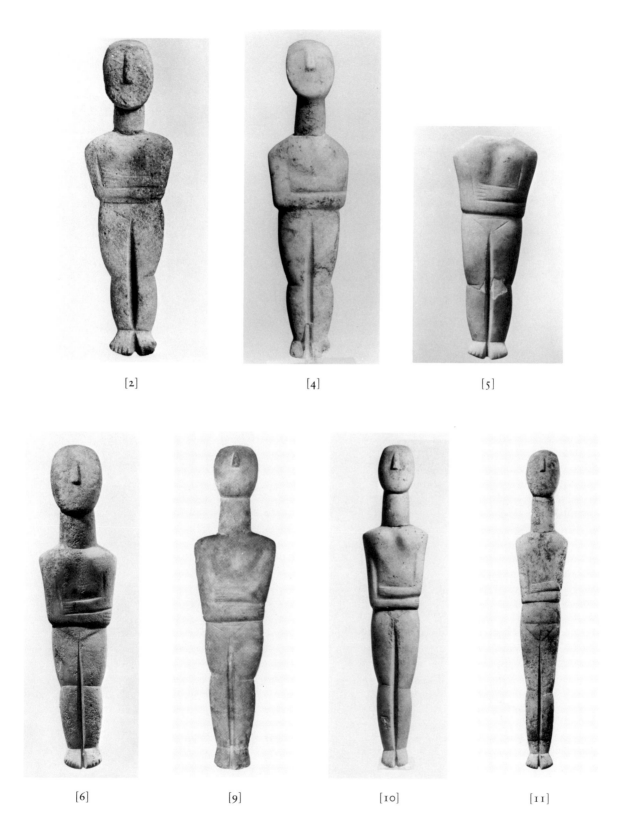

[2] [4] [5]

[6] [9] [10] [11]

PLATE 31. Works attributed to the Naxos Museum Master

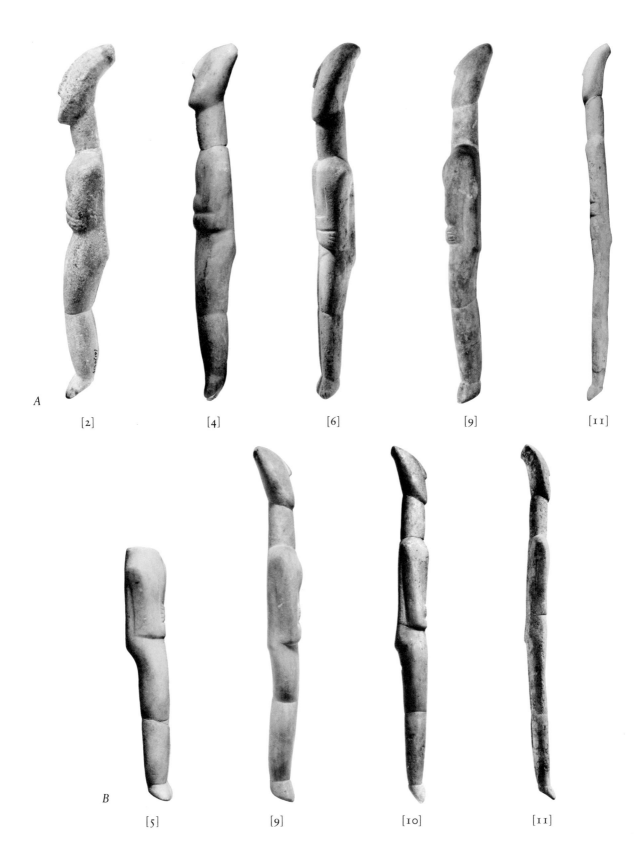

A

[2] [4] [6] [9] [11]

B

[5] [9] [10] [11]

PLATE 32. Works attributed to the Naxos Museum Master

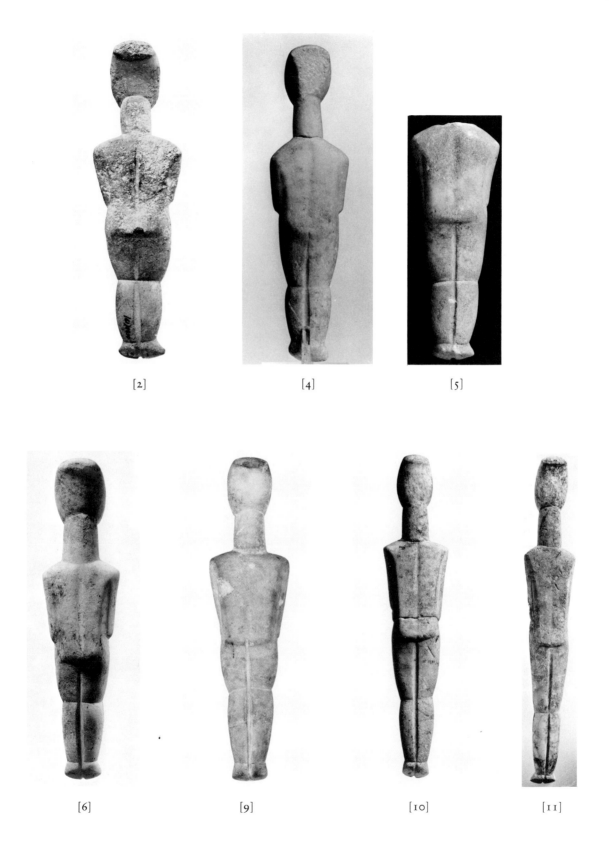

[2]   [4]   [5]

[6]   [9]   [10]   [11]

PLATE 33. Works attributed to the Naxos Museum Master

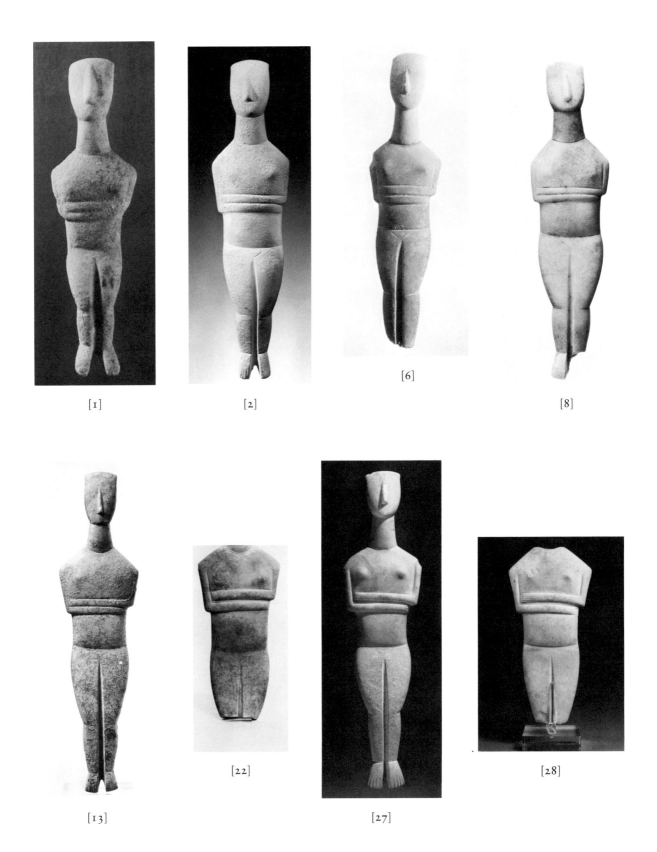

[1]   [2]   [6]   [8]

[13]   [22]   [27]   [28]

PLATE 34. Works attributed to the Goulandris Master

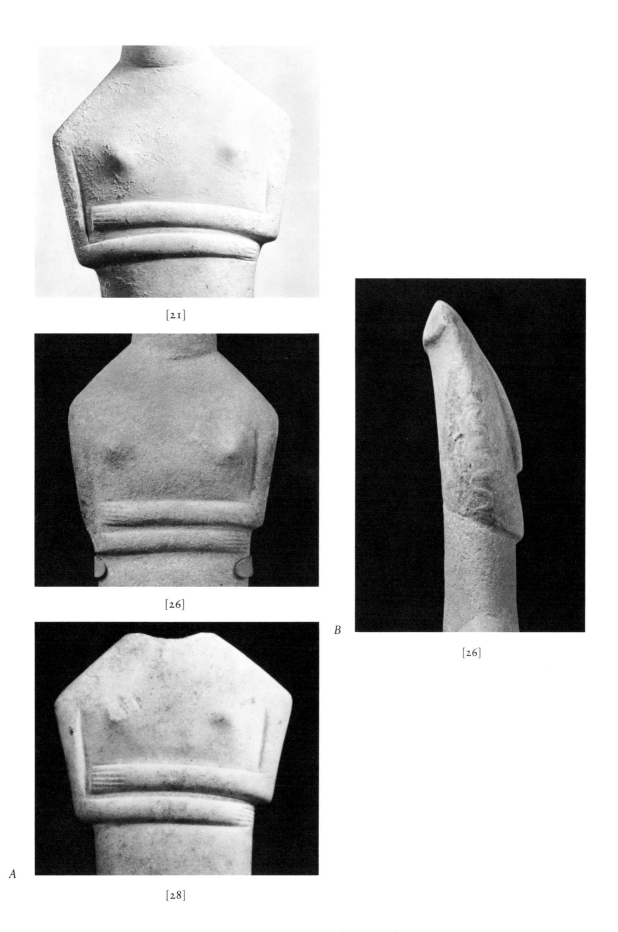

[21]

[26]

B

[26]

A

[28]

PLATE 35. Works attributed to the Goulandris Master

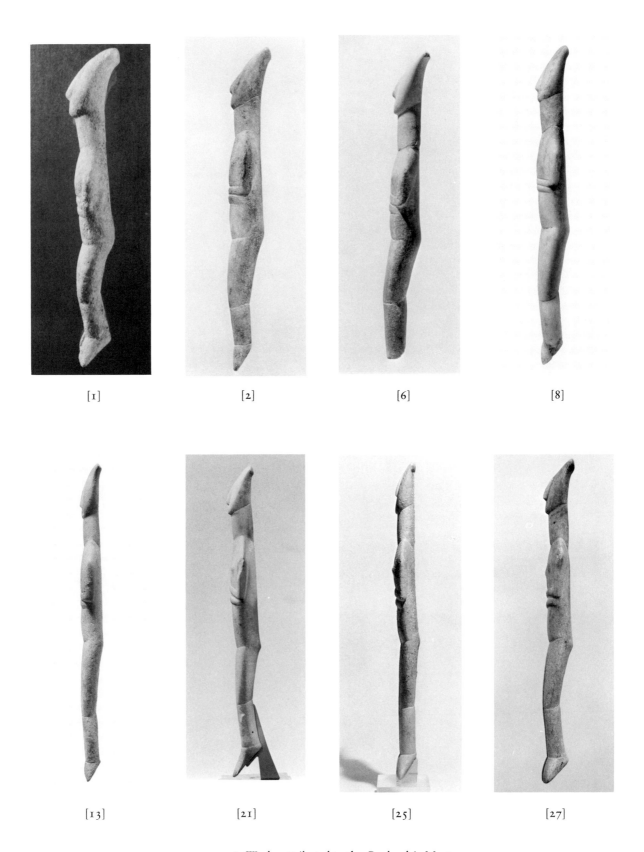

[1] [2] [6] [8]

[13] [21] [25] [27]

PLATE 36. Works attributed to the Goulandris Master

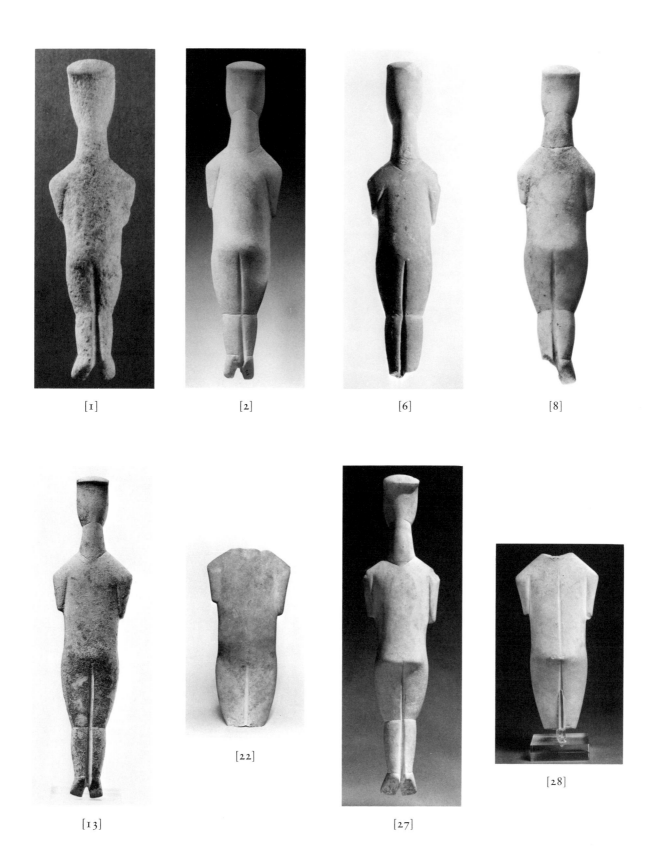

[1] [2] [6] [8]

[13] [22] [27] [28]

PLATE 37. Works attributed to the Goulandris Master

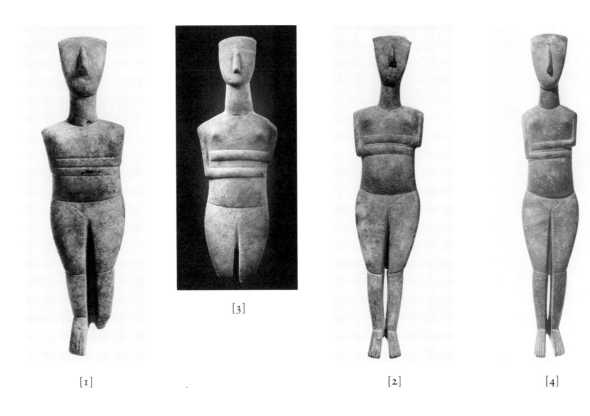

[3]

[1]   [2]   [4]

PLATE 38. Works attributed to the Bastis Master

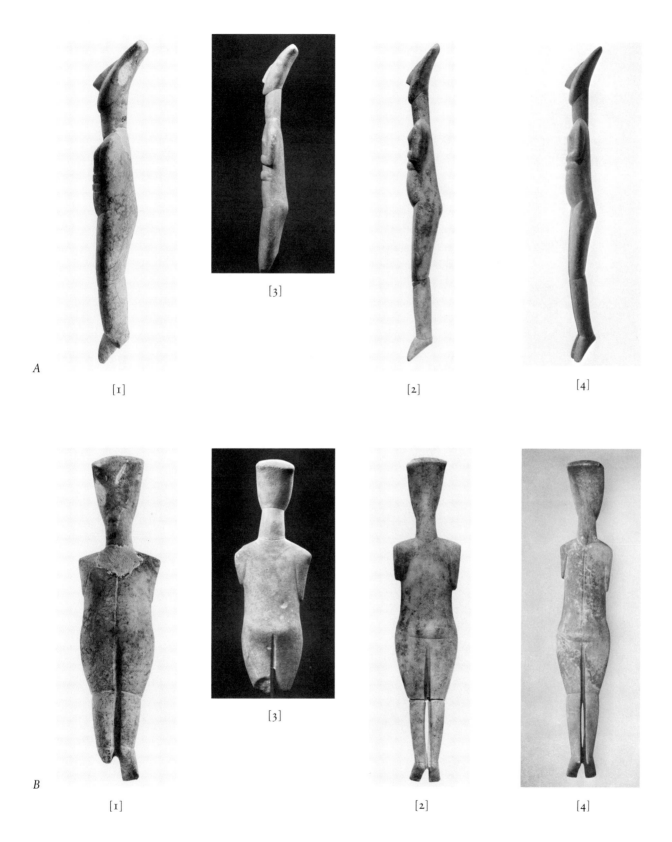

A

[1]   [3]   [2]   [4]

B

[1]   [3]   [2]   [4]

PLATE 39. Works attributed to the Bastis Master

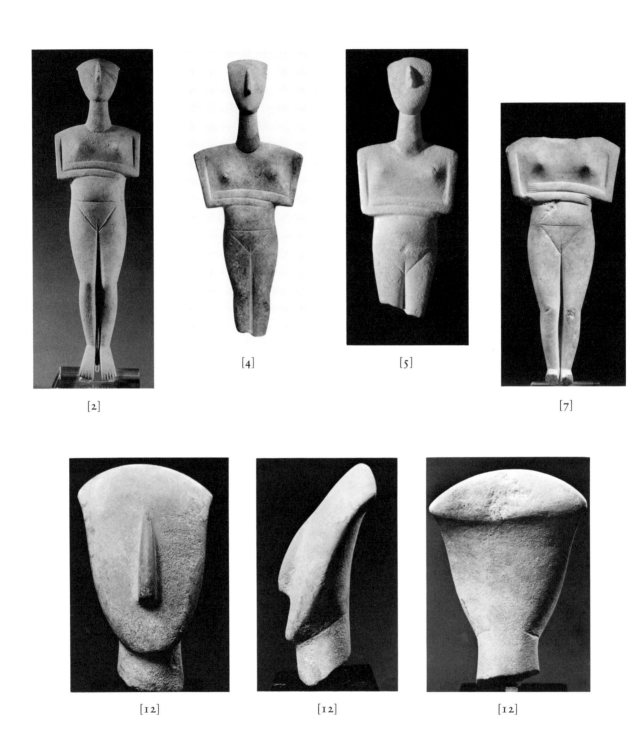

[2]　　　　　[4]　　　　　[5]　　　　　[7]

[12]　　　　　[12]　　　　　[12]

PLATE 40. Works attributed to the Schuster Master

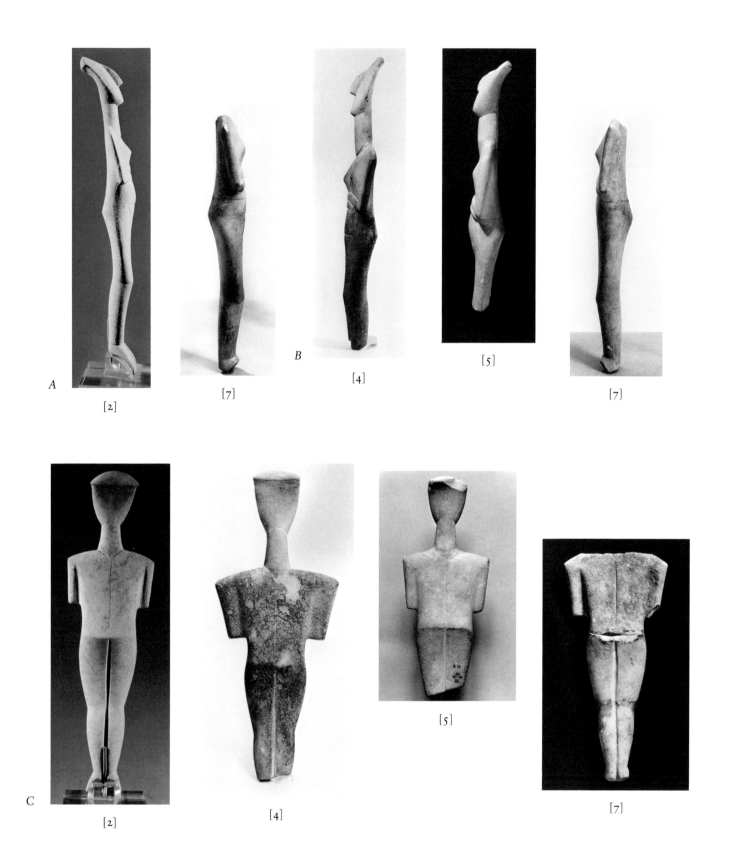

A [2]   [7]   *B* [4]   [5]   [7]

C [2]   [4]   [5]   [7]

PLATE 41. Works attributed to the Schuster Master

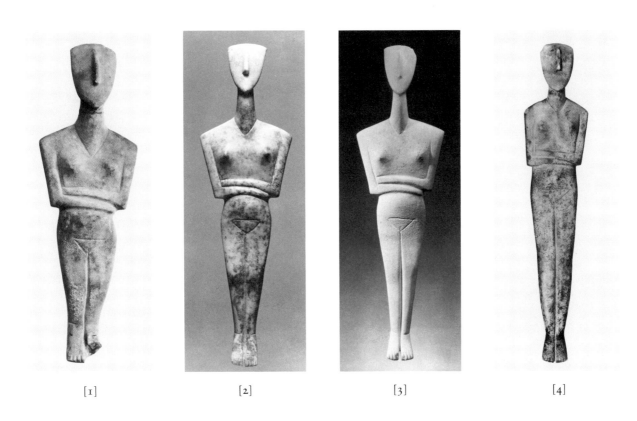

[1]   [2]   [3]   [4]

PLATE 42. Works attributed to the Ashmolean Master

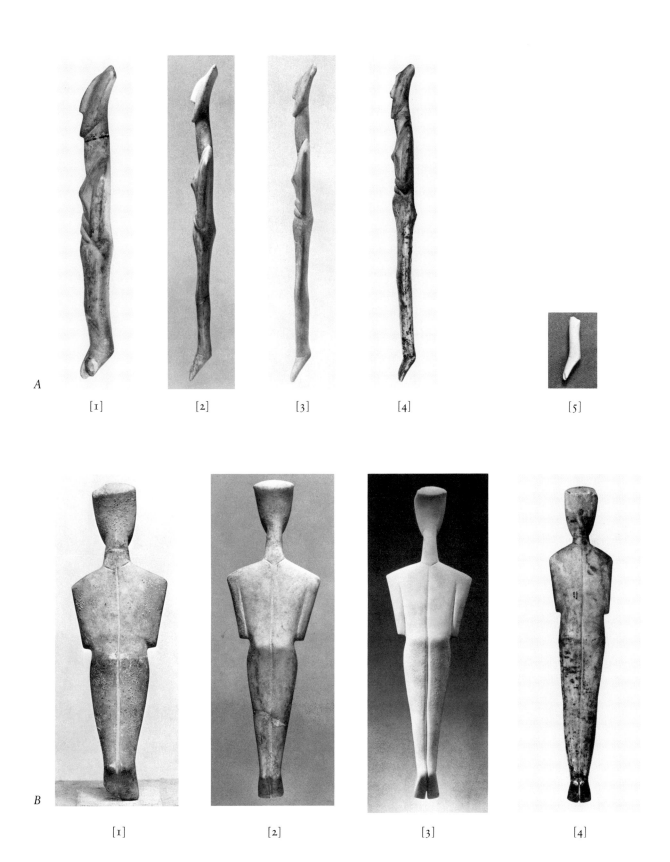

A

[1]   [2]   [3]   [4]   [5]

B

[1]   [2]   [3]   [4]

PLATE 43. Works attributed to the Ashmolean Master

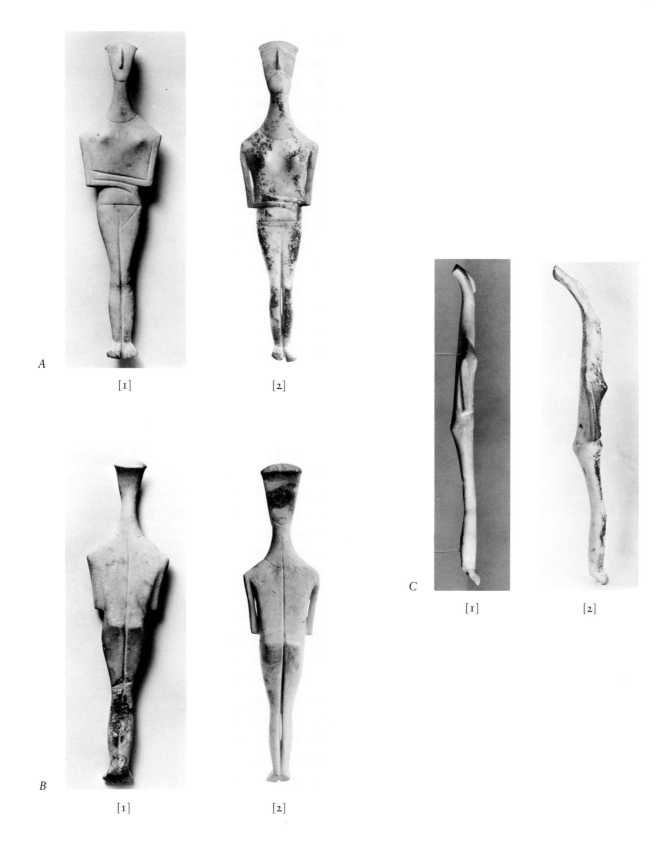

A

[1] [2]

B

[1] [2]

C

[1] [2]

PLATE 44. Works attributed to the Berlin Master

[3?]

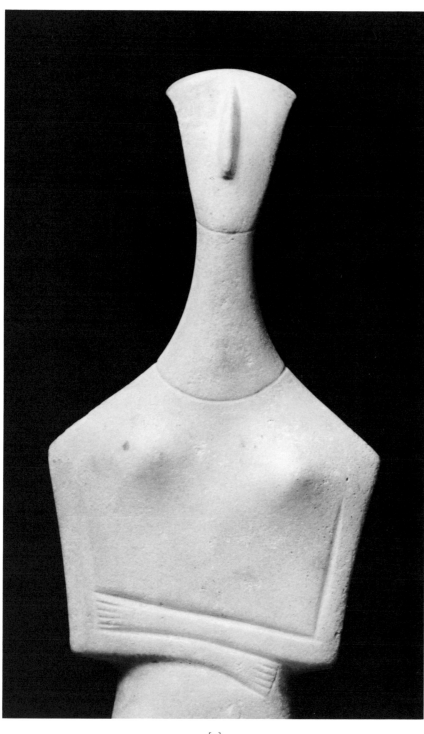

[1]

PLATE 45. Works attributed to the Berlin Master

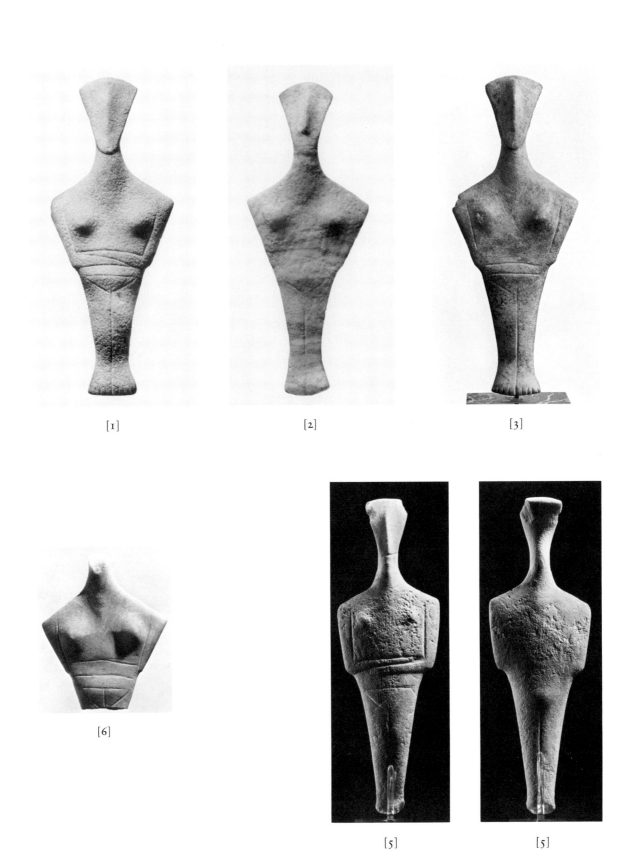

[1]

[2]

[3]

[6]

[5]

[5]

PLATE 46. Works attributed to the Stafford Master

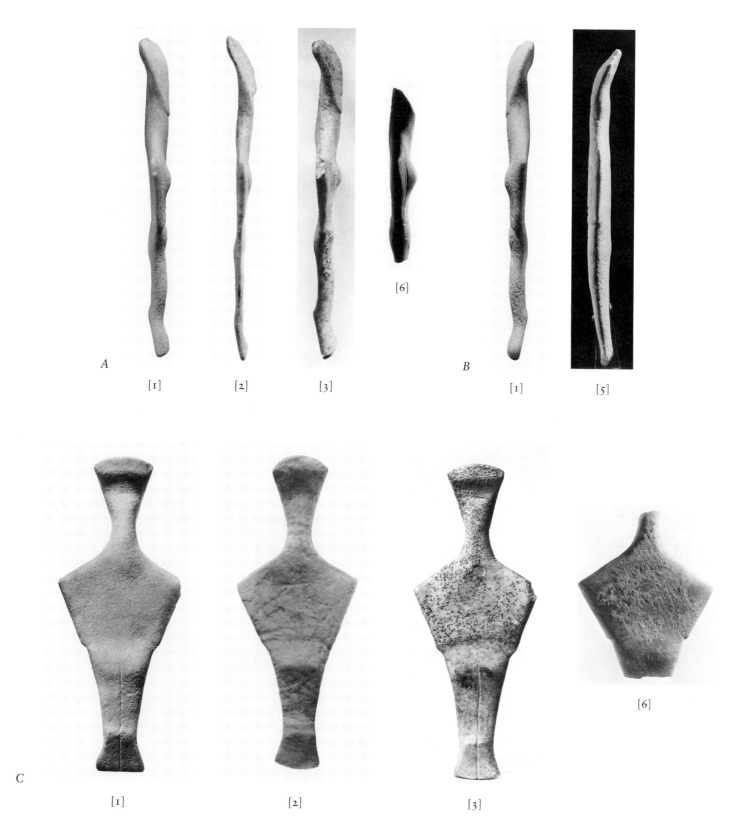

A   [1]   [2]   [3]   [6]   *B*   [1]   [5]

C   [1]   [2]   [3]   [6]

PLATE 47. Works attributed to the Stafford Master

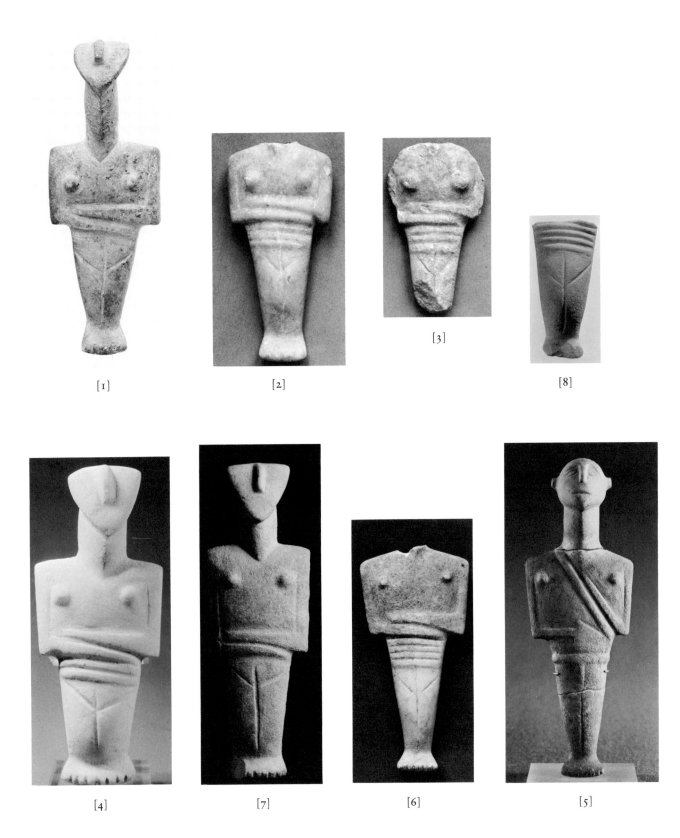

[1]   [2]   [3]   [8]

[4]   [7]   [6]   [5]

PLATE 48. Works attributed to the Dresden Master

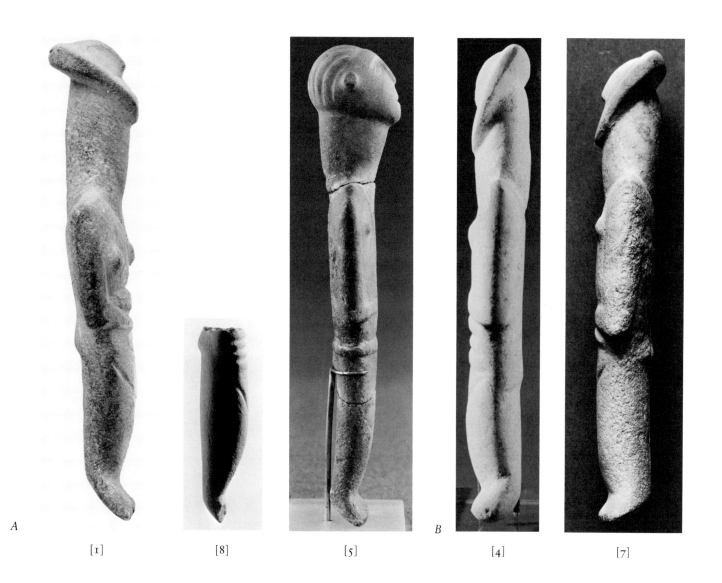

A   *B*

[1]   [8]   [5]   [4]   [7]

PLATE 49. Works attributed to the Dresden Master

[1]   [4]   [7]

[5]   [6]   [8]

PLATE 50. Works attributed to the Dresden Master

Notes on the Plates

Color

PLATE I. Plastiras-type figures of the Early Cycladic I phase.

A. Female figure. Attributed to the Metropolitan Museum Master. Geneva, Barbier-Müller Museum BMG 202-75. H. 18.3 cm. Provenance unknown. Metropolitan Museum Master [1].

A characteristic example of its type, carved with keen attention to detail, the figure shows the female in a standing posture, her legs carved separately to the crotch, her arms rendered in the old Neolithic position with fingertips meeting over the abdomen. The exaggerated proportions of such works made them especially vulnerable. This figure sustained two fractures – one in the right leg, the other at the top of the neck. Repair holes, through which a leather thong or string was drawn to refasten the broken part, were bored through the front and back of the piece for the leg break, through the sides for the neck break.

B. Male figure. Lugano, Paolo Morigi Collection. H. 29.6 cm (penis missing). Provenance unknown.

A well-developed, probably late example of its type, the figure shows the characteristic standing pose, arm arrangement, and interest in detail, but somewhat less extreme proportions than usual. The figure seems by its proportions as well as the position of the hole in the pubic area to represent a male. The penis, now missing, was added as a separate piece from the beginning or following damage. Male figures, never numerous, are more common in the EC I phase than in the EC II, and greater attention was paid on them to anatomical verisimilitude. The figure, which was executed with great care, has a number of interesting details, including almond-shaped eyes whose round eyeballs were once inlaid and, at the elbows, the beginning of perforations which were abandoned early on, apparently because they were considered too hazardous to complete.

PLATE II. Special figures of the Early Cycladic II phase.

A. Female semi-sitting figure. Early Spedos variety. Private collection. H. 19 cm. Provenance unknown.

The finest known example of a very rare variant of the standard folded-arm female, the figure is shown not in the normal reclining posture but in a near sitting position (which would be more obvious if the work were mounted with its back vertically oriented). In other respects the piece is a characteristic example of the early Spedos variety. It is unclear if it was originally furnished with a wooden seat or perhaps with a mound of earth to support it in its intended posture. Normally seated figures are carved of a piece with a simple stool or chair.

B. Cupbearer. Early Spedos-variety style. Athens, Goulandris Collection 286. H. 15.2 cm. "Keros"?

The only complete example of an extremely rare occupational type, the charming small work shows a figure presumed to represent a male even though no genitalia are indicated. The wine (?) cup is held in the outstretched right hand while the left is folded across the body in the manner of the female figures contemporary with it. The significance of the gesture and the precise meaning and function of the work are open to conjecture.

C. Harp Player. Early Spedos-variety style. Malibu, The J. Paul Getty Museum 85.AA.103. H. 60 cm. "Amorgos."

A remarkably well-conceived and unusually well-preserved example of a rare occupational type, this is the largest of the harp players known at present. It is carved in the streamlined style of the early folded-arm figures, for which reason it is no surprise that the genitalia are not indicated. The figure is assumed to represent a male both by its role and because some examples of the type are clearly rendered as males. Characteristically the musician sits on a simple four-legged stool, his instrument resting on his right thigh. He holds the harp frame with his left hand, while his right hand lies at rest along the soundbox. Unlike other examples he is not shown actively playing his instrument.

PLATE III. Musician figures.

A. Harp player. Precanonical style. New York, Metropolitan Museum of Art 47.100.1 (Rogers Fund). H. 29.5 cm. Provenance unknown. Copyright © 1977 by The Metropolitan Museum of Art.

The earliest and one of the best preserved examples of its type, the New York harper is also the most elaborately detailed member of a group now numbering only nine. The musician, seated on an intricate backed chair based on wooden models, holds his outsize harp on his right side as required by the conventions of the type. He is represented holding the harp frame with both hands, his naturalistically carved thumbs plucking the invisible strings. The figure wears a belt and vaguely indicated codpiece and has sculpted ears and facial features. (A cap or hair was originally painted.) The detailed rendering as well as the sculptor's interest in musculature combined with somewhat ungainly proportioning indicate that stylistically the piece is related to the precanonical female figures produced in the transition to or at the very beginning of the EC II phase.

B. Syrinx player. Kapsala-variety style. Karlsruhe, Badisches Landesmuseum 64/100. H. 34 cm. Provenance unknown.

The standing woodwind player is another occupational type seldom attempted by the Cycladic sculptor. Mounted on a base to enable them to stand upright, the posture of such works is clearly distinguished from that of the standard female figures of the time. In the example illustrated here the musi-

cian holds to his mouth a rectangular syrinx. In actuality the instrument would have consisted of pipes of graduated size tied together, but the Cycladic sculptor has transformed the instrument into a simple symmetrical form. The articulated rib cage shows an interest in detail reminiscent of earlier styles.

PLATE IV. Marble vases of the Early Cycladic I phase.

A. Anthropomorphic beaker. Oxford, Ashmolean Museum 1938.727. H. 7.5 cm, D. 8 cm. "Naxos"?

B. Double vase in the form of a sheep. Oxford, Ashmolean Museum 1912.71. H. 11.5 cm, L. 20.2 cm. "Amorgos."

C. Collared jar (kandili). Karlsruhe, Badisches Landesmuseum 63/103. H. 31.5 cm. Provenance unknown.

D. Beaker. Karlsruhe, Badisches Landesmuseum 63/48. H. 19.3 cm. Provenance unknown.

The stone vessels of the EC I phase are carved in marble and in a limited range of oft-repeated forms executed in a wide size range. These include the beaker (A, D), the collared and footed jar or kandili (C), the simple bowl, often with a suspension lug, and the rectangular palette pierced for suspension. The cumbersome collared jar in particular was produced in astonishing quantity in distinct contrast to the figurative images of the period. Characteristic features of nearly all stone vases of the EC I phase are the horizontally perforated vertical suspension lugs that in the case of the very rare anthropomorphic beaker (A) serve also as the upper arms of the female torso depicted on one side and in the case of the equally rare zoomorphic vase as its tail (B). Besides having a ritual function as containers, many of the vases may have served as symbols of the life force embodied in the female figures. The anthropomorphic beaker is an especially graphic example of the relationship between woman/womb and vessel.

PLATE V. Figure with "cradle and three marble vases of the Early Cycladic II phase.

A. Late Spedos-variety figure with trough-shaped palette said to have been found together. Jerusalem, Israel Museum 71.61.208 (gift of Mr. and Mrs. Isidore M. Cohen). L. 19 cm (figure), 19.7 cm (palette). "Paros."

B. Footed spherical pyxis. Karlsruhe, Badisches Landesmuseum 63/50. H. 11.5 cm (lid missing). Provenance unknown.

C. Cylindrical pyxis. New York, Paul and Marianne Steiner Collection. H. 8.7 cm, D. 9.1 cm (lid missing). Possibly EC I/II.

D. Spool pyxis. Karlsruhe, Badisches Landesmuseum 64/117. H. 8.2 cm, D. 13 cm. "Naxos."

In the EC II phase the old repertoire of shapes was replaced with a wide variety of new and for the most part smaller and lighter forms. The horizontally pierced lug was supplanted by a vertically perforated one (*B, C*) or by an unpierced oblong lug horizontally oriented. The conical pedestal of the old collared jar now took on a distinct bell shape and was used for a variety of different types usually carved without a foot (*B; see also VIIIA*). The most common type was the open bowl either spouted or plain, but lidded pyxides, either spherical (*B*) or cylindrical (*C, D*), often with parallel encircling grooves, were popular too, and multipurpose "palettes," flat or trough-shaped, are found with some frequency also. The example of the latter type (*A*), which indeed seems best suited for use as a pallet, is said to have been found with the figure shown with it, an association which, though plausible, has yet to be documented through systematic excavation.

PLATE VI. Figures with painted details.

A. Kapsala variety. Possibly a work of the Kontoleon Master. Private collection. Pres. L. 69.4 cm. Provenance unknown.

B. Early Spedos variety. New York, Paul and Marianne Steiner Collection. L. 49.5 cm. Provenance unknown.

Although originally virtually all Cycladic folded-arm figures received some painted detail, this has only occasionally survived to the present. The unusually large and beautifully modeled Kapsala-variety figure with carved ears (*A*) stands out as the single most elaborately painted figure known today. Anatomical features (ears, brows, hair, and pubis) are rendered in blue, while the nostrils, facial tattooing, necklaces, fingers, and wrists are painted red. The somewhat later figure (*B*) has similar facial tattooing, painted ears, and some of the grooves are highlighted with red paint. (See fig. 29.)

PLATE VII. Figures with painted (*A, C, D*) or unusual carved detail (*B*).

A. Detail of pl. I*B*. (Photo courtesy the collector.)

B. Precanonical type. Private collection. Pres. H. 19 cm. Provenance unknown.

C. Detail of pl. VI*B*.

D. Late Spedos variety. Attributed to the Goulandris Master [36]. Copenhagen, Danish National Museum 4697. Pres. L. 24.6 cm. "Amorgos." While painted nostrils are at present unique to the intricately painted figure shown in pl. VI*A*, incised nostrils are found only on the precanonical head with small carved ears and upturned nose seen here (*B*). Although ears were regularly carved on precanonical works and on some of the earlier true folded-arm figures (especially unusually large ones), the round red-painted ears seen on *C* are at present unparalleled. Other examples of painted detail include the red stripes seen on the neck of *A* and the striped facial decoration of *D*.

PLATE VIII. Musician groups of the Early Cycladic II phase.

A. A pair of harpers carved in the Kapsala-variety style and a table fashioned in one piece with a miniature footed bowl. Private collection. H. 20.1 cm, 17.4 cm (harpers), 7.5 cm (table with vase). "Amorgos." (See pls. 7–8.)

B. The harper and double pipes player from a grave on Keros. Early Spedos-variety style. Athens, National Archaeological Museum 3908 (harper; left leg from knee and both feet as well as a section of the harp, probably grasped originally by the musician, restored in plaster), 3910 (piper). H. 22 cm, 20 cm (See pl. 10.)

At least three cases are known in which two musician figures were found in the same grave. The charming harpers seated on simple stools and the table carrying a miniature footed bowl with spout said to have been found with them were clearly carved by a single sculptor and intended as companion pieces (*A*). The harper and double pipes player from Keros, by contrast, are carved in different scales and do not resemble each other sufficiently — this is perhaps because they represent different postural types and because the extremities of the harper are not preserved — to attribute them to one sculptor with any confidence (*B*). The Athens harper is, like the much earlier New York harper (pl. III*A*), seated on an elaborate openwork chair. The little woodwind player is at present unique for his instrument.

PLATE IX. Works attributed to the Goulandris Master, an Early Cycladic II sculptor of late Spedos-variety figures.

A. Bloomington, Indiana University Art Museum 76.25 (gift of Thomas T. Solley). L. 60 cm. Provenance unknown. Goulandris Master [25].

B. Canberra, Australian National Gallery 1982.2232. L. 55 cm (ends of feet incorrectly restored in plaster). Provenance unknown. Goulandris Master [21].

Two excellently preserved mature works of the most prolific and best known sculptor of classic folded-arm figures, these images display a calm force, a harmony of proportion, and a refinement of line which characterize the finest examples of Early Cycladic sculpture. A few of the hallmarks of the Goulandris Master's mature style seen in the two works are a lyre-shaped face with long semiconical nose, markedly sloping shoulders, small wide-spaced breasts, separated and modeled forearms, with carefully incised fingers on *B,* a small pubic triangle, and legs separated by a deep unperforated furrow.

PLATE X. A nearly life-size figure.

Early Spedos variety. Belgium, private collection. L. 132 cm. Provenance unknown.

The third largest complete (or nearly complete) Cycladic sculpture known at present, the piece is remarkable for its workmanship and surface finish and for its excellent state of preservation. It may have been deliberately broken in order to fit it into a grave which would otherwise have been too small to accommodate it.

PLATE XI. Head of an unusually large, elongated figure.

Early Spedos variety. New York, private collection. Pres. L. 22 cm. Provenance unknown.

Outstanding for its slender form and long refined nose, the head beloned to a figure measuring 120 cm or more. It retains vivid traces of red-painted facial ornamentation.

Black and White

PLATE 1. One-piece compositions with two and three figures.

A. Two-figure group. Precanonical type. Private collection. L. 46 cm. Provenance unknown.

B. Two-figure group. Early Spedos variety. Karlsruhe, Badisches Landesmuseum B839 (ex Thiersch Collection). L. 21.6 cm. "Paros."

C. Three-figure group. Early Spedos-variety style. Karlsruhe, Badisches Landesmuseum 77/59. H. 19 cm. Provenance unknown.

PLATE 2. Groups of figures from graves of the Early Cycladic I phase.

A. Thirteen of the fourteen figures from grave 103 at Pyrgos on Paros. Schematic types. Athens, National Archaeological Museum 4821.1–14 (the figures are not shown in numbered sequence). H. 3–10.5 cm (the second row of figures is shown in a larger scale than the first).

B. The thirteen figures from grave 117 at Krassades on Antiparos. Schematic types. Athens, National Archaeological Museum 4956.1–13. H. 2–15.2 cm.

PLATE 3. Groups of figures from graves of the transitional phase.

A. Five of the original seven figures from grave 26 at Louros Athalassou on Naxos. Louros type. Attributed to the Stephanos Master. Athens, National Archaeological Museum 6140.6.7.9–11. H. ca. 17.4–22 cm.

B. Six figures said to be from a grave on Paros. Louros type. Attributed to the Fitzwilliam Louros Master. Cambridge, Fitzwilliam Museum GR.8a–f.1933. H. 3–12.2 cm.

PLATE 4. Groups of figures from graves of the Early Cycladic I phase.

A. Three figures said to have been found together. Schematic and Plastiras types. Attributed to the Missouri Master. Columbia, University of Missouri Museum of Art and Archaeology 64.67.1.3.2. H. 7.6–14.1 cm. Provenance unknown.

B. The four figures from grave 9 at Plastiras on Paros. Plastiras type. 1–3 attributed to the Doumas Master. Paros, Archaeological Museum 656–59. H. 11.2 to ca. 15.3 cm. Doumas Master [6, 7, 8].

PLATE 5. Two of three figures said to be from a grave on Naxos. Early Cycladic II phase. Kapsala variety. Oxford, Ashmolean Museum 1929.27, 1929.28. L. 13.7 cm, 18 cm.

PLATE 6. The pair of figures from grave 10 at Spedos on Naxos. Early Cycladic II phase. Spedos variety. Athens, National Archaeological Museum 6140.22, 6195. L. 43.5 cm (end of left foot restored in plaster), 58.7 cm.

PLATES 7, 8. A pair of harp players said to have been found together. Early Cycladic II phase. Kapsala-variety style. Private collection. H. 20.1 cm, 17.4 cm (section of harp frame restored in plaster). "Amorgos." (See pl. VIIIA.)

PLATE 9. A pair of harpers said to have been found in a grave on Thera. Early Cycladic II phase. Early Spedos-variety style. Karlsruhe, Badisches Landesmuseum B863, B864. H. 15.6 cm, 16.5 cm.

PLATE 10. The double pipes player and harper from a grave on Keros. Early Cycladic II phase. Early Spedos-variety style. Athens, National Archaeological Museum 3908, 3910. H. 22 cm harper (partly restored in plaster); H. 20 cm piper. (See pl. VIIIB.)

PLATES 11, 12. A group of four figures said to have been found together on Naxos (A) and two related figures (B, C). Early Cycladic II Phase.

A.1. Chalandriani variety. Attributed to the Goulandris Hunter/Warrior Master. Athens, Goulandris Collection 308. L. 25 cm. "Naxos."

A.2. Chalandriani variety. Attributed to the Goulandris Hunter/Warrior Master. Athens, Goulandris Collection 312. L. 20.8 cm. "Naxos."

A.3. Late Spedos variety. Possibly an early work of the Goulandris Master. Athens, Goulandris Collection 309. L. 15.7 cm. "Naxos."

A.4. Closest to Chalandriani variety. Athens, Goulandris Collection 328. L. 14.8 cm. "Naxos."

B. Chalandriani variety. Attributed to the Goulandris Hunter/Warrior Master. Private collection. L. 16.5 cm. Provenance unknown.

C. Closest to Chalandriani variety. Athens, Goulandris Collection 108. L. 16.2 cm. "Naxos"?

PLATE 13. The pair of figures from grave 14 at Dokathismata on Amorgos. Early Cycladic II phase. Chalandriani/Dokathismata variety (1), Dokathismata variety (2). Attributed to the Tsountas Master. Athens, National Archaeological Museum 4723, 4722. L. 16.3 cm, 20.5 cm.

PLATES 14, 15. Works attributed to the Doumas Master, an Early Cycladic I sculptor of Plastiras-type figures. (Read with pl. 4B.1–3; Doumas Master checklist.)

[1] Naxos, Archaeological Museum 1990. Pres. H. 8.7 cm. Grave 5, Akrotiri, Naxos.

[2] Oxford, Ashmolean Museum AE.417. Pres. H. 8.6 cm. "Lefkes, Paros."

[3] Private collection. Pres. H. 10.1 cm. Provenance unknown.

[4] Geneva, Barbier-Müller Museum BMG 202-13. H. 13.4 cm. Provenance unknown.

[9] Athens, National Archaeological Museum 4762. H. 31.5 cm. Grave 23, Glypha, Paros.

PLATES 16, 17. Works attributed to the Metropolitan Museum Master, an Early Cycladic I sculptor of Plastiras-type figures. (Read with pl. IA; Metropolitan Museum Master checklist.)

[1] Geneva, Barbier-Müller Museum BMG 202-75. H. 18.3 cm. Provenance unknown.

[2] New York, Metropolitan Museum of Art 45.11.18. H. 21.8 cm. Provenance unknown. Name-piece.

[3] E. Berlin, Staatliche Museen, Antikensammlung 8429. H. 23.5 cm. "Delos."

PLATES 18, 19, 20. Works attributed to the Athens Museum Master, an Early Cycladic I sculptor of Plastiras-type figures. (Read with Athens Museum Master checklist.)

[1] Private collection. Pres. H. 18.2 cm. Provenance unknown.

[2] Athens, National Archaeological Museum 3919. H. 30.8 cm. "Amorgos." Name-piece.

[3] Oxford, Ashmolean Museum AE.151. Pres. H. 9.2 cm. "Amorgos."

[4] Geneva, Barbier-Müller Museum BMG 202-59. Pres. H. 13.6 cm. Provenance unknown.

PLATES 21, 22. Works attributed to the Kontoleon Master, an Early Cycladic II sculptor of Kapsala-variety figures. (Read with Kontoleon Master checklist.)

[1] Athens, National Archaeological Museum 6140.12. L. ca. 17.5 cm. Spedos?, Naxos.

[2] Dominique de Menil Collection X 084. L. 18.9 cm. "Paros."

[5] New York, Metropolitan Museum of Art 1977.187.10ab (bequest of Alice K. Bache). L. 30 cm. Provenance unknown.

[6] Private collection. L. 31 cm. Provenance unknown.

PLATE 23. Works attributed to the Israel Museum Master, an Early Cycladic II sculptor of Kapsala/early Spedos-variety figures. (Read with Israel Museum Master checklist).

[2] Washington, D.C., Hirshhorn Museum and Sculpture Garden HMSG 1966.5186. L. 22.9 cm. Provenance unknown.

[3] Athens, National Archaeological Museum 6140.15. Pres. L. 19 cm. Spedos?, Naxos.

[4] Jerusalem, Israel Museum 74.61.206. L. 29 cm. Provenance unknown. Name-piece.

PLATES 24, 25. Works attributed to the Copenhagen Master, an Early Cycladic II sculptor of early Spedos-variety figures. (Read with Copenhagen Master checklist.)

[1] Private collection. L. 56.2 cm. Provenance unknown.

[2] London, private collection. L. 57.2 cm. Provenance unknown.

[3] Copenhagen, Danish National Museum 1624. Pres. L. 49.7 cm. "Amorgos." Name-piece.

[4] Athens, Goulandris Collection 257. L. 70.7 cm. "Naxos."

[5] Private collection? Pres. L. 15.6 cm. "Keros."

[6] Private collection. Pres. L. 13.6 cm. "Keros."

PLATES 26, 27. Works attributed to the Fitzwilliam Master, an Early Cycladic II sculptor of early Spedos-variety figures. (Read with Fitzwilliam Master checklist.)

[1] Stockholm, Medelhavsmuseet 62.10. L. 19.6 cm. Provenance unknown.

[2] New York, Christos G. Bastis Collection. L. 20.6 cm. Provenance unknown.

[3] Herakleion, Archaeological Museum 122. L. 23.8 cm. Communal tomb, Koumasa, Crete.

[4] Cambridge, Fitzwilliam Museum GR.33.1901 (gift of R. C. Bosanquet). L. 25.6 cm. "Amorgos." Name-piece.

PLATES 28, 29, 30. Works attributed to the Steiner Master, an Early Cycladic II sculptor of late Spedos-variety figures. (Read with Steiner Master checklist.)

[1] Tokyo, National Museum of Western Art S.1974-1. L. 34.5 cm. Provenance unknown.

[2] Naxos, Archaeological Museum 4674. L. 42 cm. "Naxos."

[3] Basel, Erlenmeyer Collection. Pres. L. 22.7 cm. "Keros."

[4] Athens, Goulandris Collection 654. L. 48 cm. Provenance unknown.

[5] Private collection. L. 51 cm. Provenance unknown.

[6] New York, Paul and Marianne Steiner Collection. L. 60.2 cm. Provenance unknown. Name-piece.

PLATES 31, 32, 33. Works attributed to the Naxos Museum Master, an Early Cycladic II sculptor of late Spedos-variety figures. (Read with Naxos Museum Master checklist.)

[2] Athens, National Archaeological Museum 6140.19. L. 19.8 cm. Grave 28, Phyrroges, Naxos.

[4] Munich, Staatliche Antikensammlungen und Glyptothek, von Schoen Collection 262. L. 27.8 cm. Provenance unknown.

[5] Private collection? Pres. L. 25 cm. "Keros."

[6] Private collection. L. 39.5 cm. Provenance unknown.

[9] New York, Woodner Family Collection. L. 50.8 cm. Provenance unknown.

[10] Naxos, Archaeological Museum 4676. L. 55 cm. "Naxos." Name-piece.

[11] Athens, Goulandris Collection 598. L. 72 cm. "Naxos."

PLATES 34, 35, 36, 37. Works attributed to the Goulandris Master, an Early Cycladic II sculptor of late Spedos-variety figures. (Read with pls. VIID, IX; Goulandris Master checklist.)

[1] Norwich, University of East Anglia, Sainsbury Centre for Visual Arts, 1955 UEA 343. L. 16.5 cm. Provenance unknown.

[2] Athens, Goulandris Collection 251. L. 33 cm. "Naxos." Name-piece.

[6] New York, Mrs. Allan D. Emil Collection. Pres. L. 32.4 cm. Provenance unknown.

[8] Private collection. L. 38.2 cm. "Keros."

[13] Private collection. L. 42 cm. Provenance unknown.

[21] Canberra, Australian National Gallery 1982.2232 (ex Maurice Bonnefoy Collection). L. 55 cm. Provenance unknown.

[22] Private collection. Pres. L. 29 cm. "Keros."

[25] Bloomington, Indiana University Art Museum 76.25 (gift of Thomas T. Solley). L. 60 cm. Provenance unknown.

[26] New York, Christos G. Bastis Collection. L. 62.15 cm. "Paros."

[27] Athens, Goulandris Collection 281. L. 63.4 cm. "Naxos." Name-piece.

[28] Private collection. Pres. L. 34.3 cm. "Keros."

PLATES 38, 39. Works attributed to the Bastis Master, an Early Cycladic II sculptor of late Spedos-variety figures. (Read with Bastis Master checklist.)

[1] Naxos, Archaeological Museum 168. L. 22.5 cm. Phionta, Naxos.

[2] Naxos, Archaeological Museum 166. L. 50 cm. Phionta, Naxos.

[3] Fort Worth, Kimbell Art Museum AG70.2 (gift of Ben Heller). Pres. L. 41.8 cm. "Keros."

[4] New York, Metropolitan Museum of Art 68.148 (gift of Christos G. Bastis). L. 63.5 cm. "Naxos." Name-piece.

PLATES 40, 41. Works attributed to the Schuster Master, an Early Cycladic II sculptor of late Spedos/ Dokathismata–variety figures. (Read with Schuster Master checklist.)

[2] New York, private collection (ex M. Schuster Coll.). L. 29.2 cm. Provenance unknown. Name-piece.

[4] Zürich, Mr. and Mrs. Isidor Kahane Collection. Pres. L. 28.5 cm. "Keros."

[5] London, British Museum 1854.12–18.23. Pres. L. 26.9 cm. Provenance unknown.

[7] Norwich, University of East Anglia, Sainsbury Centre for Visual Arts 1977 UEA 668. Pres. L. 33 cm. "Keros."

[12] Jerusalem, Israel Museum 74.61.217. Pres. L. 12 cm. Provenance unknown.

PLATES 42, 43. Works attributed to the Ashmolean Master, an Early Cycladic II sculptor of Dokathismata-variety figures. (Read with Ashmolean Master checklist.)

[1] Budapest, Musée des Beaux-Arts 4709 (ex Paul Arndt Collection). L. 23.7 cm. Provenance unknown.

[2] Dominique de Menil Collection CA 6326. L. 36.7 cm. "Naxos."

[3] Athens, Goulandris Collection 206. L. 39.1 cm. "Keros"?

[4] Oxford, Ashmolean Museum AE.176. L. 75.9 cm. "Amorgos." Name-piece.

[5] Private collection. Pres. L. 9.7 cm. "Keros."

PLATES 44, 45. Works attributed to the Berlin Master, an Early Cycladic II sculptor of Dokathismata-variety figures. (Read with Berlin Master checklist.)

[1] W. Berlin, Staatliche Museen Preussischer Kulturbesitz, Antikenmuseum 1978.4. L. 43 cm. Provenance unknown. Name-piece.

[2] Athens, National Archaeological Museum 9606. L. 68.6 cm. Provenance unknown.

[3?] Private collection. Pres. L. 4.1 cm. "Keros."

PLATES 46, 47. Works attributed to the Stafford Master, an Early Cycladic II sculptor of Chalandriani-variety figures. (Read with Stafford Master checklist.)

[1] Cambridge, Mass., Fogg Art Museum L.63.1984 (on loan from Frederick Stafford Collection). L. 27 cm. "Paros." Name-piece.

[2] New York, Woodner Family Collection. L. 27 cm. Provenance unknown.

[3] Paris, Musée du Louvre MA 3093. L. 27.5 cm. "Naxos."

[5] Private collection. Pres. L. 26.1 cm. "Keros."

[6] Private collection. Pres. L. 10.3 cm. "Keros."

PLATES 48, 49, 50. Works attributed to the Dresden Master, an Early Cycladic II sculptor of Chalandriani-variety figures. (Read with Dresden Master checklist.)

[1] Athens, National Archaeological Museum 3916. L. 11.3 cm. "Ios."

[2] Keos, Archaeological Museum K9.55. Pres. L. 12.1 cm. Ayia Irini, Keos.

[3] Keos, Archaeological Museum K3.1. Pres. L. 9.4 cm. Ayia Irini, Keos.

[4] Private collection. L. 19 cm. Provenance unknown.

[5] Dresden, Staatliche Kunstsammlungen, Skulpturensammlung ZV 2595. L. 22.8 cm. "Amorgos." Name-piece.

[6] Basel, Erlenmeyer Collection. Pres. L. 16.1 cm. "Keros."

[7] Geneva, Barbier-Müller Museum BMG 202-62 (ex P. Geneux Collection). L. 26.7 cm. Provenance unknown.

[8] Private collection. Pres. L. 11 cm. "Keros."

Illustration Sources

Plates: Museums and Private Collections

Athens, National Archaeological Museum: VIII*B* (photo courtesy of the Archaeological Institute of America), 2, 3*A*, 6, 10, 13, 14−15[9], 18−20[2], 21−22[1], 23[3] (reproduced courtesy Éditions Cahiers d'Art, Paris), 31−33[2], 44[2], 48−50[1]

Athens, N. P. Goulandris Collection: II*B* (photos courtesy of the Photographic Archives of the National Gallery of Art, Washington, D.C.), 11*A*.1−4, 11*C*, 12*A*.1 (photos courtesy of the British Museum, London), 12*A*.2−3, 24−25[4], 28−30[4], 31−32[11], 34[2, 27], 36−37[2, 27], 42−43[3]. (Copy photos courtesy of the Photographic Archives of the National Gallery of Art, Washington, D.C.: 11*A*.1−4, 11*C*, 12*A*.3, 24−25[4 rear], 34[2], 42−43[3])

Basel, Erlenmeyer Collection: 28−30[3], 48[6], 50[6] (photos courtesy of the Badisches Landesmuseum, Karlsruhe)

Berlin (East), Staatliche Museen, Antikensammlung: 16−17[3]

Berlin (West), Staatliche Museen Preussischer Kulturbesitz, Antikenmuseum: 44−45[1]

Bloomington, Indiana University Art Museum: IX*A*, 36[25]

Budapest, Musée des Beaux-Arts: 42−43[1]

Cambridge, Fitzwilliam Museum: 3*B*, 26−27[4]

Canberra, Australian National Gallery: IX*B*, 35−36[21] (photos courtesy of M. Bonnefoy)

Columbia, University of Missouri Museum of Art and Archaeology: 4*A*

Copenhagen, Danish National Museum, Department of Near Eastern and Classical Antiquities: VII*D*, 24−25[3]

Dresden, Staatliche Kunstsammlungen, Skulpturensammlung: 48−50[5]

Fort Worth, Kimbell Art Museum: 38−39[3]

Geneva, Barbier-Müller Museum: I*A*, 13−14[4], 16−17[1], 19−20[4], 48−50[7]

Herakleion, Archaeological Museum: 26−27[3] (photos courtesy of I. A. Sakellarakis)

Houston, Dominique de Menil Collection: 21−22[2], 42−43[2]

Jerusalem, Israel Museum: V*A*, 23[4], 40−41[12]

Karlsruhe, Badisches Landesmuseum: III*C*, IV*C*−*D*, V*B*, *D*, 1*B*−*C*, 9

Keos, Archaeological Museum: 48[2, 3] (photos courtesy of the late J. L. Caskey)

London, Trustees of the British Museum: 40−41[5]

Lugano, Paolo Morigi Collection: I*B*, VII*A*

Malibu, J. Paul Getty Museum: II*C*

Munich, Staatliche Antikensammlungen und Glyptothek: 31−33[4]

Naxos, Archaeological Museum: 14−15[1], 38−39[1, 2] (photos courtesy C. Doumas), 28, 30[2], 31−33[10] (photos courtesy C. Doumas and P. Zapheiropulou)

New York, Metropolitan Museum of Art: III*A*, 16−17[2], 21−22[5], 38−39[4]

New York, Christos G. Bastis Collection: 26−27[2], 35[26]

253

New York, Mrs. Allan D. Emil Collection: 34[6], 36–37[6]

New York, Frederick Stafford Collection: 46–47[1]

New York, Paul and Marianne Steiner Collection: VC, VIB, VIIC, 28–30[6]

New York, Woodner Family Collection: 31–33[9], 46–47[2]

Norwich, University of East Anglia, Sainsbury Centre for Visual Arts: 34[1], 36–37[1], 40–41[7]

Oxford, Ashmolean Museum, Department of Antiquities: IVA–B, 5, 14–15[2], 18[3], 20[3], 42–43[4]

Paris, Musée du Louvre: 46–47[3]

Paros, Archaeological Museum: 4B (photos courtesy of C. Doumas)

Stockholm, Medelhavsmuseet: 26–27[1]

Tokyo, National Museum of Western Art: 28–30[1]

Washington, D.C., Hirshhorn Museum and Sculpture Garden, Smithsonian Institution: 23[2]

Zürich, Mr. and Mrs. Isidor Kahane Collection: 40–41[4]

Private collections: 14[3], 31–33[6], 34[13], 37[13] (photos courtesy of Münzen und Medaillen AG)

Private collection: 24–25[2] (photos courtesy Sotheby's, London)

Private collection: 34–35[28], 37[28] (photos courtesy of Michael Ward)

Plates: Photographers

Roger Asselberghs: X

H. Bloesch: 24[5]

Gad Borel-Boissonnas: 1A, 31–33[5], 34[8], 36–37[8]

Geoffrey Clements: VC, VIB, VIIC, 29[6 right profile]

Christopher Danes: 24[6], 34[6], 36–37[6], 46–47[6], 48–50[8]

A. Emmerich: 15[3]

P.-A. Ferrazzini: 1A, 13–14[4], 16–17[1], 18–20[3], 48[7]

David Heald: 34–35[28], 37[28]

John Hoffstot: 4A

Ino Ioannidou–Lenio Barziotis: 18–20[2], 11A.1–4, 11C, 12A.2–3, 18–20[2], 24–25[4], 34[2, 27], 36–37[2, 27], 42–43[3]

Bob Kieffer: 35[26]

C. H. Krüger-Moessner: 31–33[4]

Lennart Larsen: VIID, 24–25[3]

Werner Mohrbach: IIIC, IVC–D, VB, D, 1B–C, 9, 28–30[3], 48[6, 7], 50[6, 7]

E. Oustinoff: 43[5]

Pfauder: 48–50[5]

Eric Pollitzer: 11B, 12B

Istvân Râcz: 7, 8, 40–41[2], 48–50[4]

P. Rheinfelder: 28[6], 29[6 left profile], 30[6]

Stella Shackle: 34[1], 36–37[1]

Klaus Sommer: 34[22], 37[22], 41[4]

Ken Strothman and Harvey Osterhoudt: IXA, 36[25]

Taylor & Dull: 21–22[2]

Spiros Tsavdaroglou: 31–33[10], 38–39[1, 2]

John Webb: 40–41[5]

Saul Weinberg: VIIIB

Sarah Wells: XI, 18[1], 20[1], 21–22[6], 26–27[2], 31–33[9], 36[13], 46–47[2]

D. Widmer: IXB, 14[3], 31–33[6], 34[13], 35–36[21], 37[13]

Text Figures

Eugenia Joyce Fayen: 3–12, 25–30, 42–44

after Eugenia Joyce Fayen: 1–2, 14, 31, 48, 53

PGP: 15–24, 32–41, 46–47, 49–52

after John Hoffstot: 42e

after Annelis Schwartzmann: 13, 43b

after Danaë Thimme: 45

LIBRARY OF CONGRESS CATALOGING-IN-PUBLICATION DATA

Getz-Preziosi, Pat.
Sculptors of the Cyclades.

"Published in association with the J. Paul Getty Trust."
Bibliography: p.
Includes index.
1. Sculpture, Cycladic.   I. Title.
NB130.C78G44   1987   733'.3'093915   85-20887

ISBN 0-472-10067-X